SLIM JIM

SIMPLY THE BEST
THE JIM BAXTER STORY

TOM MILLER

BLACK & WHITE PUBLISHING

First published 2014
by Black & White Publishing Ltd
29 Ocean Drive, Edinburgh EH6 6JL

1 3 5 7 9 10 8 6 4 2   14 15 16 17

ISBN: 978 1 84502 783 4

Typeset by Iolaire Typesetting, Newtonmore
Printed and bound by Gutenberg Press, Malta

To Patricia, who showed enormous patience as I took my obsession with Jim Baxter to new levels.

ACKNOWLEDGEMENTS

Thanks to all of Jim's former teammates and opponents who gave such a fascinating insight into Baxter the footballer and Jim the man.

Special mentions to Jim's only sister Elizabeth and to his partner Norma for sharing a closely guarded family secret with me and affording me the privilege of telling the true story of James Curran Baxter, just as he wanted it told.

Tom Purdie's supply of some unique pictures tells the Baxter story better than I could in a million words, while sharing memories with legends such as Denis Law and Ian McMillan will leave me with lifetime memories any football fan would dream about.

Willie Henderson may now be long past the age of collecting his first state pension payment, but he remains fit as a flea and powerwalks ten miles most days. His charity work has raised many thousands of pounds for the Michelle Henderson Cervical Cancer Trust, in memory of his daughter. Willie and his wife Veronica lost Michelle when she was only twenty-eight years old. I thank Willie for his time and his contributions to the text.

Bill McCarry and his wife Sandra still live under the ramparts of Stirling Castle. They made me very welcome when I called to talk about their great friend. Sadly, Bill at the age of seventy-five has been diagnosed with the early stages of dementia. Frontal lobe dementia is the medical term, a problem believed to have been brought on by heading a football over the years. As a young man, Bill was a true athlete, a footballer who looked as if he had been carved out of granite. I wish Bill and Sandra well in their battles ahead.

Thanks to my colleagues in broadcasting and in journalism: Archie Macpherson, Alan Herron and Rodger Baillie. I hope I did justice to your wonderful tales of a sensational period in Scottish football. My thanks to Chick Young, who chaired and organised Jim Baxter's benefit dinner, for sharing great memories and great stories from times in the great man's company.

Kevin Raymond kindly gave his permission to reproduce the poem 'A Working Class Hero? Is Jim Baxter to me!' You can check out more of Kevin's work and other fantastic football poems at www.footballpoets.org.

Finally, thanks Terry, for your magnificent support in getting my efforts over the line, and for Campbell and his team at Black & White Publishing for giving me the opportunity.

Contributions from the proceeds of this book will go to the Former Players Club at Rangers FC, and to the Michelle Henderson Cervical Cancer Trust.

CONTENTS

AN APPRECIATION OF JIM BAXTER
BY GORDON BROWN

JIM BAXTER had personality on the field. He had tremendous character, he was assertive, he could dominate a match with his ability and it all looked so effortless. It has often been said that Jim thought that training was for other people. I'm not sure if he ever actually said that, but he was just so natural on the field. He was a born footballer.

It was long after he retired that I got to know him. He was a constituent who became a friend. Even then he radiated the mischievous nature that characterised his play.

The Right Honourable Gordon Brown MP entered Parliament in 1983. He was appointed Chancellor of the Exchequer in 1997 and became the longest-serving holder of that office in modern history. In 2007, Gordon Brown replaced Tony Blair as prime minister and in May 2010 he resigned. Gordon was born in Renfrewshire but was raised in Kirkcaldy. He remains a Raith Rovers fan.

FOREWORD BY CRAIG BROWN

SOME players just make you smile. Whether it was watching his fantastic playing skills or having the privilege of being in his company, Jim Baxter brought a smile to everyone's face. His fantastic football skills could induce spontaneous happiness, while his off-the-field demeanour was full of fun.

One couldn't fail to engage with his infectious humour and gregarious nature when you were with him. He had not always been like that, though. On his visit to Ibrox in June 1960 to sign for Rangers, Jim was a shy, nervous lad from the Kingdom of Fife. And slim indeed!

How do I know? Well, not for the first time was I in the treatment room when that gentleman of a manager Scot Symon appeared, accompanied by the new signing. I had read the Jim 'Jolly' Rodger 'exclusive' in the morning newspaper about a new recruit from Raith Rovers costing all of £17,500.

Having introduced him to trainer Davie Kinnear, the manager then had Jim Baxter shake hands and chat with me, so when he reported for training I was the only player he had already met. The fact that we were pegged alphabetically, and that there was not a differentiation between first-team and reserve players, meant that we were comfortably together – Baird, Baxter, Brown, Caldow . . . What was I doing there, I often wondered.

I think Jim was happy to have someone he knew in the camp, and although never bosom pals we were good friends for the remaining two years I was at Ibrox before I went, initially on loan, to Dundee.

I have already referred to one of Slim Jim's admirable attributes: his sense of humour. Sometimes mischievous, but never nasty, Jim could have us all in stitches. A perfect example was provided one Friday morning before an important home match. There being no substitutes in those days, the actual team, with a 12th man, was printed on impressive Rangers Football Club headed notepaper and pinned to the noticeboard while we were out training.

Although he knew he would be in the team – first pick in the eyes of the supporters, as well as the manager – Jim liked to provide an opinion on the selection. This particular Friday, the morning papers had carried the headline, 'Henderson to get contact lenses!' It was well known that the brilliant right winger Wee Willie Henderson had deficient eyesight, so the club was investing in this relatively new provision. The regular outside left at the time, Davie Wilson, was injured and his replacement was Bobby Hume, who was well known to be one of the first players ever to wear contact lenses.

That morning Jim read the forward line out loud in that distinctive lilting Fife accent: 'Henderson, McMillan, Miller, Brand and Hume. Two blind wingers! I'm gonna tell Davie [McLeod, the groundsman] not to bother lining the park the morra, just to put kerb staines alang the side!'

We used to train often at the main stadium and run lap after lap on the cinder track, wearing spikes. That did not go down too well with Jim, who was known to jump the terracing wall on occasion. When challenged by Davie Kinnear, he would respond, 'I'm up here practisin' to catch wan o' Bobby Shearer's cross-field passes.' That was not an original shout, as it was previously used by the inimitable Johnny Hubbard when referring to the quality of Sammy Baird's long passes.

Hurtful? No one could take offence, not even when he used to mimic the manager, or when he would ask me, 'Did you win a competition to train with the team?'

If another player had said that, it would have been insulting, but such an accusation could never be levelled at Jim Baxter. Young and old players in the dressing-room used to gravitate towards him to hear his cheeky one-liners and his stories of the pride and togetherness of the mining communities in his native Fife.

In the modern day, his transfer value would be at least £25 million, so I hardly need to eulogise about the man's playing ability. That has been well, and justifiably, recorded.

In the days when fans used to throw toilet rolls onto the park, I remember in a big European tie Jim was in possession of the ball and was getting fankled with one of these rolls. A frustrated fan shouted, 'Haw Jim, surely you can beat that Andrex. You've already beaten everyone else on the park!'

Often it was the case that he would beat everyone on the park, and anyone who did what he did against England will always be a hero to the Scots and respected among his peers.

Indeed, so loved was he among his colleagues that unique, and unsolicited, tributes to a remarkable and most likeable true Scottish footballing legend are easy to come by. Johnny Hubbard, eleven years with Rangers, and sixty-five goals from sixty-eight penalties, told me that Jim had said to him that there was only one soup: Baxter's tomato soup. To show the regard he still has for the late Jim Baxter, to this day Johnny still heeds Jim's jocular advice and it's the only soup he'll ever eat!

Although Baxter made the headlines sometimes for the wrong reasons, he has a captivating story, wonderfully extolled by Tom Miller in this brilliant biography.

Craig Brown CBE,
Former Rangers player and Scotland manager

PROLOGUE

MEET YER MAMMY

AT fifty years of age, James Curran Baxter's football career had been over for the best part of twenty years, but he was still an icon. A football legend in the eyes of so many, he had been a Wembley winner twice, offering 'man of the match' displays on the pitch. Not just this, but he had been a ten-man Scotland's two-goal hero in 1963 and was tormentor-in-chief to England's World Cup-winning side in 1967. He was the stuff of legend.

The tales of excess from probably Scotland's finest ever footballer were unlikely to have been exaggerated, as Baxter had had it all, enjoyed it all and almost blown it all. Jim Baxter was a larger-than-life character: he lived each day as if it was his last.

However, the halcyon days of 'Slim Jim' were little in evidence beyond his middle age. Quick with a quip, a glint still in his eye, he was always ready for that bit of devilment that was just in his manner, but a sustained lifestyle of partying and excess was much tamed: the years had left their mark on him.

Baxter could still walk down Sauchiehall Street in Glasgow and turn heads. Autograph hunters – from callow teenage youths to octogenarian ladies – would recognise him and request his signature. He was still box office, the most popular of all the ex-player hosts for the Rangers faithful. Even non-Rangers football fans on corporate visits to Ibrox on matchdays enjoyed his patter. He had time and stories for everyone.

1

It wasn't, however, while walking the streets of his adopted city of Glasgow that James Curran Baxter experienced an unexpected life-changing moment. It was on a November day in 1990 back home in his native Cowdenbeath – and it was to have a profound effect on him.

Jim was back in Fife to visit his parents, Agg and Wee Rab. Before heading home for his mother's famed steak pie dinner, he took a detour past a bookmaker's to have a wee punt, as he was prone to do on a daily basis. As he approached the shop doorway, a small woman in her seventies looked up at Fife's most famous son and said candidly, 'Are you not going to say hello to your wee mammy?'

Yet it wasn't his mother Agg who was asking the question.

His experience that winter's day changed Baxter forever. As the story unravelled, it would also go some way to explaining why this genius of the football field was such a complex and wayward character off it.

THE EARLY YEARS

'Get that notion out yer head'

Born in the village of Hill of Beath in Fife, it was almost inevitable that in James Curran Baxter's life there would be a spell working down the pits. However, this diamond in the coalfield was bound for bigger things, and indeed a much bigger stage. It was usually a case of the bigger the stage, the bigger the performance from the man from the Kingdom of Fife who went on to be a Wembley Wizard not once but twice in the heady days of Scottish football in the 1960s.

Baxter was actually a reluctant footballer in his teens, first with Cowdenbeath Royals, then Halbeath Boys Club. He had a total disdain for training and the discipline that was expected in organised games. The lure of the Hill of Beath Institute card room and a kick-about on a Sunday were his preferred ways to relax after knocking nails into wood as an apprentice cabinet maker in Dunfermline, which was his job before he moved into coal mining.

That said, the support and persistence of family and friends paid off and the qualities of Jim Baxter were soon spotted by local junior side Crossgates Primrose, which reportedly offered him £50 to join their ranks, albeit that figure may well have been exaggerated, given that Baxter had recently been earning only £1 per week as a cabinet maker and then £7 a week as a miner at Fordell Colliery. His move to join the thriving mining industry was based on the higher rewards available in that industry, though the risks were higher, too, and Jim's decision to take up the job at Fordell was totally against the wishes and advice of his parents, Rab and Agg, who were concerned about young Jim's safety.

It took constant cajoling from his best friend Malcolm Sinclair for Baxter to join Crossgates. Sinclair had been close to Jim since their days at primary school – albeit Malcolm attended the Catholic school, while Jim went to the Protestant school. Religion meant nothing to Baxter even then, though as the boys played football Malcolm would pretend to be Willie Bauld, the hero of Heart of Midlothian at that time, and the greatest header of a ball in that era, while Jim was Hibs daft and was always Gordon Smith, who was a central part of that Famous Five front line at Easter Road.

Malcolm was on a mission to have Jim play organised football rather than the twenty-a-side, or sometimes even more, down the local park, which was pretty rough-and-ready, to say the least. So much so, in fact, that Malcolm was influential in Halbeath Boys Club being formed.

Despite Baxter saying he was finished with football, Malcolm kept at him. When he found Jim deep in a game of cards one Saturday while he had half an hour to spare before a match, he held off to see if his pal had the winning hand. When the cards were turned over, Jim lost to a hand of three aces and he was skint. He had lost his money. Baxter decided that football wasn't such a bad way to spend the afternoon, so he headed home for his boots, then set off with Malcom to Kingseat, where the match was to be played.

It begs the question: had Jim been packing the winning hand, would he ever have played that day at Kingseat and kept on playing until Crossgates Primrose offered him terms to join the ranks of the juniors? Whatever, the losing hand that day was a turning point.

In 1956, when James Curran Baxter signed for Primrose, £50 was more money than he had ever seen in his life.

In a strange quirk of fate, during 1948–49 journalist Allan Herron – father of the future Rangers news editor Lindsay – was on national service with the Royal Air Force at Leuchers and regularly turned out at inside right for Crossgates Primrose. At inside left, and team captain at that time, was Mickey Denholm, who just happened to be Jim Baxter's uncle. In 1960, when the Baxter transfer from Raith Rovers to Rangers was confirmed, despite the twelve-year gap, Denholm immediately put a call in to Allan Herron, who was then a top football reporter with the now defunct *Glasgow Evening Citizen*. Herron was later to write Baxter's column for that daily paper, which was presented as a balance to their regular 'Tully Vision' feature that was effectively the diary of Celtic's ultra-talented and equally charismatic Charlie Tully. It was a small world indeed, but so much of Baxter's life stemmed from those early events in Fife.

Eric Caldow, who was Rangers and Scotland captain, had been the sports editor's choice originally, but very quickly after Baxter's dream move to Glasgow Herron recognised something in the nephew of his former teammate that was worthy of the limelight. How right he was. Herron recalls Baxter's reaction to the news that he would be paid £10 per week for his column: 'Christ, Allan, ya beauty ye . . . I'm rich!'

We should remember, of course, that Baxter was by now earning around £25 per week at Ibrox and, with his newspaper income on top, it eclipsed his Raith Rovers and Fordell Colliery earnings by quite some way. However, it may well be that the possibility of supplementing his reasonable miner's wage was the motivation for pulling the boots back on and turning out for Crossgates, rather than any dreams he may have had of glory and global fame. That would come later.

Allan Herron is in the almost unique position of having known and worked with Baxter at close quarters both as a shy and easy-going youngster before he grew in confidence, then later, after he had established the on-field arrogance that saw Baxter established as a genuine football icon in Scotland and beyond.

When the call came that day from 'Uncle' Mickey Denholm, he asked Allan to 'look after my nephew in the big city'. I doubt if anyone ever truly understood the size of that task.

It may have been destiny that on Bank Holiday Monday, 1 April 1957, Raith Rovers invited the seventeen-year-old Baxter to play a trial but it took the vision of Raith Rovers' chief scout Jim McDermid to make it happen. At this stage, Baxter was a skinny youth and, given his lack of physical presence, many had doubts whether he had what it took to make the step up from the juniors. But Jim McDermid, father of bestselling novelist and lifelong Raith Rovers fan Val McDermid, had spotted Baxter's talent and is the man widely credited with this crucial move in his career. McDermid alerted Raith manager Bert Herdman and Baxter was on his way. It was surely one of the greatest ever spots by a football scout.

Ironically, in opposition that day were Rangers Reserves. However, before Jim could mix it up with the second eleven of Scotland's reigning Division One champions, he had to negotiate an early release from his work commitments at the pit. Securing an early 'pass out', or 'tug' as it was known, necessitated gaining the foreman's stamp of approval. The foreman took a bit of convincing and refused to believe Baxter's reason for wanting to leave work early.

It was reported he said, 'Fitba player? You, a fitba player? You're too skinny, so you should get that notion out your head!'

But Baxter persisted and pleaded his case, explaining how important getting away early that day was to him. The foreman relented, and although it cost a young Jim Baxter half a day's pay, it worked out well for him in the end. So Baxter washed his face, grabbed his haversack, with the sandwiches Agg had made for him that morning, and headed off on the bus to Stark's Park and what was to prove a date with destiny.

In the light blue of Rangers that day were Ralph Brand, Billy Ritchie and Harry Melrose. Brand would later become one of Jim's closest friends; indeed, he would introduced him to the future Mrs Baxter when he set Jim up with Jean Ferguson.

6

Rangers were to win 3–0, but Stark's Park boss Bert Herdman saw enough in the skinny kid to offer him a contract, with an immediate six-month loan back to his junior side at Crossgates to help toughen him up.

To be fair to the Raith manager, he had a very strong half-back line at that time, with Andy Young, who made 621 appearances for the Stark's Park side, as the powerhouse; Willie McNaught, who was capped five times by Scotland and had a twenty-year career with Raith, as the commanding central figure; and the wily and visionary Andy Leigh, who later became the club's groundsman, playing in Baxter's favoured left-half position.

Raith Rovers had finished a very respectable fourth in the campaign the season before Jim signed, albeit they were a distant sixteen points behind Rangers, who again won the championship, which was contested over thirty-four games. In 1957–58, a respectable mid-table position was achieved, with Heart of Midlothian pipping Rangers to the title and Celtic finishing third.

Baxter, however, had to learn his craft in the reserves until an injury to Jackie Williamson gave him his top-team chance against Airdrie at Stark's Park on 12 April 1958.

With fifteen minutes on the clock, the eighteen-year-old Baxter slammed the ball beyond Diamonds' keeper Jock Wallace (who would later manage Rangers with distinction) to open the scoring in a match that saw Rovers run out as 4–0 victors. It's a strange quirk of fate that many years later, with Baxter's Rangers career all but over and him facing a free transfer, Wallace was joining the Waddell revolution at Rangers as his right-hand man.

The *Kirkcaldy Times* had this to say about Baxter, the debutant:

The scoring of the opening goal made it something of a dream debut for this young reserve player. Not because of his goal, mind you, but because it set the seal on a performance that was full of promise and full of intelligence. Although he was less prominent in the second half, which was hardly surprising for an eighteen year old on his first senior game, Baxter did enough in the first half, when he controlled and used the ball quickly and effectively, to suggest that he is a young player with a future.

It's hard to believe that only twelve years later in the month of April Baxter's career was over. In between, Baxter lived life to the full, a maverick with a genius that set him apart from others when it came to ninety minutes on the football field.

Hill of Beath is a village with a population of less than 2,000 residents. It is also home to current Scotland international captain Scott Brown, who happens to be skipper of Rangers' great rivals, Celtic. Brown was raised no more than a short corner kick from the statue erected in 2003 to commemorate Baxter; he knows the legend of Slim Jim, which has been handed down from generation to generation in the Fife community. As a youngster, Brown dreamed of emulating the feats of the local hero on the international stage.

'Everybody in the village had a story to tell about Jim Baxter,' says Brown. 'My grandad was a pal of his, and he often talked about not just what a player Jim Baxter was, but also what a home-loving and family guy he was. How he just wanted to play football . . . but it seemed like he did like a drink or two and was happy in anyone's company.

'I used to play with my ball in the streets and look at his statue and wonder, was he as good as the legend that he carried? I wanted to be just like him.'

Baxter sported Scotland's national colours on thirty-four occasions and captained the side a couple of times.

Brown continues: 'Obviously I never saw Baxter play, but I knew all about him, and to think he captained Scotland, an honour I also have now experienced. It speaks volumes for the village of Hill of Beath and how we were all brought up, despite a gap of fifty years. I would love to have seen him at his peak. It's not about Celtic or Rangers, it's about one of Scotland's greatest-ever players. And, yes, his statue outside my parents' house was definitely an inspiration to me.'

Scott Brown has already overtaken Jim Baxter's cap tally, although in the modern game the international football calendar is much busier than in the 1960s. Brown will go on and rack up many more Scotland appearances, but I am sure Slim Jim would have approved of the way he has developed and matured as a player and of him being another son of Fife.

Just over half a century earlier, Baxter was an unassuming youth who showed no inclination for the good life, bright lights and distractions that surely shortened his career. At this stage in his life, Baxter was still very much a home bird. He was Rab and Agg Baxter's only child and they adored him. The feeling was mutual, despite an underlying tension that in later years would reveal itself and show that perhaps all was not what it appeared to be by way of happy families.

Raith Rovers knew they had a precocious talent on their hands, one who was starting to get itchy feet for a bigger stage for his skills. It was no surprise that the list of clubs showing an interest in his services was growing by the week. On 31 October 1959, the *Kirkcaldy Times* reported that Blackpool, Birmingham, Everton and Aston Villa had noted interest in Baxter – all alerted to the fact that he had asked for a transfer. A move to a bigger club was inevitable.

Less than a month later, on 21 November, Raith Rovers were visitors to Ibrox and found themselves two down with only thirteen minutes played. However, prompted by the skinny, quixotic figure in midfield, Rovers got a goal back through Jim Kerray. Baxter himself pulled Raith level, dancing past three challenges before rifling the ball into the net from twenty yards. Baxter was running the show and Rangers had no answers to his promptings and dazzling close control. When Kerray scored again at fifty-six minutes, it gave the Kirkcaldy side their first victory at Ibrox since March 1924. Kerray had scored twice, but he confirmed it was a 'masterclass' from his young teammate.

It was a performance that left a huge impression on the Rangers' hierarchy. Jim Baxter was clearly destined for bigger things and manager Scot Symon was determined to get his man. Baxter was viewed by Symon as the missing link at Rangers, the crucial last part of his jigsaw, and money was not a consideration.

Scot Symon saw Baxter as the keystone in his Rangers squad of that period and although Baxter's first two seasons at Ibrox coincided with his national service as a soldier in the Black Watch regiment, Rangers were soon to experience a period of unrivalled success in the domestic game, while really establishing themselves as genuine contenders in the European arena. Symon's vision of how Baxter would enhance his team could not be questioned.

The question then was, how would the new star player in light blue adapt to life in the big city, away from his parents, away from his roots, away from his friends?

The answer to that question was that Baxter took to life in Glasgow like a duck to water. The Maestro had found his stage, both on and off the park.

2

MOVE TO RANGERS

'Pure gold dust'

In February 1960, before his big money move to Rangers, Baxter was selected to appear for the Scottish League against a Scotland XI to add to his single Under-23 cap, which had been gained against Wales at Tynecastle.

By the spring Rangers were stepping up their interest in securing his talents. When Rangers increased their original offer of £12,000 to a then astronomical £17,500 in June, Baxter was Glasgow bound. The transfer fee was a record between two Scottish clubs; indeed, it stood for fully three years, until 1962, when Rangers eclipsed it themselves when they paid St Mirren £26,500 for George 'Dandy' McLean. McLean could play as an inside forward or straight up top as a centre-forward. As it developed, McLean too had his wayward moments during his time at Ibrox.

The deal to sign for Rangers was completed on 22 April 1960. Bizarrely, negotiations were played out on the eve of the Scottish Cup final, in which Rangers were going head-to-head with Kilmarnock in search of the only trophy that remained available to them that season.

When manager Scot Symon ultimately got his man, he was quoted at the time as making reference to Baxter's sublime performance at

Ibrox in that match of November 1959: 'When I watched you that day, I knew that I had to sign you. You ran the game, the whole show. You controlled everything and that was in a Raith Rovers jersey, and I wondered just what you would be capable of in a Rangers jersey.'

However, the directors of Raith Rovers had no wish to lose their prize asset and placed a substantial bounty on his head, with the Stark's Park manager Bert Herdman saying, 'He [Baxter] is real class. Pure gold dust.'

When the deal was finally agreed, Herdman had again earned his club a healthy profit on the £200 they had paid Crossgates Primrose just three years earlier.

For Baxter, it was not a transfer driven by financial greed. His £10 wage from Raith Rovers as a part-timer, on top of his National Coal Board £7 per week, was a sizeable income for a twenty-year-old living at home with his parents, who by now had moved to Cowdenbeath.

Symon had been relentless in his pursuit of the man (albeit Baxter was still only the tender age of twenty) who he saw as the cornerstone of his Rangers side: despite many suggestions that it was a risk, the Rangers manager was confident it was a gamble he had to take.

Baxter was not a wing-half in the Rangers tradition of power, strength and presence. He was not noted for his heading, he couldn't tackle, his right foot bordered on being redundant, and he was untried at the top level, while his physical shape suggested he was of the lightweight category.

The man in possession of Baxter's preferred left-half slot in the Rangers side of the day was Billy Stevenson, who had racked up almost one hundred appearances in the two seasons prior to Jim Baxter joining the club. With one League title, one Scottish Cup and a European Cup semi-final place on his record as a Rangers player, Stevenson was a more than capable midfielder of his day. So much so that when Baxter did join up, he was shuttled to either inside right or inside left, as Symon tried to shoehorn his young prodigy into his side, with Stevenson retaining the coveted left-half role.

But Baxter was Symon's blue-eyed boy, a fact that became more than obvious as Rangers swept all before them in the coming years, despite the indiscretions that were to become part of the baggage that came with the talented ex-miner from Hill of Beath.

Rangers went on to win the Scottish Cup final at Hampden Park against Kilmarnock, with a crowd of 108,017 in attendance. Jimmy Millar notched a double, but that very morning the *Daily Record* carried the headline that Jim Baxter was Ibrox bound. The story was on the money, although the paperwork wasn't to be finalised until two months later. Respected Scottish sports journalist Rodger Baillie was the man in the know who broke the story: 'It wasn't a case of a super gumshoe story, if I am honest ... I was in the middle of a teenage romance with Carolyn Symon, whose father just happened to be Rangers' manager, Scot!

'I was a young staff journalist on the *Daily Record* at the time and on the eve of the cup final was dispatched to cover Ayr United against Hibs. Being a Friday night, I asked Carolyn to come with me, and when we met she said, "Dad told me to tell you ... Jim Baxter is signing for him!"

'Now, this was a big story and when I phoned it in I was told to check it out with the Rangers' manager myself. So I built myself up for the call to Mr Symon's Ralston home and asked him for confirmation on the Baxter signing. Quite candidly and in a matter-of-fact style, he replied, "Of course. I told Carolyn to tell you."'

This was quite un-Symon-like, or indeed un-Rangers-like, as transfer dealings in those days were not conducted in the public domain. Why was it done? Rodger Baillie picks up the tale: 'I honestly think Symon was just so excited to have got his man. Baxter had been a long-term target and Rangers had been frustrated when previous bids had been rejected by the Raith board. By going public with the story on the eve of a cup final, I think it was also a message to his players that a wind of change was brewing.

'It may have been to send a rocket up Billy Stevenson in particular, and remember, Rangers had already relinquished their league title to Hearts and Symon was already planning for next season.'

Sadly for Baillie, he was not credited with the scoop, as politics in the inky game meant that the editor pulled rank. The byline to the story carried 'Exclusive by Willie "Waverley" Gallagher ... the *Record*'s top football writer of the day'.

That aside, Baillie and Baxter were to combine on an equally important day in the life of Slim Jim five years later, when Rodger was best man for the player's marriage to Jean Ferguson.

The record transfer fee was high in relative terms for a young player with limited experience. Consider that one year earlier Tottenham Hotspur had paid £30,000 for Dave MacKay, while in October 1958 Newcastle United signed the established Welsh internationalist Ivor Allchurch for only £20,000.

In March 1960, Denis Law's move across the Pennines from Huddersfield Town to Manchester City saw a cheque go in the opposite direction for £55,000, becoming the highest fee paid in the British game for a footballer of that era.

Transfer fees were escalating, especially on cross-border exchanges, with Alex Young going from Hearts to Everton for £41,000. George Herd went from Clyde to Sunderland for £45,000 and Ian St John moved from Motherwell to Liverpool for £35,000.

Did Rangers bag a bargain?

Lifelong Rangers fan and unofficial historian of the Ibrox club Robert MacElroy recalls Baxter's signing and says little was made of the weighty transfer fee involved: 'The cup final was still to be played and a potential barren season for Rangers probably dominated the thoughts of fans, who also positioned his purchase as another youngster being bought for the future.

'Although the impact of the Baxter signing wasn't long in kicking in when the new season got started, the fans quickly took him to their hearts.'

From a players' perspective, soon-to-be teammate Davie Wilson knew Rangers were getting a unique talent. That had been highlighted to Wilson the day Rangers had visited Stark's Park to take on Raith Rovers. As the Light Blues emerged from their team bus at the stadium door, a motorbike roared up and it was only the young Baxter arriving to play for Raith.

Eccentric? You bet! But it was nothing compared to some of the bold boy's escapades, which Wilson would witness on a regular basis for years to come.

Winger Wilson couldn't believe this skinny youth with the heavy Fife accent was to be the keystone in the team. He says: 'Jimmy would have blown over in a wind and his right foot was genuinely for standing on, but the left was a gift from God. It was a wand, and Jimmy himself often referred to it as "the Glove". He could put a ball on a tanner from eighty yards.

'I quickly realised playing in front of him was like nothing I had experienced before. He just used to shout, "Wee Man, get on yer bike … I'll find ye," and with uncanny consistency he certainly did.'

Some of the other players were sceptical about the new signing, as the old guard of Alex Scott, Billy Simpson and a few others tended to rule the roost, but Wilson confirmed: 'The youngsters were finding their feet and Jim's confidence was sky high after the transfer. He was ready to take on all-comers.'

Davie also recalls that cracks soon started to appear in the Baxter professionalism. 'I used to room with him on away trips. Curfews were something for others, not for Jimmy Baxter! I remember in one Continental hotel Jimmy going through all the exercises, stretches, star jumps, the lot, under our room window at 5 a.m. I thought that's dedication, then I realised he was trying to get my attention to open the window and let him back in after a night on the tiles! What a character … what a player … but authority – not for Jimmy.'

Despite a reputation for off-field waywardness that would grow, on the field he delivered the goods.

Scot Symon wanted Baxter's subtlety in his side, and his first two appearances for the Light Blues were in the old inside-forward position – on the left on his competitive debut against Partick Thistle; on the right in his next game, against Third Lanark. That match against the now defunct Cathkin Park side saw Rangers lose by two goals to one. When the next fixture paired Rangers with Celtic, James Curran Baxter was allocated his favoured position of left-half. Thereafter, for the duration of his first spell with Rangers, that was his role.

Baxter suffered disappointment in his first Old Firm fixture, with Rangers going down 2–3 to their great rivals, despite home advantage in the League Cup sectional tie. Incredibly, in a further seventeen matches against Celtic, he was only on the losing side on one other occasion.

A king was born.

A king who was to become for Celtic their tormentor-in-chief.

The way the new King of Ibrox was leading his life suggested that he himself might have been carrying some kind of torment – or was it just the newfound wealth and fame, and the opportunity to enjoy it?

This torment of Celtic in particular was not quite enough for well-known Bluenose Scottish comedian Andy Cameron, who wanted more, much more. And Andy was firmly of the belief that Slim Jim was the guy to make it happen. He takes up the story: 'It was well documented that Rangers had been turned over by Celtic 7–1 in the 1957 Scottish League Cup final. A real black day in our history, and nearly sixty years on that scoreline still hurts.

'After Baxter came to us, we could have and should have wiped that result out with a similar or even bigger margin of victory over Celtic. We had numerous chances, but "Stanley" [a nickname given to Baxter by his great friend and teammate Ralph Brand after the Glasgow comedian and actor of that period with the same surname, the great Stanley Baxter] would rather have a wee game of keepie-uppie and give his hooped opponents some verbal than go on and stick more goals in the pokey!

'It infuriated me … it really did! I, and many other Bears on the packed terracing, wanted eight or nine in revenge for that 1957 final.

'We had the opportunities to put that result behind us big time, but Jim just didn't see it that way. As fans, we wanted Celtic humiliated the way we were not that many years before.'

* * *

16

Scot Symon may have got his man, but Rangers had to share him, as even the most talented of footballers were not exempt from national service. It was a case of Jim Baxter, number 6 at Glasgow Rangers, but also Private James Curran Baxter of the Black Watch Regiment.

It was during his national service that Baxter further developed a real bond with another serving soldier who also doubled as a professional footballer. Bill 'Buck' McCarry, a rugged, no-nonsense wing-half in the old-fashioned style with St Johnstone, was a regular 'square basher' with the emerging Rangers icon and a friendship was forged that was to last a lifetime.

McCarry was also captain of the Black Watch regimental football team – and he had the audacity to drop Baxter from his side.

'He was my mate,' Bill recalled, 'but he just hadn't tried a leg in a game played on a Stirling public park, so I left him out for the next match. I suppose he had a good excuse, though. Two days after that army game, he was due to play in a European tie for Rangers!'

On another occasion, and on the eve of a battalion game between the Black Watch and the Cameronians based in Edinburgh, both barracks were excited about Baxter playing. The Cameronians were contacting everyone they knew in the Stirling camp to find out how best to 'take care' of one of Scotland's most talented professional footballers. They need not have bothered! Apart from losing by eight goals to two, Baxter's total involvement in the game was to act as a linesman.

The Black Watch's *Red Hackle Magazine* of April 1961 carried the story of Private Baxter being on a charge for the late return to his army unit after a three-week period of sick leave spent at his parents' home in Hill of Beath. He was given a further seven days' grace, but when that period expired the army phoned Ibrox Park to determine the whereabouts of their AWOL sapper. Baxter returned the next day, thirty hours late. Commanding Officer Major J.V. Parnell was quoted in the publication, saying: 'The trouble is that we have so many soldiers coming in with bogus medical certificates.

17

I pointed out that if he did it again, he [Baxter] might be sent to serve in Cyprus.'

Baxter did have a genuine medical certificate issued by the Rangers' doctor, but it would have been interesting if Cyprus had been the next posting for Rangers' prodigal son.

Jim was also known to regularly miss Tuesday and Thursday games afternoons during his national service (well, he never did like training ...). This coincided with an investigation into regular spikes on Tuesday and Thursday afternoons, resulting in excessive government telephone bills of that period from outgoing calls from the Quartermaster's Office. Further research determined that the most repetitive numbers called were to a couple of well-known Glasgow bookmaker's. However, Baxter's standing with his Battalion mates ensured it was a case of no name, no pack drill.

It's incredible to think that Scotland's most expensive footballer was playing almost alternate games between the Black Watch XI and one of Britain's top professional sides, and sometimes playing for both in the same week.

National service was being phased out from 1957, and both Baxter and McCarry were among the last of the 'less than willing' recruits before call-ups were abolished on 31 December 1960.

Suggestions remain that the two professional footballers had been deliberately targeted by a Senior Officer who wanted his Black Watch football side to be the best in the British Army.

Based at Stirling Castle, McCarry and Baxter became inseparable. McCarry was also from mining stock, born and raised in Tillicoultry. The uncanny parallels didn't just end at the similarities between the Clackmannanshire town and Baxter's home in Hill of Beath. They both enjoyed a night at the dancing, both half-backs in the professional game, and both had more cash in their pockets than most lads of a similar age. McCarry was content to spend almost all of his career at St Johnstone, however, and reflects on Baxter's moves after Rangers with sadness.

'If Sunderland was wrong for Jim, it got even worse at Nottingham

Forest,' he recalls.'Jim was a naturally fit guy, much fitter than people realised, but he only liked training when the balls came out. It had to catch up with him eventually. I didn't have Jim's ability, but I made a career in the game by hard work and effort.'

That hard work and effort almost won McCarry a dream move to partner his best friend at Ibrox, but it didn't materialise. McCarry confirms: 'Jim tipped me the wink that I was being mentioned in dispatches as a potential signing target for Rangers, but somebody didn't do their research properly, and with my surname an assumption was made that I didn't fit the criteria for Rangers signing policy at that time.'

When Bill McCarry announced to Jim that he was to marry his girlfriend Sandra, he asked Baxter to be his best man. The bold Jim, by this time enjoying the trappings of his Rangers success, immediately offered to buy the couple their first house.

'That was typical Jim,' says Bill. 'He made the offer and he would have delivered on it, too. He would have given you his last penny, but Sandra wouldn't hear of it.'

When, as part of his best man duties, Jim then said that he would pick up the tab for a slap-up reception, it was an offer the happy couple were more than delighted to accept.

Bill advised Jim of the intended date for the wedding, but Jim said that day wasn't suitable and so the event was pushed back by seven days.

The wedding party enjoyed an especially memorable evening in Glasgow's St Enoch Hotel, a venue Jim knew well. In fact, it was often considered to be his second home during his time in Glasgow.

In its day the St Enoch was one of the city's finest hotels. It also happened to be the venue of choice for Rangers' directors, senior staff and players, who all regularly dined there before home matches across the River Clyde at Ibrox.

On the original date for the McCarry wedding, Rangers were scheduled to be playing away from Ibrox. The new date, initiated by their best man, coincided with a home game. This change was not

19

just more suitable in terms of the busy diary of James Curran Baxter, but also much more convenient, as the wedding reception bill could be added to the Rangers lunch account from earlier in the day.

Indeed, the King was in his castle.

Glasgow belonged to Baxter and he was in his element.

McCarry admitted that the discipline expected in the Black Watch didn't sit easy with Jim. He reflects: 'Maybe Jim could have changed, but that was just the way he was. A one-off. A diamond. He was a very special friend and I still miss him to this day.'

3

GLASGOW BELONGS TO ME

'The man about town'

When Jimmy Baxter arrived in Glasgow, it was the start of the Swinging Sixties. He was young, single and had money in his pocket. Life was for living and he was without a care in the world – he just wanted to play football. Give me the ball, was all he asked.

He had been elevated to superstar status, living a life that was light years away from his humble Fife roots. Glasgow was the big city. It presented opportunities to party and drink every night of the week, if he was so inclined, and Baxter accepted every such opportunity without a thought towards religious, sectarian or footballing divisions, the like of which have forever blighted the Scottish game when it comes to the Old Firm.

Jim was often found in the company of players from his employer's biggest rivals. He had built a strong bond with Pat Crerand before the Hoops' half-back was sold to Manchester United, and a number of Crerand's Parkhead teammates were in Baxter's regular social set, including Billy McNeill, Mike Jackson and Duncy McKay, with Ferrari's in Sauchiehall Street their regular meeting joint midweek after training. On Saturdays after the match, they were all usually together in the bar of the George Hotel.

Jim's party habits and company of choice brought about issues in the Rangers changing room, however, as others were not so easily accepting, and these became a constant source of irritation to the club's directors and hierarchy.

Crerand still remembers some great nights back in Glasgow in Baxter's company and has nothing but praise and admiration for his old on-field adversary. Off the field, he claims, 'Jimmy was never bigoted in any shape or form, but he was a Rangers man through and through. He loved the club, but he never at any time avoided building friendships with anyone from Celtic Park. It just wasn't the way that Jimmy was built. Let's face it, the Celtic fans loved him too because they knew he was a special talent, and they recognised what he did for the country when he pulled on that dark blue shirt.'

At one time, Jim was romantically linked with Crerand's sister and, had that relationship developed, you would have to question the reaction and fallout that might have ensued from the Blue Room, with Rangers still operating a very transparent sectarian signing policy at that time. Indeed, it was more than twenty years later that Graeme Souness broke the mould, with the controversial signing of former Celtic star Maurice Johnston. Johnston was eventually accepted by the Rangers support, particularly after scoring a late winner in November 1989 against their biggest rivals and against his former team in the white hot atmosphere of an Old Firm derby.

Another Rangers player of a slightly later era claimed to have found life much more difficult at Ibrox after marrying a Roman Catholic. In 1976, Graham Fyfe was shipped out to Hibernian after seven years with Rangers. Fyfe was later hugely critical of the Rangers' board and policy of that time, claiming his marriage cost him his career at Ibrox.

Alex Ferguson, meanwhile, in his autobiography, dismissed any suggestion that his 1966 marriage to Cathy Holden, who was Roman Catholic, was the reason that he was transferred to Falkirk. Derek Johnstone and Robert Russell also married Roman Catholics and their choice of partners had absolutely no negative effect on their Rangers careers.

However, it remains questionable how the Rangers directors in those days, in the early 1960s, would have viewed a Baxter–Miss Crerand tryst.

It was doubtful, though, that Jim Baxter was ready to settle down. He was never short of female company and he enjoyed having the freedom to have his pick of the girls on a night out – and there were plenty of nights out. Maybe his Ibrox teammate Ralph Brand recognised this, as he was the man who actually introduced Jim to the girl who was later to become Mrs Baxter.

Again, Sauchiehall Street after training forms part of the story.

Rangers legend Brand takes up the tale: 'Jim and I were walking down Sauchiehall Street and "Stanley" was *the* man about town. We had lunch and were doing a bit of window shopping, when two stunners were walking towards us. Jimmy was captivated, immediately smitten even, with the tall, immaculately dressed girl in the pencil skirt, high heels and a hairstyle that just set off her natural head-turning looks. I felt his elbow in my ribs: "Ralphie, Ralphie, speak to her, go on, go on, find out her name and where she works." I was meant to be the quieter one in this partnership, but Jimmy insisted. So I plucked up the courage and went over to make conversation. Immediately, his smile was switched on and the Baxter charm flowed after that.

'Three days later at training, Stanley was lying in the bath after a far from strenuous shift and he said, "Ralphie boy ... where do you think I was last night?"

'I said, "No idea."

'"I was only at the pictures with that bird from Sauchiehall Street!"

'It was the first date for Jim with Jean Ferguson the baker's daughter from Coatbridge and they later married in Jean's home town in 1965.'

Before then, Jim was still the maverick, playing the field with the fillies and not just those at the racetrack. Gambling clubs were now also a haunt and chemin de fer and poker had taken over from the pontoon schools and pitch-and-toss of his days at the pit.

Ian McMillan was a huge fan of Jim Baxter as a teammate, but he couldn't believe the life his star midfield partner was living off the field. McMillan, who doubled as a full-time quantity surveyor the whole time he played for Rangers, is still bemused as to how Baxter got away with it. He recalls: 'I would turn up for the game on a Saturday and Jim would come in, clearly the worse for wear after a night on the tiles, but he still delivered the goods in the ninety minutes.'

McMillan goes on: 'It was even suggested on one occasion that he had been arrested the night before a home game at Ibrox and had spent the night in the cells, but Mr Symon just turned a blind eye and stuck with his usual team talk of *just give the ball to Jim* and that was a huge frustration for others, trainer Davie Kinnear and Harold Davis in particular.

'More often than not, Jim was still reeking of booze but even the club captain at the time, Bobby Shearer, gave up on lecturing him about his errant ways, as he knew he was just wasting his breath.'

Harold Davis was appalled at how Jim Baxter conducted his life. 'Jim would come in and the smell of drink on his breath was obvious, even only a couple of hours before a match. You just knew he had been out all night on another bender. How did he get away with it? Well, he was Symon's blue-eyed boy.'

The St Enoch Hotel was Jim Baxter's regular haunt and he treated it as if it was his own private drinking club. Many late nights and early morning sessions saw huge bills for the best of caviar, smoked salmon, Havana cigars, Bacardi, champagne and cases of beer routed to Rangers Football Club and not all carried the J.B. signature. Sometimes he would sign it in the name of a teammate! Davie Wilson was one whose autograph Baxter had perfected, and his name was used to authorise many expensive party purchases, while in reality he was leading a strict teetotal lifestyle, which he continues to this day.

Despite Baxter racking up a host of similar bills, most of which carried his own signature of approval, 'Wilsongate' was investigated by manager Symon. While the others had been totally ignored and the accounts settled, Davie Wilson was told that he was to pay for the lot from his wages. Wilson was horrified. 'I didn't drink and everybody knew who the real culprit was, but it took a bit of convincing before Symon told me to *have a word with Jim!* Jimmy continued to use the St Enoch as his Glasgow base, and the bills kept coming in, and the club kept paying them.'

Roll on twenty-three years and John Brown reminded me of a similar situation he had faced when he'd joined Rangers. 'Bomber' Brown was living in the Marriot Hotel in Argyle Street after his move from Dundee. Like Davie Wilson all those years before, Brown was summoned up the marble staircase to the office of Graeme Souness, where the manager was waiting with Campbell Ogilvie, the SFA President, then the secretary at Rangers, and a sizeable bar bill was presented to Bomber with signatures on the various dockets approving the purchases that bore no resemblance to his own. As a new boy at the club, Brown was horrified and was quick to plead his innocence. Further investigation of the handwriting suggested that the calligraphy skills of Messrs. McCoist and Durrant needed to be developed further.

That was pretty much a one-off and, of course, Rangers settled the account. In the days of Baxter and the St Enoch, it was more than a weekly occurrence, but again Rangers always picked up the tab.

Willie Henderson remembers those days well: 'Jimmy treated the St Enoch Hotel as if it were his own house, and the staff loved him. There was a Polish waiter and he was like Jimmy's personal butler.'

Jim Baxter was a betting man and had been from his days in the Institute card room back in Hill of Beath. Now living in Glasgow, a host of wider betting options were open to him. Jim was a member of most of the Glasgow gambling clubs and was a regular visitor to the Queens Club and the Chevalier Casino. Billy McNeill recalls one particular evening when Jim was lucky: 'We were due to head off with Scotland for a tour that involved games in Norway, Spain and Ireland, and the squad was to assemble at the North British Hotel in

Glasgow. Rooms were available for those that needed them on the night before we were supposed to meet. I wasn't married and just lived at Bellshill, but Jimmy insisted that I should come into town and have a "wee night out"!

'I should have known better. Jimmy didn't do "wee nights". Anyway, we had something to eat and then moved on to one of Jimmy's regular haunts, which was a private club near Central Station. I'm no gambling expert and just watched, but Jimmy was having a lucky night and he had a pile of chips in front of him at the card table. When he cashed up to go back to our hotel, the chips turned into £2,000. That was a lot of money in those days.

'We were away the next day and Jimmy just gave me his winnings and asked me to keep them for him. When we came back, Jimmy took his winnings and headed back to the same club. Unbelievably, within half an hour, it was gone. Two thousand pounds! Gone! Jimmy wasn't bothered: easy come, easy go.'

On another trip to Spain with Rangers in 1963 after losing 6–0 to Real Madrid, Baxter was around £5,000 in front in the casino of the team's hotel. When it was announced that the casino was closing for the night, Baxter wagered and lost the lot on the last spin of the roulette wheel. Baxter flew back to Glasgow the next day more annoyed about the drubbing from Real than losing a fortune in the casino.

Jim Baxter was most definitely a man about town, living a life of luxury. He had no regard for Rangers dress code, which was a policy of shirt and tie, even when reporting for training. Rangers were the establishment club and the players were expected to be ambassadors. But Baxter would regularly turn up for training in a casual sports shirt and slacks. Invariably, trainer Davie Kinnear would ban him from training, but Jim was more than happy to accept such punishment.

In a footballing sense, without doubt Glasgow did belong to Baxter, especially when it came to Old Firm games. In his first spell at Rangers, Baxter's influence was obvious, as Rangers dominated their Glasgow rivals. In eighteen matches against Celtic, which were made of ten league games, five League Cup clashes and three Scottish Cup ties, Jim Baxter was on the losing side on only two occasions. A remarkable record.

Those two defeats were a League Cup tie at Ibrox in August 1960, when Celtic were 3–2 winners, with Carroll, Divers and Hughes on target, Millar and Brand replying for Rangers. It took four years before Celtic enjoyed Old Firm success again: this time they ran out 3–1 winners in a league match at Celtic Park on 5 September 1964. Remarkably, Baxter managed only one goal against Celtic in those eighteen fixtures: a late strike to give Rangers a share of the points in a 2–2 thriller in September 1961. One year before that draw, in September 1960, Rangers probably had their best opportunity to avenge the 1957 League Cup final embarrassment, with a 5–1 win at Celtic Park. Millar, Brand, Wilson and a double from Alex Scott humiliated Celtic on their own patch and, with Baxter pulling the strings in Rangers' midfield, many thought the margin could have, and should have, been greater, as Rangers scorned a number of chances.

Even when Jim Baxter returned for his second spell in blue, Celtic couldn't get the better of Rangers in Old Firm games. In the two games in that short period that involved Baxter, they both won one game each.

Back in that period of the early '60s, Rangers were most certainly the team to beat. Jim Baxter collected his first senior winners' medal, with a 2–0 win over Kilmarnock in the League Cup final within only four months of his transfer, and by the end of that season Rangers were crowned League champions, Heart of Midlothian having claimed the title twice in the preceding three seasons.

During his first stint at Ibrox, there was never a season when Jim Baxter failed to lift silverware. Baxter would add League Cup winners' medals in 1961, 1963 and 1964 to his first in 1960. A trio of Scottish Cup successes in 1962, 1963 and 1964 enhanced his medal tally, while the big one – the champions of Scotland title – was secured in 1961, 1963 and 1964. Baxter's influence was obvious: if it was a gamble taken by Scot Symon to bring the finest footballer Fife has ever produced to Rangers, the return on the record transfer fee he invested was enormous.

For Baxter, the transfer had been an awakening. He was quoted at the time as saying: 'You trained from ten until twelve noon and that was your day's work over. After that, you could choose from drinking, betting, golfing, snooker or shagging! Hey, some days you could do all five if you wanted!'

Yes, Glasgow belonged to Jim Baxter. And, my goodness, he knew how to make the most of it.

4

EUROPEAN DISAPPOINTMENT

'We had no master plan'

The 'gold dust' that Baxter's former manager at Raith Rovers, Bert Herdman, had talked about was soon in evidence. Scot Symon's vision and expectations of Baxter in light blue were soon surpassed, as Jim hit the ground running from day one of his Ibrox career. Symon had made Baxter his number one signing target to take Rangers forward, not just in terms of competition on the home front but also in light of emerging opportunities presented by European football.

Rangers were heading for domestic supremacy – with Baxter their talisman and their most influential figure on the park by the length of Paisley Road West. In front of Baxter in the Rangers line-up, Ralph Brand, Jimmy Millar and Davie Wilson were thriving on the promptings and precision passes from their new playmaker. Baxter was providing goal-scoring opportunities galore and his mates playing in advanced areas revelled in the service.

Slim Jim was King and he was reigning in style, both on and off the park.

In 1961, within a year of Baxter signing, Rangers were to contest their first-ever European final, having missed out at the semi-final stage of the European Cup the season before.

In 1959–60, pre-Baxter, Rangers had been taught a very harsh lesson. The final was scheduled for Hampden Park, Glasgow, that year, but Rangers' hopes of an appearance in the most prestigious competition were dashed when they were comprehensively beaten home and away by crack German outfit Eintracht Frankfurt. Before going head-to-head with the German champions, Rangers had flown the flag for Scotland with distinction.

Their European Cup campaign had started with a 7–2 aggregate demolition of Anderlecht. A 5–2 win at Ibrox just about sealed the tie, with Jimmy Millar and Alex Scott putting Rangers two in front in the opening two minutes. Andy Matthew chipped in with a double and one from Sammy Baird completed the scoring. Rangers were on easy street with a 2–0 win in Belgium, with Matthew again on target and Ian McMillan also on the scoresheet, something that became a feature of that campaign.

Next up it was Cervena Hviezda of Bratislava, with the first leg again at Ibrox. It didn't take long for Rangers to hit their stride and score in the first minute through Ian McMillan. But then the Iron Country side responded with three goals in a thirteen-minute spell to book a two-goal advantage. However, the ever reliable Wilson, Scott and Millar all hit the target in the second half, allowing Rangers to take a slender single goal advantage from a 4–3 win into the second leg. A feisty ninety minutes in Bratislava saw the teams tied at 1–1, with Alex Scott on target to take his tally to three in four games in the tournament, and Rangers were through to the quarter finals.

The draw for the last eight paired Rangers with Dutch giants Sparta Rotterdam. After two games, the teams were locked together 3–3 on aggregate. Rangers won 3–2 away in Holland, with goals from Davie Wilson, Sammy Baird and Max Murray, but lost 1–0 in the return leg in a nail biter at Ibrox in front of a crowd of 85,000.

A play-off was the order of the day and Arsenal's neutral Highbury was the chosen venue. The game was arranged for 30 March 1960 and Rangers progressed with a 3–2 win. It did, however, take two Dutch own goals and a strike from Sammy Baird to put Rangers into the hat for the last four.

Rangers were again drawn to play the first leg away from home, and the Waldstadion in Frankfurt was a less than welcoming arena, despite a huge presence of British servicemen posted in Germany. Rangers were shredded by the slick passing and clinical finishing of Eintracht, who scored six on the night, with Rangers only reply coming from an Eric Caldow penalty kick. It was going to take a monumental effort for Rangers to come back from this hiding in Frankfurt, if they were to make that Hampden final.

It didn't get any better under the Ibrox floodlights. Rangers shipped six again, and only consolation goals from Davie Wilson and a double from Ian McMillan brought a degree of respectability to the scoreline. It wasn't to be.

Scot Symon, who had pretty much used the same tactics he would have adopted were it Falkirk in opposition and not Frankfurt giants Eintracht, knew he needed to improve the squad to add a different dimension to his team and to build on the harsh lessons of this campaign. It had made him all the more determined to make Jim Baxter part of Rangers.

For the record, the final at Hampden remains in football folklore as one of the greatest football matches ever played. A crowd of 127,621 squeezed into Hampden Park and were enthralled by a game that was end-to-end open and entertaining football, finishing Real Madrid 7 Eintracht Frankfurt 3. A certain Alfredo Di Stefano scored three, with Ferenc Puskas going one better than his Real teammate and notching four.

Both Di Stefano and Puskas became great friends of Jim Baxter, and Willie Henderson too. They met again and teamed up together in Rest of the World selects on more than one occasion.

What would Real Madrid have done to Rangers if they had been in the same form that put seven behind Eintracht that night at Hampden? When you consider that that same Frankfurt side had taken twelve off Rangers over two games, we can only wonder.

However, Symon was ambitious. He wanted to go one better in Europe and he believed, with Baxter on board, it was possible.

The following season Rangers were one of ten clubs that entered the inaugural European Cup-Winners' Cup tourament. The campaign to the final saw the first phase of Symon's transforming side grow and gel together.

The campaign started with a preliminary round double header against Ferencvaros of Hungary on 1 August 1960, just weeks after Baxter's arrival.

In the first leg at Ibrox, Orosz put the visitors ahead after only seventeen minutes, but a four-goal power play in the second half from Rangers, with strikes from Harold Davis, Ralph Brand and a Jimmy Millar brace, all but made the tie safe – although Friedmanszky pulled a late goal back for the Hungarians to give Rangers a 4–2 lead going into the second leg.

Symon had sent out his strongest 'first pick' starting side that evening: Ritchie, Shearer, Caldow; Davis, Paterson, Baxter; Scott, McMillan, Millar, Brand; Wilson.

If Jim Baxter lacked experience in the European arena, or even in big games in general, it was far from obvious: he took to the European stage as if he had been born for it.

Ten days after the Ibrox win, and with a two-goal advantage over in Budapest, Rangers fielded the same starting eleven and again the pairing of Orosz and Friedmanszky were on target to put the Magyars two up and level on aggregate. Just after the hour mark, however, the ever reliable Davie Wilson scored to book Rangers' passage into the next round.

After two very eventful legs, it finished 5–4 in favour of Rangers on aggregate.

Next up would be German opposition in the form of Borussia Mönchengladbach. With memories of the previous season's going-over at the hands of Eintracht Frankfurt still fresh in the minds of players and fans alike, confidence was understandably low.

The first leg of the quarter-final tie was in the Rheinstadion in Dusseldorf, but Rangers were quick to take the game to their German opponents and were two up in the first twenty-five minutes, with goals from Jimmy Millar and Alex Scott. Early in the second half, Ian McMillan made it three and Rangers looked on target for their second European semi-final in consecutive seasons.

If the second leg against Mönchengladbach was a formality, Rangers went about their business in spectacular fashion, recording what is arguably their greatest-ever European result. That November night in 1960 the scoreline finished Rangers 8, Borussia Mönchengladbach 0.

Baxter claimed his first European goal with just two minutes on the clock. The rout was under way. The mercurial Ralph Brand grabbed a hat-trick, Jimmy Millar chipped in with his customary double and Borussia defender Pfeiffer turned one into his own net before Harold Davis finished off the scoring. Eight goals scored and none conceded against top quality German opposition showed that Rangers had learned from the previous season in Europe and that by bringing Baxter on board Rangers had a player of genuine class who could run a game in any company, at home or abroad. The wily Symon had made only one change in his side for the second fixture of the campaign, with George Niven replacing Billy Ritchie in goal, and it was the same again for the return leg, which ended with that sensational 11–0 aggregate score.

Wolverhampton Wanderers had knocked out FK Austria Wien in their quarter final, and it now set up a battle of Britain for a place in the first final of the European Cup-Winners' Cup.

The tournament had gone into cold storage for the winter and resumed with Rangers welcoming the Wolves to Ibrox on 29 March 1961.

Rangers were forced into changes, with Bobby Hume, who had turned twenty just two weeks before, given a rare starting jersey, while Dougie Baillie (who went on to carve out a superb career at the *Sunday Post* as a sports writer) came in to offer some steel to the mid-line. Baillie's inclusion saw Baxter in a slightly more advanced role, with licence to unpick the well-drilled Wolves defence.

With regular front man Jimmy Millar missing with a slipped disc,

Alex Scott played in the centre-forward position in a team that lined up: Ritchie, Shearer, Caldow; Davis, Baillie, Paterson; Wilson, Brand, Scott, Baxter; Hume.

A goal in each half from Scott and Brand put Rangers in a strong position for the second leg, which took place almost a month later.

For the match in the Black Country, Dougie Baillie made way for Ian McMillan, as Rangers set out their stall to make the ball a prisoner. When the final whistle blew with the score at 1–1, and after Billy Ritchie's goal had had to withstand some late home side pressure, Rangers had their first European final to look forward to.

Scott, who would later experience English football at Everton, put Rangers one up and the best Wolves could muster was an equaliser from Peter Broadbent. A crowd of 80,000 witnessed this first-ever Anglo-Scottish meeting in European competition, with over 10,000 considered to be of a Rangers persuasion.

The key to success was the McMillan–Baxter partnership in midfield. They were experts at keeping the ball, or protecting their defence when they didn't have it and creating chances at the other end when they did. It was a stunning Rangers victory and, of course, it gave Scotland the bragging rights over their old foe England.

Rangers knew Fiorentina of Italy were to be their opponents, as they had booked their place in the final the week before, despite losing 2–1 away to Dinamo Zagreb. Their 3–0 victory in the first leg was enough to see the Italians progress.

On 17 May 1961, the attendance once more reached 80,000, but this time the venue for the first leg of the final was Ibrox Park. Again, Rangers were on familiar lines. Throughout the entire campaign, Rangers used a total of only fourteen players, which is hard to comprehend when you consider the demands and intensity of European games played over two legs, with travel in those days not nearly as quick or as comfortable as today. Add into the mix the long-term injury that ruled out first-choice centre-forward Jimmy Millar for much of the campaign.

The chosen eleven, who were given the opportunity to be

history-makers – not just for Rangers but for Scottish, and indeed British, football read as follows: Ritchie, Shearer, Caldow; Davis, Paterson, Baxter; Wilson, McMillan, Scott, Brand; Hume.

The Italians were fleet of foot and mind, with the ability to frustrate but hit on the counter-attack with style and precision. Typical Italian disciplined football. Rangers lost the first leg 2–0, with Luigi Milan scoring both goals for the Viola.

Ten days later in the second leg in the Stadio Comunale in Florence, Rangers had a mountain to climb. Millar was back in the side for youngster Hume, who, incidentally, would be tragically shot dead at the age of fifty-six in a car hijacking incident in South Africa.

The task got even more difficult when Milan opened the scoring in thirteen minutes. Alex Scott got Rangers back on terms in the tie, but Fiorentina's flying Swedish winger Kurt Hamrin (who remains Seria A's seventh all-time top scorer) put the game beyond doubt. He ensured it was the Italian side's name that was inscribed on the shiny new silver trophy, as first-ever winners of the European Cup-Winners' Cup.

Jimmy Millar, recalling the run to the final, says: 'It was a fantastic time, with European football in its infancy, but Jimmy Baxter took to it like a duck to water. He loved mixing it with the Continentals. The only down side was the game plan!

'We had no master plan. We went in to games in Europe against the likes of Real Madrid the way we would prepare for a game against Raith Rovers. Although it was around this time Scot Symon started to send us out with the simple instruction – *just give the ball to Jim ... he'll make things happen!*'

Millar was one of the most committed players ever to wear Rangers colours, arriving from Dunfermline as a wing-half but converted to centre-forward. He would have played anywhere for the jersey and enjoyed huge domestic success in his twelve years at Ibrox, but not winning that first Cup-Winners' Cup still frustrates him

'We had a great team at that time, a match for anybody, but we were maybe a wee bit gung-ho. We weren't cute enough!'

After further disappointment in the final of the same tournament in 1967, when Rangers lost to emerging giants Bayern Munich, the Ibrox club finally lifted the trophy in 1972 – their third appearance in the final. Sadly, by that time Jim Baxter was pulling pints for a living. Under different circumstances, he could easily have still been pulling the strings as Rangers midfield general. When the final took place in Barcelona, Baxter was still only thirty-two years of age.

Though Rangers had failed to gain European glory in 1961, the Ibrox trophy room was adorned with the League championship trophy, sitting with the League Cup, which had been secured before the turn of the year. It was this tournament that gave Baxter his so important and cherished first winner's medal.

The league had been won by the narrowest of margins, with Rangers pipping Kilmarnock by a single point. Interestingly, Third Lanark finished third in the table, with the highest number of goals scored in the league – with one hundred in the *for* column – while they had the second-worst goals against in the same period – with eighty conceded from thirty-four games played. It is incredible to think that Third Lanark would cease to exist just six years later.

James Curran Baxter's influence on the Rangers side was recognised in November 1961, when he was called into the national side and gained his first Scotland cap, against Northern Ireland. Another chapter in his life was about to unfold.

5

A HAT-TRICK OF TITLES

'Witnessing an artist at work'

Celtic were totally revitalised after the appointment of Jock Stein in 1965. Stein had been a Celtic player of no particular note, but had delivered success despite his tender age when he moved into management, first with Dunfermline, then at Hibernian. He guided Celtic to nine-in-a-row success between 1966 and 1974, a feat that Rangers would match many years later. However, back in the early 1960s competition was fierce, especially with consideration to the quality of other ambitious top-flight clubs, including Aberdeen, Dundee, Hearts and Kilmarnock, before you even factored in the presence of Glasgow's other big club, so three championships in a row was at the time a sensational achievement.

In 1961–62, Rangers came extremely close to achieving that three-in-a-row holy grail for the first time since 1935 but were pipped at the post by a wonderful Dundee side under the management of Bob Shankly, whose brother Bill's record at Liverpool remains legendary. Two amazing brothers born in another mining community, this time in Glenbuck, East Ayrshire. Bill and Bob had three other brothers, and all five played football professionally. Bill won three English First Division titles at Anfield, while Bob has a Dens Park stand at Dundee, named in his honour from that solitary title success.

The cornerstone of that Dundee side was Ian Ure, who was first to admit it took something very special to wrestle the championship from Rangers. Ure was another Ayrshire man, a modern centre-half, standing six foot five inches tall and built like a tank. Ure remembers the league-winning campaign well.

'The Dundee side that season were a one-off, a quirk of nature, a blip, it just all came together with a wonderful group of players. We had the two Alans, Gilzean and Cousin, up top, and Gordon Smith may have been thirty-eight years of age but that pair thrived on his deliveries from the wing.'

Ure, whose career was later dogged with injury during his time south of the border with Arsenal and Manchester United, picked up eleven caps for Scotland along the way, including the one he earned on the most memorable day of his international career, playing centre-half alongside Baxter at Wembley in 1963. Ian admitted, on occasion watching Slim Jim in action was like 'witnessing an artist at work ... I would rather be in his team than playing against him.'

He recalls fondly: 'I remember one match against Rangers at Dens, and Bob Shankly gave a very young Andy Penman, who was later to play with Rangers, the job of marking Jim Baxter. His instruction was clear: get tight and follow him everywhere, he is their main threat. Don't let him play!

'Well, Baxter could be lazy, as could Andy, but when Jim decided enough was enough of the close attention he was getting from Andy, he just strolled off the pitch in the middle of the game. Sure enough his shadow followed him onto the cinder track. Baxter stood, hands on hips, laughing and shaking his head, while Penman looked bemused and embarrassed that he had just become another victim of Slim Jim's wicked sense of humour.'

Rangers had been crowned champions the season before, and took the crown in the two seasons to follow, but in 1961–62 Dundee had assembled a side that not only excelled in the Scottish championship but also went all the way to the semi-final of Europe's foremost club competition before losing to AC Milan.

Before going out to Milan, Dundee knocked out Germany's FC Koln, the tie secured with a sensational 8–1 win in the first leg at home. They then saw off Sporting Lisbon and Anderlecht of Belgium before losing 5–2 on aggregate to the Italian masters, despite winning the first leg 1–0 at home.

Other than Ure, they had top quality as mentioned in Alan Gilzean, who became a legend at Tottenham Hotspur; Andy Penman, who later swapped the dark blue of the Dees for the light blue of Rangers; Bobby Seith, who hung up his boots to become part of Scot Symon's back-room team at Ibrox; and legendary winger Gordon Smith, whose league success with Dundee set a record – he was the only player to win a championship medal with three different clubs. The Dundee honour was added to those collected from his time in Edinburgh, with both Hearts and Hibs.

Meanwhile, down Ibrox way, a quiet revolution was being affected in the playing squad under the focused management of Symon. Phase 2 of his squad changes were under way.

Stevenson made way for Baxter, and Jim Forrest displaced Max Murray in the squad, while Jimmy Millar was converted from a half back to a genuine number 9. The teenage Henderson's form soon saw Alex Scott sold on to Everton. Ronnie McKinnon was preferred to Paterson, while John Greig, who was later to be recognised as the greatest-ever Rangers player, was starting to force himself into the manager's plans.

Perhaps this period of transition gave the initiative to Dundee, as they lifted the title – the only time they have done so in their history. The league was won by garnering three more points than Rangers, who finished in second place, with Celtic a long way behind in third.

The League Cup again proved kind to Rangers, but it took two games to see off the challenge of Hearts. Jimmy Millar's strike in the first game of the final was cancelled out by a John Cumming penalty, meaning a second Hampden match was required. This time Rangers made no mistake, with Millar again on target, as was strike partner

Ralph Brand. The 3–1 victory was completed with a rare counter from playmaker Ian McMillan.

Millar recalls: 'The League Cup was always good to us and although we didn't take anything for granted, Hampden was like our second home. In that replay, Jimmy Baxter was spraying passes all over the ground. Every one better than the one before. As front players it was service that you dreamt about.'

Rangers brought the curtain down on the season with another win at the National Stadium, beating St Mirren 2–0 in the Scottish Cup final. A crowd of 127,940 saw that deadly duo of Brand and Wilson scoring to make it a cup double, but the treble was allowed to slip through their grasp.

The league campaign took an unusual twist and notice was posted that Dundee might just have been the shock side of the season, especially when they won 5–1 at Ibrox in conditions that suggested the game should never have been played.

It was a typical Glasgow pea-souper in November. Thick fog restricted vision to around twenty-five yards, and a huge travelling support from Tayside had been advised by the police to turn back some twelve miles from Glasgow at Stepps, as the game had been cancelled. Rangers probably wished it had been.

Ure again picks up the story: 'How the game went ahead was a mystery. You just couldn't see, so I just lumped the ball long into the gloom and hoped for the best. We won 5–1 and my most vivid memory was standing on the halfway line when I saw "Gilly" running towards me with his arms in the air. He was around twenty yards away and he was celebrating a Dundee goal, a goal that I doubt anyone in the stadium actually witnessed. Five-one? We only have the word of the referee for that!'

By Christmas, the Dens Parkers had build up what appeared to be an unassailable lead, but Rangers, with Baxter in inspirational form, took advantage when Dundee went on a poor run early in the new year. Rangers capitalised and displaced them at the top of the table. However, in the closing weeks of the season, Rangers lost at Dundee

United and Aberdeen, giving impetus to Bob Shankly's side, who regrouped and won the title with a 3–0 win twenty miles down the road at St Johnstone. That result also relegated the team from Perth.

It was frustration for Rangers, but the fans were confident the loss of the title was merely a blip and they accepted that changes in the playing staff were for the better. A youthful squad was being assembled to take the club forward for competition both at home and in Europe. Symon's squad was being equipped for the challenge.

Normal service was to resume the following season, as Rangers reclaimed their champions crown. For Jim Baxter, it was time to prove he was indeed 'Simply the Best'.

Not everyone in Rangers colours was completely enamoured with Jim Baxter, however. Eric Caldow was a Bill Struth capture in 1952 and had skippered the side with distinction up until the start of 1962–63 season.

When Rangers came back for pre-season after their Russian tour in the summer of 1962 and the squad lined up for the official photograph, Scot Symon handed the ball to Bobby Shearer and told him he would be leading the team out that season. Symon never spoke to Caldow or explained why he was being stripped of the captaincy. Suggestions were that Caldow had been a ring leader in Russia, where a few of the players had revolted about the standard of food that was being served and had headed to the British Embassy in search of a decent meal. It was not an act that Symon appeared to appreciate. So Shearer, or 'Captain Cutlass' as he preferred to be known, was promoted as his successor.

Baxter and Caldow were a good blend; other than in the blue of Rangers, they were also regular teammates in the national side. Caldow was blessed with blistering pace and he knew he had responsibilities when playing behind Slim Jim. 'Jim was some player, but he wasn't the quickest,' said Caldow. 'In fact, he was actually quite slow. I had to do a lot of his work for him. Going forward he was great, but he didn't much fancy the defending part of the job. Nobody could deliver a pass like Baxter, but I don't know how many times I was left on my own against the other team's half-back and winger, with Jimmy posted missing.'

Caldow broke his leg in that 1963 Wembley clash where Baxter scored both goals. It took him a long while to get back to his previous form, having missed almost a full season with that injury. But he did come back and rediscovered that sensational speed that had served him, and Baxter, so well both at home and in Europe.

Caldow remembers: 'I played against that great Spanish winger Francisco Gento and in three matches against him he never ran away from me once. I don't remember getting much help from Jimmy, though.'

6

CHEQUEBOOK RANGERS

'The genie was out the bottle'

When Rangers wrote the cheque to the value of £17,500 in favour of Raith Rovers, thereby acquiring Jim Baxter, the genie was well and truly out of the bottle. High-value transfers were still very uncommon between Scottish clubs, although deals such as the one that sent Dave MacKay south to Tottenham from Hearts with a reported fee in the region of £32,000 were becoming more prevalent. However, while English clubs were considered to be cash rich, the exchange of vast sums between two clubs north of the border was unheard of.

Baxter's move actually signalled a new signing policy at Ibrox and perhaps gave an indication of Symon's vision for the future: he was driven to make Rangers a serious consideration in the developing European arena.

Looking back at that Rangers team of the early 1960s, the line-up almost trips off the tongue: Ritchie, Shearer, Caldow, Greig, McKinnon and Baxter, Henderson, McMillan, Millar, Brand and Wilson.

RITCHIE signed from Bathgate Juniors
SHEARER, a 1955 Symon capture from Hamilton Accies, for £5,000
CALDOW joined from Muirkirk Juniors

GREIG straight from school
McKINNON straight from school
BAXTER £17,500 from Raith Rovers
HENDERSON straight from school
McMILLAN recruited for a nominal fee in 1958 from Airdrie
MILLAR on board as a half-back in 1955 for £5,000 from Dunfermline
BRAND signed by Bill Struth as a schoolboy
WILSON joined as a sixteen-year-old

There were other examples, too: Alex Scott came from Bo'Ness United; Kirkintilloch Rob Roy provided Bobby Hume; Willie Stevenson arrived from Dalkeith Thistle; and George Niven had previously been with Coupar Angus Juniors.

Rangers had a habit of breeding their own. Once they had identified talented youngsters, they signed them and farmed out to junior sides to help them grow up fast and learn their craft. But with European football emerging, Rangers were now looking to supplement their squad by signing the best players of other clubs.

Baxter's transfer fee eclipsed anything Rangers had previously paid for any of Jim's new teammates.

This new signing 'philosophy' – it may not quite have been 'policy', but it was a trait that certainly crept into Rangers' transfer dealings and continued through a succession of Ibrox managers – also meant that players could showcase their talents in matches against Rangers and be signed by them.

John 'Bomber' Brown and Davie Kirkwood were both signed by Graeme Souness after catching the manager's eye in competitive action against his team.

Like Baxter, Kirkwood was with a Fife club. He was only nineteen when he left the East Fife dressing-room for a career at Rangers in 1987. Kirkwood was a talented and tidy midfielder who, twelve months before signing for Rangers, had held his own against a Light Blue midfield that contained Cammy Fraser, Derek Ferguson and Ian Durrant, as the men from Methil battled out a 0–0 draw. It took a penalty shoot-out for Rangers to progress to the next round of the League Cup that night.

St Andrews-born Kirkwood remembers the game well: 'East Fife were a well-organised side and we had good experience throughout the team. We weren't overawed by the Rangers visit because at the old Bayview ground we were a handful and had already beaten Hibs there that season. I had actually turned Rangers down when their former manager Willie Waddell, then running the scouting network, wanted me to sign as a sixteen-year-old. I also turned down Celtic and Manchester City to sign for East Fife and go to college. That night we lost on penalties but had given Rangers a huge fright and as we left the field Graeme Souness shook every East Fife player by the hand and he took me aside and told me to "stick in and we will be monitoring your progress"!

'He was as good as his word and I was aware, as were the club, that I was on Rangers' radar and they were represented at a lot of our games over the next few months. Did I raise my game against them that night? Not so sure. I think I reacted to the atmosphere and the intensity of the game, but it certainly went a long way to helping me further my career and become a Rangers player.'

Kirkwood suffered a horrific knee injury soon after joining Rangers that curtailed a potentially fine career and he moved on to Hearts in 1989. He later returned to Rangers to coach the Murray Park youngsters and in between also had a successful spell as a player, including being a League Cup winner with Baxter's old club, Raith Rovers.

Within six months of Souness signing Kirkwood, he was back in the market, signing John Brown from Dundee forty-eight hours after the flame-haired self-confessed Rangers fan had given a fantastic performance against his heroes in a league match at Dens Park. John – or 'Bomber', as he became known at Ibrox (he had been plain 'Broony' at Dundee) – had a glittering career at Rangers and remains one of a select few who have league winners' medals from all nine-in-a-row seasons, 1988 to 1997. Bomber couldn't believe it when he got the call from Souness the day after he had played against his team and was even more shocked to be invited to join Souness's Rangers revolution.

John recalls: 'We had lost 1–0 to an Ally McCoist goal at home and the next day I got a call from the club saying Rangers wanted to speak to me. I thought it was a wind-up. I had been for a walk on the beach at Broughty Ferry to loosen up from the game the night before and the office staff at Dens were going mad trying to find me. I was told to phone Rangers and speak to Graeme Souness! You can imagine how I felt. I was from a family of Rangers diehards, so this was a dream come true. I knew I'd had a good game the night before, as Souness gave me a wink and a nod as I left the field, but I thought nothing of it.

'I don't know if Rangers had been watching me before that night in January 1988. In that game I cemented Souness and was immediately surrounded by his players, with Terry Butcher in particular letting me know in no uncertain terms that my challenge was out of order. I was surrounded, but Souness got up and pushed everybody away. I thought that was strange, nearly as strange as me only getting a yellow card when it really should have been a straight red for the challenge! It was all much clearer the next day in my conversation with Graeme Souness, when he told me he had made up his mind to sign me as soon as I had laid him out with my challenge and determination to win the ball. But remember, I had scored all three of our goals while playing at full-back when we beat them 3–2 at Dens Park in November 1985. In between the time, I nearly moved to Hearts, but it wasn't to be. I certainly enjoyed playing against Rangers, who I had supported as a kid, but did I try harder with a view to getting a move there? I don't think so. Not knowingly. But maybe deep down there was something that made me give that wee bit extra, not so much to win a move there but maybe just to show everybody that I was a good professional, and good enough to compete with anyone in the Rangers side.'

Others who also fall into this category include George McLean, recruited from St Mirren in 1962 – his fee eclipsing Baxter's two years previously. Junior McGillvray was a one-game wonder from Third Lanark in 1965, while the following year Tottie Beck came from St Mirren and Alex Smith joined from Dunfermline, having impressed with the Pars at Ibrox. With Smith, a new Scottish transfer record was established, as it took a fee of £55,000 to secure his signature.

One year later Rangers again broke their own transfer record and once more it was Dunfermline who made a profit. Rangers paid out £65,000 for Alex Ferguson, who, to be fair, had scored forty-five goals in fifty-one appearances for the East End Park side the season before. The days of Rangers grooming their own talent were most definitely on the way out.

Let's also not forget another legend, now sadly passed away, who had as terrific a left foot as his hero, Jim Baxter – winger Davie Cooper. Signed from Clydebank for £100,000, Cooper was outstanding as the Ibrox side replayed two games to defeat the lower league side. Baxter would have appreciated the present Coop received from his Ibrox teammates at his testimonial dinner: a prosthetic 'right leg'. More of him shortly …

Going into that historic 1959 Raith win at Ibrox, the Stark's Park side's form had been patchy, but as two-goal hero Jim Kerray confirms, 'It was perhaps the first time we realised that Jim Baxter was best motivated to play on a big stage. I got two goals, but Jim was the best player on the park. It was no surprise Rangers signed him. I think we saw for the first time that day that the bigger the game, the bigger the performance Jim gave. We saw that many more times before his career ended. He was a big game player, of that there is no doubt, and worth every penny of the transfer fee Rangers paid. In comparison to the money clubs pay for players nowadays, it was pennies.'

Derek Johnstone was an exception to what were by the mid- and late '60s regular buying sprees by Rangers. He joined the club straight from school, debuting in the first team before his 17th birthday. Derek saw a succession of players come and go in his time at Ibrox, and highlights the late great Davie Cooper as another player whose dream came true when he was offered a move to his boyhood favourites after turning it on against them while in the colours of Clydebank. In June 1977, Jock Wallace plundered the Bankies and paid £100,000 for the winger, who went on to be a Rangers legend in his own right.

The previous year, in September 1976, Rangers paired with the now defunct Clydebank in the League Cup at the quarter-final stage. The first game was a 3–3 thriller at Ibrox, with Cooper scoring a last gasp equaliser for the Bankies; in fact, it took two replays before Rangers marched on to book their place in the semi-finals. Cooper had made his mark. Next stop in his football career: Ibrox.

Derek Johnstone formed a great friendship with Cooper but remembers those cup ties when Davie was on the other side. 'Greigy was at left-back and Coop turned him inside out in all three games. We nearly had to untangle John's legs. Davie Cooper had been the outstanding player in each of the games and he had made it known he was a "bear" and fancied a move to Rangers.

'He was the talk of our own dressing-room after the games, as he had ripped us apart, and we all agreed he would be a terrific signing. My goodness, how right we were. Watching how some opponents performed at Ibrox was a great yardstick to see if a player had what it took to play for Rangers. You needed to be able to stand up and be counted.'

Back in 1960 Jim Baxter, unlike John Brown or Davie Cooper, was not a Rangers fan, with his allegiances most definitely nailed to the Hibernian mast. His decision to support Hibs was influenced by their exciting Famous Five forward line of Gordon Smith, Bobby Johnstone, Lawrie Reilly, Eddie Turnbull and Willie Ormond, who had lit up Scottish football in the '50s.

Perhaps even more important was the way Baxter became a real Rangers man after he had signed for the club – even after he moved on to play in England, his passion was undiminished. In Raith Rovers colours, he had grabbed that game at Ibrox by the scruff of the neck; with hindsight, he may well have been destined to join Rangers, when you recall that his first trial for Raith was also against the Ibrox giants.

Baxter earned his move to Rangers, but his legacy – of stepping up from a smaller club and becoming a 'great' – was not embraced by many of those who experienced similar transfer moves. Bomber Brown, Davie Cooper, perhaps Ian Ferguson (from St Mirren), Colin Stein and Gordon Smith were the absolute exceptions. Kris Boyd would certainly qualify from a twenty-first-century perspective.

No transfer fee was involved when Rangers took out-of-contract Darren McGregor from St Mirren in the summer of 2014, as Ally McCoist tooled up for the championship campaign. McGregor had scored for the Buddies at Ibrox three years earlier in a 2–1 win for Rangers and from that day the rumour mill went into overdrive.

McGregor remembers the period when he joined Rangers: 'It was my first season with St Mirren and scoring at Ibrox was the pinnacle of my season. Rangers fans wouldn't have thanked me then, but for me it was great. Lo and behold, I'm here now and I'd love to add a few more goals over the season for Rangers to help get us to the Premiership. In that first season at St Mirren, I got four or five goals. I've never forgotten Ally McCoist made a point of speaking to me after that game, then talk started about me getting a move to Ibrox. After scoring, I had come off with a hamstring injury, and he knew I had missed the previous St Mirren game against Rangers as I had just lost my dad.

'Ally McCoist remembered that and also said I had done really well since coming up from Cowdenbeath. It was a pat on the back. I took a lot of heart from it. However, when the photo of Ally speaking to me with an arm round me appeared in the papers the speculation of a move to Ibrox increased. The whisper was misconstrued that I was being tapped up! If that was the case, he was trying to tap me in front of 50,000 fans. I appreciated McCoist's words massively. If you'd said to me six years earlier when I was sitting in the wee pokey dressing-room in Gorebridge on the outskirts of Edinburgh that I would go from Arniston Rangers to Glasgow Rangers, I'd have said NO CHANCE! But just maybe that goal and that brief conversation was enough to help me get that massive move.'

On the flip side, Rangers still develop some top talent of their own, as can be demonstrated by players such as Allan McGregor and Alan Hutton from the 2014 Scottish international group, while the next crop coming through include Fraser Aird and Lewis MacLeod. They will ensure Rangers are back competing for trophies at the top end of the Scottish game sooner rather than later.

However, looking back to those days of Rangers' domination in the early '60s and to have a virtually home-grown team, with talents such as Henderson, Brand, Wilson and McKinnon to name but a few, it was some achievement. But at £17,500, Baxter must still have been the bargain of the century.

7

A WEMBLEY LEGEND IS BORN

'Dressing-room torture if Scotland lost'

Jim Baxter had just turned twenty-one when he was first called up for his country in November 1960. He had been with Rangers for a matter of weeks.

Through injury and selection issues, Baxter played in only one game of the six that formed the 1960–61 Home International Championship, which was memorable for much more than its incredible statistics, though they are revealing: forty goals were scored in a tournament of only six games.

Scotland overall had an unsuccessful tournament, the hopes and dreams of a nation systematically dashed as Scotland launched themselves from success to failure of incredible proportions.

Baxter took his international bow in a seven-goal thriller against Northern Ireland at Hampden Park on 9 November midway through the tournament, and it was his influence and promptings from midfield that set up his Light Blue buddy Ralph Brand to score twice. Skipper Eric Caldow converted a penalty, while Denis Law was also on target, as was Hearts front man Alex 'Golden Vision' Young, who later that month made the move from Scotland's capital to Everton. Scotland ran out 5–2 winners and the result went some way to recover a disasterous start to the campaign, which had seen

Scotland go down 2–0 to Wales at Ninian Park less than three weeks before.

When Scotland went to Wembley on 15 April 1961, they were royally thrashed 9–3. A crowd of 97,350 had gathered, with more than half of them ensuring Wembley was a sea of tartan. These were the days when football fans north of the border saved up for two years between fixtures for their Wembley pilgrimage.

Jim Baxter was not part of the Scotland squad that took a thrashing at the hands of the Auld Enemy that day. A hamstring injury ruled him out of selection. His time would come and on future visits he would make sure Scotland gained revenge – and how.

It was this result that forced Scotland international manager Ian McColl to turn to Baxter to try and turn around the fortunes of the national side. Though he would have to wait for two years, McColl was eventually rewarded with a phenomenal 2–1 win at Wembley, with Slim Jim scoring both goals. When Baxter returned to put by now World Cup winners England to the sword in 1967, McColl had been replaced in the Scotland hot seat by another former Rangers man, Bobby Brown.

Many are of the belief that Baxter's performances in 1963 and 1967 under the famous twin towers were his finest on the football field, but it's a debate that still goes on – even Jim himself could recall other games when he had felt he had performed even better. One thing is for sure: Jim Baxter loved that lush green Wembley surface and the arena was the perfect theatre for his magnificent talents.

It could also be suggested that, when he returned in 1967, Baxter wasn't motivated enough to go for revenge by racking up as big a scoreline as possible to confirm Scotland's domination, having not played in the 1961 humiliation. Denis Law wanted it badly and was frustrated that not for the first time in major games Baxter preferred to showcase his own talents rather than pile on the agony by way of goals!

The nightmare result in 1961 left its mark on Law. He recalls: 'Playing in England meant you had at least a year of dressing-room torture if Scotland lost to them. You can imagine what stick was flying about after the 1961 humiliation. I wanted to win and to exorcise that demon.'

Eccentric Celtic goalkeeper Frank Haffey picked up his second and last Scotland cap during that nightmare match. The scoreline launched the gag:

'What time is it?'

'Nearly ten past Haffey!'

Haffey was later to leave these shores for a new life in Australia. Many Scottish football fans say that was not far enough!

Also on the wrong side of the nine-goal mauling were Davie Wilson, Ian St John and Eric Caldow, all of whom were to exact revenge two years later.

From the starting whistle on 6 April 1963, Baxter ran the show. He scored twice and had not just a Scottish but a worldwide audience captivated by his skills.

With only six minutes on the clock, Caldow suffered a broken leg, leaving Scotland to play the bulk of the match with only ten men, as the days of substitutes were still some way off. It was an horrific tackle from Spurs front man Bobby Smith, a reckless challenge, and it ended Caldow's match.

England scorer Bryan Douglas, then of Blackburn Rovers, remembers the challenge. 'Bobby Smith was a real old-fashioned, fearless battering ram of a centre-forward who loved to rough up defenders. The game was more physical back then, of course, and the referees were maybe a bit more lenient, but that day Bobby just got the timing all wrong and the obvious crack of bone breaking as he hit Caldow was pretty sickening.

'Going into the game, England were in fine form, having beaten Mexico and Ireland by five goals, and we also beat Spain by four, but that day we maybe didn't account for the Baxter factor.'

Slim Jim went on to convert a crucial match-winning penalty with ease, despite the fact that he was neither the nominated team penalty taker at international or club level. It was Willie Henderson who had been downed as he cut into the English penalty box, with a scything challenge from Wolves midfielder Ron Flowers.

The penalty was awarded, and with captain and regular penalty taker Eric Caldow off the field with his leg broken, stand-in captain Dave MacKay just threw the ball to Baxter. Henderson knew it was the right decision.

Wee Willie recalls: 'Stanley was flying and had scored just two minutes before. He was cool as a cucumber as he stepped forward to place the ball on the spot, lifted his head, then tucked the ball into the net.

'Pressure? Jim Baxter didn't do pressure! It was just one of those days when Jimmy was in the mood and nothing in the world could upset him or knock him out his stride.'

It was a stunning Scotland performance. Baxter was still only twenty-three, collecting his tenth international cap, but it was the perfect stage for his talents and, as was often the case in the years that followed, Jim had a habit of saving his big performances for the big games.

Denis Law still holds that victory dear. 'Oh, how I enjoyed that one,' he remembers. 'When we lost Eric, nobody fancied our chances, but they didn't bargain on Jimmy Baxter grabbing the game by the scruff of the neck. He scored a sublime goal from Wee Willie's delivery that put us in front. We never really looked back after that, and we have Davie Wilson to thank too for an incredible performance, when he slipped back to left-back with Eric off. You wouldn't have known we were a man down such was the energy Davie displayed.'

Jimmy Armfield was captain of the English side that day and had a torrid afternoon trying to nullify Willie Henderson, who was turning Liverpool full-back Gerry Byrne inside out with his trickery.

Armfield said, 'Baxter got the credit and quite rightly so, but it was a real team effort by Scotland. They almost drew inspiration from the loss of Eric Caldow. I remember the opening goal clearly and the ball coming in from a wide area. I saw Baxter coming, but just as I thought it was my ball to clear, he took a touch and created a half yard for himself, then just passed the ball into the net between Gordon Banks and the post.

'Wembley was a stadium that could bring on an attack of nerves to the best of players, but not Baxter. His performance that day took him to a different level and everyone now knew he could play and hold his own, and more, in any company.'

Denis Law remembers the penalty. 'There really was no other candidate to take the spot kick, although I don't think Jimmy would have parted with the ball anyway after Dave MacKay threw it to him. I also remember manager Ian McColl patrolling the touch line up and down, up and down, talking Davie Wilson through the game. At the same time, Jim was shouting at him to pay no attention to the manager and just to give the ball to him!

'I played in a lot of great Scottish international teams, including 1967, but for a team performance it had to be 1963, even if Jim Baxter was a maverick that just wanted to play his way.'

If it was a great day for Baxter, it was terrible day in the career of club mate Eric Caldow. The challenge from Smith ended Caldow's international career. He managed just over forty appearances for Rangers in the next three years before being given a free transfer from Ibrox towards the end of the 1965–66 season.

For the record, England scored a consolidation goal with ten minutes of the match remaining, with Dundee defender Ian Ure shouldering the blame. 'I should have just launched it out the park,' he said, 'but I thought I could play it out of defence. Instead I delivered it straight to Bryan Douglas, who whipped it into the net.

'Despite that mistake, 1963 remains my best football memory ever and probably the best team I was ever part of.

'I think it was the first time Jim Baxter played in the same team as Dave MacKay and they were a natural partnership. They just complemented each other so well. Dave had the discipline and defensive awareness, Jim thrived when he had the ball at his feet, and he loved playing passes to create so many chances for his front players.'

When the sides met again one year later at Hampden Park, Scotland won again, recording three in a row against the Auld Enemy for the first and only time in the twentieth century. The team were dubbed the 'Hat-Trick Heroes'.

That match in April 1964 delivered a number of firsts. Tottenham hitman Alan Gilzean scored his first international goal, Rangers legend John Grieg gained the first of his forty-four Scotland caps and Billy McNeill of Celtic captained Scotland for the first time, while soon-to-be World Cup winners Bobby Moore, Roger Hunt and Gordon Banks played on the Hampden pitch for the first time.

A mighty crowd of 133,245 were inside the Scotish national stadium to see Scotland continue where they had left off at Wembley the season before, running out 1–0 winners, with Gilzean's header in the 72nd minute enough to separate the sides.

Kilmarnock goalkeeper Campbell Forsyth, making his first appearance for his country that day, remembers the big occasion and build-up before the thrill of walking out on Hampden's lush turf: 'Over 130,000 fans were in the stadium and the pitch was slippy from morning drizzle. I told my defenders I wanted an early touch. Some hope! With Slim Jim running things, we went straight on the attack and I didn't get that early touch.'

Only three men played in all three consecutive matches against the English: Denis Law, Davie Wilson and, of course, Jim Baxter.

Baxter represented Scotland on thirty-four occasions only. It is a travesty when compared with the way caps are handed out now – albeit international games feature much more regularly in the footballing calendar than they did in the 1960s.

His first recognition was that 5–2 win over Northern Ireland, his last coming only months after his Wembley virtuoso performance in 1967. He bowed out with Scotland beating Wales 3–2, with Ronnie McKinnon on target and a double from Tottenham's Alan Gilzean.

In 2004, Baxter's contribution and his efforts on the football field for his country were recognised when he was nominated to become the inaugural member of Scottish football's Hall of Fame. Sadly, it was a posthumous award, presented just three years after his death.

His fame was such that the Tartan Army hijacked a website poll in 2005, commissioned by the London Development Agency, to determine a name for a new footbridge at the rebuilt Wembley Stadium. They asked the question: 'What significant name or moment in Wembley history should be recognised by naming the new footbridge as a memory?'

It was suggested 90 per cent of the 80,000 votes cast were for Jim Baxter Bridge; Nationalist MP Pete Wishart even backed calls for it in a parliamentary motion to the Commons. But it didn't happen.

The bridge was finally christened the White Horse Bridge after a police horse named Billy that had been used to restore order during the 1923 FA Cup final, when a huge number of fans of Bolton Wanderers and West Ham United, who were contesting the final, spilled onto the pitch. The Baxter Bridge would never have been accepted by the English football establishment.

8

SUCCESS AT HOME

Prime Minister's Question Time

The early '60s were a magical time for Rangers, with Slim Jim the lynchpin in Scot Symon's team. In season 1963–64, for only the second time in the club's history, the domestic treble was secured. It would take another eleven years before Rangers managed to repeat the feat, under Jock Wallace, who had been in goal for Airdrie all those years before when Jim Baxter made his Raith Rovers debut. Wallace delivered the treble again in 1977–78 before resigning to manage Leicester City. Walter Smith, Dick Advocaat and Alex McLeish remain the only other Rangers managers in that exclusive club to have achieved domestic treble success.

It was in 1948–49 that Bill Struth's Rangers created history by becoming the first team to win all three major trophies in the same season. Struth, of course, had a remarkable record in his thirty-four years and twenty-six days in charge before handing over the reins to Scot Symon. His trophy haul at Ibrox amounts to eighteen league titles, ten Scottish Cups and two League Cup trophies. It's impossible to imagine any football manager having a tenure anything like Struth's in the modern game. In fact, the average lifespan of an Old Firm manager in recent years is between three and four years.

It was a huge achievement to emulate Struth's feat; however, given his performance at Wembley in the 2–1 victory over England, Baxter knew he had no peers in the Scottish game and his confidance soared – and that confidence transmitted itself right through the team. This can be seen by the way only one month after Baxter's Wembley virtuoso performance Rangers won the Scottish Cup – even without the qualities of Eric Caldow, who had been stretchered off the field in that Wembley classic.

On 4 May 1963, Hampden was set for an Old Firm showdown, with the Scottish Cup the prize. Rangers had beaten Dundee United 5–2 in the semi-final at the same venue, while Celtic had beaten Raith Rovers by the same scoreline at Ibrox to book their place in the final.

A crowd of 129,643 packed into the national stadium to see the sides finish 1–1 after ninety minutes, with Ralph Brand scoring for Rangers and Bobby Murdoch on target for Celtic. Hoops goalkeeper Frank Haffey had been in inspirational form and stood defiant with Rangers in control of the game. His numerous saves somehow kept the Light Blues from scoring a winner.

Extra time and kicks from the mark to determine a winner had not been invented then, so eleven days later the teams were back at Hampden for the replay. Celtic left out Frank Brogan and Jimmy Johnstone amid controversy that chairman Robert Kelly was interfering in team selection. Their replacements were Stevie Chalmers and Bobby Craig, with Rangers making one change from the previous game. Twenty-year-old George McLean made way for thirty-two-year-old playmaker Ian McMillan.

McMillan had been given the nickname the 'Wee Prime Minister' after his namesake Harold, who was in residence at No. 10 Downing Street at that time as leader of the Conservative Party.

One thing Rangers were not in that replay was conservative. Baxter was majestic. Celtic were turned over 3–0, with Brand opening the scoring in seven minutes. Wilson made it two just before half-time, and when Ralph Brand made it three in the 71st minute, thousands of fans of Celtic streamed out of the ground in frustration.

When the chips were down and you were looking for a goal scorer on the big occasion, Brand and Wilson were beyond reliable; in fact, Brand established a record by scoring in three consecutive cup finals, with a goal against Dundee in the cup final the following season. He had been on target against Kilmarnock the previous season, as Rangers pretty much made the Scottish Cup their own.

You could not get two more opposite characters in life, or even on a football field, than Baxter and McMillan, but they both had immense respect for each other. Baxter was determined to ensure his more experienced teammate had some special memories from this cup final replay. McMillan was approaching the veteran stage of his career and, in fact, returned to Airdrie the following season.

McMillan takes up the story: 'We had won the match comfortably, with Jimmy at his sublime best, and as we sat in the Hampden dressing-room letting the moment sink in, Jim came over to me and handed me the match ball that he had left the field with stuck up his jersey! He said, "I know you are coming to the end of your career, so this is for you!"

'In the '60s, match balls were the property of the SFA and, within minutes, referee Tiny Wharton appeared at the dressing-room door to demand the return of the ball. Jim told him in his own style that he wasn't getting it back, but when a couple of other blazers arrived I relented and gave them the match ball, despite the protests from Jim.

'Unbeknown to me, Jim had not given up and around three weeks later the ball was delivered to Ibrox for me. Jim had phoned and visited the offices of the SFA nearly every day since the final and eventually the hierarchy relented. That was the measure of the man and a side to Jim Baxter people didn't see.

'It was a wonderful gesture from a magnificent player and I will never forget his one-man campaign to get that ball for me. To this day, it's still one of my most precious possessions.'

In his six years at Ibrox, McMillan combined his job as a quantity surveyor with his role playing for Rangers, and he only ever met his teammates on matchdays. He trained two nights midweek with the kids. McMillan was even recognised during his time at Ibrox with six appearances for Scotland. McMillan later managed his hometown team Airdrie and was given the role of Honorary President for his services to the club.

That 1963 Scottish Cup final replay is another game that gets added to discussions that still go on about Baxter's best-ever display for Rangers, but long after this dramatic cup win Baxter himself confirmed that his preparations for the midweek replay were far from orthodox.

The night before the game, Baxter found himself in a Glasgow shebeen that doubled as a gambling club. It was one of Jim's luckier nights – he was alleged to have pouched winnings to the value of nearly £2,000. The downside was it took him until almost 7 a.m. to make his winnings, though it was a very happy Light Blue who headed home to his parental home in Fife a couple of grand richer. Remember, too, he was only earning about twice that in a year from the Ibrox club.

When he arrived home in Cowdenbeath, his mother Agg was waiting in the kitchen with the frying pan on. Jim then proceeded to scoff a traditional full Scottish breakfast before going to bed for two hours. He then returned to Glasgow in the afternoon for the evening match.

The smile on his face for the ninety minutes was influenced by much more than just the game that was unfolding. He had a vision of greenbacks in his eyes: for ninety minutes, the green-hooped opponents on the field were little more than a distraction, as Baxter planned how to celebrate.

Before his death Baxter recalled a night at Firhill against Partick Thistle when whatever he tried came off. Most followers of the game look to 1963 or 1967 at Wembley as illustrations of his brilliance, while others remember his imperious night in Vienna before that horrific leg break. Allan Herron, who reported on most of these outstanding matches and witnessed some sensational individualism from Slim Jim on a regular basis, cites the Scottish League Cup final of October 1964 as Baxter's most illuminating performance. 'For me, that day topped the lot,' he recalls. 'Baxter skippered Rangers in that final and Celtic were soundly beaten 2–1 in front of 91,423 witnesses at Hampden. It was the most stunning, accomplished period of play that I have seen from any Scot anywhere in the world, and I have been watching our game for well over seventy years. I might add that this was one of the best Old Firm games of all time. Baxter was the supreme architect of what some people call the beautiful game!

'He revelled in his role of captain, controlled the midfield, made the delayed and damaging passes with the precision of a surgeon's scalpel. Sure, we know he couldn't tackle a fish supper. He was rarely required to do so. But he wanted the ball and made it talk his language.

'Against Celtic that day I realised I was watching a genuine soccer genius. When Celtic tried to salvage the game by switching their wingers, Jimmy Johnstone and John Hughes, Baxter immediately switched his full-backs Eric Caldow and Davie Provan. Yep, he did know a little bit about tactics. Two goals from Jim Forrest gave Rangers their victory on paper, but that final belonged to Baxter.'

Herron could also recall a discussion he had with Alex Ferguson before he received his knighthood. Ferguson commented: 'Not only was Baxter the best left-midfield player ever to wear a Rangers jersey, I think he was probably their most talented player ever.'

It's an interesting fact that Ferguson's superb Aberdeen team of the early 1980s were the last to lift the Scottish Cup three times in succession in seasons 1981–82, 1982–83 and 1983–84. Before those memorable days of Rangers in the '60s, it was only the Light Blues who had held that record, with hat-tricks of wins in 1933–34, 1934–35 and 1935–36, and in 1947–48, 1948–49 and 1949–50.

Allan McGraw never played for Rangers despite being born only a throw-in away from Ibrox, but in a stellar career with Greenock Morton and Hibernian (where he scored fifty-eight goals in 1963–64) he knew the Rangers team of that period was very special indeed. McGraw, who became a Rangers season-ticket holder after retiring from football management, and was a regular golf partner of Jim Baxter's in his heyday, recalls: 'I played in the Morton side against Rangers in the 1963 League Cup final and it was five going on ten. Jim Baxter teased and tormented us throughout.

'He must have been a dream to play with and it's the biggest regret of my career that I didn't get to work with him in the same team because nobody weighted a pass like Jimmy … I bet Ralphie Brand, Jimmy Millar and the other front players of that great era for Rangers just thrived on the service they enjoyed. Don't get me wrong, Rangers were a great team, but Baxter made them that extra bit special!

'Jim was also ultra competitive. He hated getting beat. That was also the way he approached his golf. He loved a wee side bet, too, and as a leftie he was a bit unorthodox, but he was great company, with a heart of gold. I suppose he was pretty unorthodox on the football field, too.'

One man in particular saw more of Baxter than anyone else while he was on the football field: his goalkeeper, Billy Ritchie. From his goal line, Ritchie loved to watch the game unfold in front of him.

'Scot Symon used to tell me just to roll it out to Jim,' he remembers. 'I don't know how many times I did that and just stood back and watched as he took the ball comfortably, then headed off for the opposition's half. He wasn't the quickest, but he had swivel hips. In fact, you could see it from behind him, he had a wee wiggle, with that shirt hanging out. He would show the ball to his opponent, then with a shimmy he had flat-footed him and he was away.

'Didn't matter how many players were round him or how much pressure he was under, Jim just wanted the ball. Well, actually no, he demanded the ball! No doubt he was the man that made that great Rangers team tick.'

It was a fantastic period for the Ibrox club, of that there is no doubt, but surprisingly they were within a whisker of losing their talismanic midfield general before a ball had been kicked that season.

Baxter believed he had been underpaid for his efforts since his first season at Ibrox and made no bones about it to anybody who would listen. It had been a summer of discontent for Baxter. He had cajoled, coaxed and come right out and demanded a review of his Rangers wage, as he believed he was the mainstay of the team. Rangers stuck to their guns, with the policy of the club at that time that all first-team players received the same wage, which was capped at £35 per week and £5 per appearance. There were no exceptions.

Baxter was vociferous in his demands and it was reported his stance was 'pay me an increase or sell me to a club south of the border'. Rangers reaction was that they would listen to offers for their star performer – despite him being a fans' favourite.

As the previous close season drew to its end, Baxter's contract was due to expire on 30 June. An impasse was obvious and the Rangers' directors ceased paying his wages. The tactic was to try and force his hand, while to the bemusement of many no serious offers were received for his services.

Ostracised at Ibrox, and left training alone back in Fife, Baxter had no income, and when Rangers players reported back for pre-season training Slim Jim was not part of the group.

However, with limited options open to him and the start of the season just around the corner, Baxter went back to Ibrox to play in an open trial match that he was only allowed to take part in after he had put pen to paper on a new contract.

Baxter signed.

That new contract was on the exact same terms as the previous season.

Again, the Ibrox power brokers had held their nerve and flexed their muscle to dictate the terms to keep Baxter in blue.

Jim was frustrated but never let those frustrations affect his performance on the park. As has been well documented, his impact on the success the club enjoyed was sensational. But Baxter's memory was long and his desire to increase his earnings in line with his own perceived and high-held esteem remained. A transfer to England was still the move he craved, and he was determined to get it.

9

BEST OF THE WORLD

Waiting for Puskas

The 2–1 win over England at Wembley in 1963 and the Scottish team's performance did indeed capture a worldwide audience. In particular the qualities of Jim Baxter and Denis Law were noted by the highest footballing authority when they were both named in the UEFA Rest of the World squad to take on England under the twin towers on 23 October in celebration of the centenary of the Football Association.

On the day, it turned out that three Scots were involved. Other than Baxter and Law, who turned out in the Rest of the World ranks, Airdrie's Bobby Davidson was the match referee. It was, unusually, a Wednesday afternoon kick-off, with the 23rd being the closest suitable date to the actual centenary, the FA's incorporation having taken place on 26 October one hundred years earlier. Two star-studded line-ups enthralled the fans, and whilst Law started, Baxter had to settle for a place on the bench.

The galaxy of stars who were teammates to Baxter for one day only included Russia's Lev Yashin in goal, the Brazilian Djalma Santos and West German Karl-Heinz Schnellinger as full-backs, with the trio of Jan Popluhar, Josef Masopust and Svatopluk Pluskal from Czechoslovakia ahead of them. French idol Raymond Kopa was on the right wing, with Real Madrid's Francisco Gento on the left. The main goal threat was carried by Denis Law in partnership with Argentinian Spaniard Alfredo di Stefano and Benfica's Black Panther Eusabio. It is not surprising that a boy from Hill of Beath did not get a start in the side.

Joining the Rangers maestro on the bench were Serbian keeper Milutin Soskic, Luis Eyzaguirre from Chile, and West German and Hamburg icon Uwe Seeler. The line-up completed by Ferenc Puskas.

England started with Gordon Banks, Jimmy Armfield and Ray Wilson, with Gordon Milne, Maurice Norman and Bobby Moore as half-backs. Terry Paine, Jimmy Greaves, Bobby Smith, George Eastham and Bobby Charlton were the front five who carried the goal threat.

The nucleus of Alf Ramsey's side went on and won the World Cup three years later, when they again enjoyed home advantage.

Denis Law was delighted to be part of such a massive game, recalling, 'It was a special era for Scottish football, and Jim Baxter and myself being in the World squad was just incredible. We were just kids! In fact, Di Stefano was my hero and here I was lining up with him in the same team. It was incredible.

'Jimmy was in his element and just played the game the way he always did. He had that trademark corner of his shirt outside his shorts that was loved by the Rangers fans but despised by the management, while I probably had the cuffs of my sleeves pulled down and clasped in the palms of my hands.

'We were living the dream – and we were looking forward to the after-match social gathering as much as we were looking forward to the match itself. We worked hard and played hard, but maybe Jimmy didn't quite have them in equal proportions.'

England ran out winners against the Rest of the World, with Southampton's Terry Paine opening the scoring in sixty-six minutes. Denis Law got the World back on terms with eight minutes left, then with almost the last kick of the ball Jimmy Greaves claimed the winner after substitute goalkeeper Soskic spilled a Bobby Charlton shot.

Jim Baxter got a taste of the action, but it's fair to say he was frustrated that he didn't get the time on the pitch to dictate play the way he had six months previously on his last visit to the twin towers stadium.

It was reported that on his return to Glasgow, when asked about his experience with the Rest of the World squad, the Scot said that there were 'too many chiefs and no enough Indians'! A typically dry Slim Jim reply.

By this time, Baxter was earning around £40 per week at Ibrox and perhaps this particular 'native' was getting restless. Having rubbed shoulders with the elite of world football, and having the talent to hold his own in such exalted company, he knew the disparity between his earnings and that of his international teammates was massive.

As time passed, Baxter had moved on from his *Evening Citizen* column to doing one at the *Sunday Mirror* for a fee four times that of the original payment that had made him feel rich within months of his arrival in Glasgow.

Journalist Rodger Baillie, who had broken the original transfer story, from Raith to Rangers, was now tasked with putting Jim Baxter's views into print for their tabloid readers. To finalise the deal, chief football writer for the *Sunday Mirror* Sam Leitch was dispatched from London to Fife.

Baillie recalls: 'Sam booked a hotel in Edinburgh and took a ferry across the Forth to meet Jim. Remember, there was no Forth Road Bridge in those days. The contract was quickly signed for an agreed fee of £40.'

It was then decided that they should head to a local hostelry to toast the arrangement. At 5 a.m. the next morning a bedraggled and slightly worse for wear Leitch was at the quayside, waiting in the first ferry back to the capital, with an expenses claim to be submitted that was way in advance of Baxter's weekly fee. It had been a memorable night.

The *Sunday Mirror* arrangement almost doubled Baxter's earnings and was viewed by Scot Symon as a real gift – he knew he was struggling to meet the financial demands of his top performer.

Rodger Baillie again confirms: 'The Ibrox board were next to useless. They thought that playing for the jersey was enough and were oblivious to the changing times they were operating in. Scot Symon saw the *Sunday Mirror* income as a great way to supplement Baxter's salary and it also kept the directors onside.'

Rodger Baillie ghosted Jim's column for two years and was quick to sing his praises. 'Jim was wonderful to work with and he never caused any problems other than when I drove to Cowdenbeath for our very first meeting and he wasn't there. He had forgotten.

'Scot Symon also gave Jim incredible leeway, more than I can ever imagine anyone else at Ibrox enjoyed. No restrictions were placed on our copy and if we needed Jim to go down to London for an event, Symon never refused him a day off from training to be there.

'Jim also had a natural feel for a good news story and when he received a telegram before Rangers played Red Star Belgrade in 1964 in a European preliminary round decider at London's neutral Highbury ground, he knew it would make a great story. The telegram said: "All the best from James Bond, 007". It was Sean Connery who had sent it, and it maybe tells you a bit about the star status that Baxter had at the time.'

Baillie continues: 'George Best was known as the fifth Beatle, but Jim was there before him. Leather hats and jackets, mohair suits … he was a trendsetter. Even Glasgow restaurateur Reo Stakis recognised his lure when he offered to set Baxter up in a new top restaurant to be opened on the corner of Glasgow's Union Street and Argyle Street. Fifers were often considered to be dour, but Jim was the exception. He was great company and full of life.'

The *Sunday Mirror* ran a monthly competition, with the winning prize being dinner with Jim.

'It was a phenomenon,' remembers Baillie. 'It was incredibly successful. Whoever he was asked to share the evening with, Jim was always charm personified. He made everybody feel special. Jim was also Rangers through and through, but his personality crossed any religious divide and he was welcomed in pubs and clubs throughout Glasgow without any problems.'

Later Baillie was asked by Baxter to be his best man at his wedding to Jean Ferguson. When Rodger asked, 'Why me?', Baxter told him, 'You are the only buggar I know that can make a fucking speech!'

With his off-field romance with Jean gaining pace, Baxter was even more determined to secure a Rangers contract worthy of his talent – and worthy of his value to the team – while he was firmly of the belief his love for Rangers was being tested to the limit. Every year the grind to have a salary review was waived away by the Rangers directors and every year Baxter threatened to ask for a transfer.

It may have been the Swinging Sixties, but despite huge crowds coming through the gate and Rangers sweeping all before them, the cash wasn't swinging Jim's way quickly enough.

It is also fair to say that Jim's off-field socialising at that time meant expensive habits. As journalist Allan Herron recalls: 'His obvious skills opened many doors for him and I saw less and less of him, and you can guess the direction he was taking.'

During one conversation with him, Allan says, 'I asked Jim how he got on with his manager Scot Symon and what did Symon expect of him. I was taken aback when he told me that Symon told him that he had the freedom to play as he saw it. I suggested this could be a mistake. Surely some sort of tactical arrangement should have been made involving a positive role that would benefit the overall team work. No, Symon gave him complete freedom to play as he saw it. Maybe Symon just got it right. Jim was most definitely on a pedestal.'

Herron continues: 'I recall the legendary Bob McPhail, who was in charge of the Rangers' Reserve players once, drawing Baxter aside and suggesting that he start releasing the ball earlier rather than tantalising the opposition with his skilful touches. Jim Baxter replied that he would continue to play the way he did, as he wanted to show the fans and the opposition that he could play "a bit o' fitba"!

'Bob, who had played in front of two great left midfielders, Tully Craig and George Brown, during his career before the war, just shook his head. It should be remembered that Symon himself had been a left midfielder when he had played for Rangers and just maybe he saw in Baxter the way he would have liked to have played in his day.'

While Baxter might have had the full support of his manager, the directors were not so comfortable with Symon's blue-eyed boy, and it was with them that the real power lay. It's unlikely that the manager had the strength to oppose the boardroom.

The directors also showed that they were ruthless when it came to finance. This can be illustrated with a situation that occurred in April 1965, when Bobby Shearer, who had been signed from Hamilton Accies in December 1955, was handed a free transfer rather than be paid a fee of £750, due as recognition for the former skipper's ten-year service.

Baxter was again recognised as a true footballing great, with his inclusion in a World select that had been assembled to pay tribute to Stanley Matthews. The match, on 28 April 1965 at Stoke City's Victoria Ground, celebrated Matthews' thirty-five-year playing career, with Stan's XI taking on an International XI. The game attracted a galaxy of stars and Scotland were represented by Baxter's Ibrox teammate and close friend Willie Henderson in the International side, while Denis Law led the line for Stan's select.

They travelled far and wide that night, and a crowd in excess of 35,000 looked on as some of the finest players in the world took centre stage. Other than Baxter and Henderson in the International squad, the German superstars were out in force, with Karl-Heinz Schnellinger, Wolfgang Weber, Hans Tilkowski, Uwe Seeler, Hans Schafer and Wolfgang Overath.

Spain were represented by the incredible Francisco Gento, while 'the Blond Arrow', Alfredo Di Stefano, was still representing his native Argentina. From Hungary, Laszlo Kubala, while Real Madrid offered Ferenc Puskas. Legendary Russian giant, goalkeeper Lev

Yashin was there, as was Czechoslovakian magician Josef Masopust and French World Cup sensation Raymond Kopa.

Eusabio was the man who led the International side's attack. Wee Willie from Baillieston and Slim Jim from Hill of Beath were in exalted company, footballing royalty in fact, and the King of Ibrox was in his element.

Henderson was just twenty years old, and Baxter was a mere twenty-five. Lining up in opposition alongside Law were Matthews himself, Jimmy Armfield, Jimmy Greaves and Bobby Charlton, representing the English legends. Tottenham and Scotland front man Alan Gilzean played with his club mate, flying Welsh international Cliff Jones who operated on the left flank. Johnny Hayes, Roger Hunt, George Cohen and Ray Wilson were also involved, as was Danish international and soon-to-be Rangers player Kai Johansen, who was then at Greenock Morton.

The game finished with a 6–4 win for Baxter's side, with Willie Henderson on target. At the end of the ninety minutes, Matthews was carried shoulder high from the field by Puskas and Yashin.

Willie Henderson remembers the night well. 'I must have been doing something right to be in that team,' he laughs. 'A front three of Henderson, Di Stefano and Puskas! After the game we were heading for the bus to head back to the hotel when I got the shout from Stanley: "Go on and keep us a seat on the bus, wee man. I'll be along in a minute … I need to wait here, Puskas and Di Stefano want my autograph!"

'That was Jimmy to a tee. Nothing phased him, and do you know what? He wasn't kidding – that's exactly why he was holding up the bus. Jimmy was holding court with two of the finest players the world will ever see, and I mean EVER!'

Blackpool and England legend Jimmy Armfield played against Baxter and his stellar international teammates in both of these matches – to commemorate the centenary of the FA and the testimonial for his good friend Stanley Matthews. Armfield racked up forty-three caps for England and captained his country on fifteen occasions, so he knew a player when he saw one.

In an interesting aside, Armfield had been part of the World Cup-winning squad of 1966 but didn't play because of injury. At that time not every member of the squad was given a winners' medal. FIFA agreed in 2009 that Armfield should be presented with a World Cup medal and he was awarded it at 10 Downing Street by none other than number one Baxter fan Gordon Brown.

Of Baxter, Armfield recalls: 'He was up there. A special talent, but one that must have been a nightmare to manage. At Blackpool, I played a couple of seasons alongside another Fifer, Allan Brown, who went to the 1954 World Cup with Scotland, and he had a similar dry sense of humour to Baxter. But to be selected not once but twice to play in such exalted company as Di Stefano, Puskas, Kopa and others you needed to have confidence in your own ability and a unique talent. For Baxter, it was that cultured left foot that made him so very special.

'I, of course, came up against him when his career took him south of the border. It was such a shame to see his qualities diminish when he should have been winning cups and medals in a team more worthy of his skills.'

10

BROKEN IN EUROPE

'Crack . . . it was like a gun had been fired'

Many Rangers fans will remember 8 December 1964 – and not for positive reasons. That evening Jim Baxter was imperious as Rangers marched on in Europe, but it came at a price. A 2–0 victory at Austria's famous Prater Stadium was marred when Baxter suffered a broken leg.

The pitch was a quagmire of snow-slush and mud, but Slim Jim glided over the surface like he was demonstrating his own version of a Viennese waltz. It was thirty seconds short of the full ninety minutes and the quarter finals beckoned. Jim Forrest and Davie Wilson had scored to leave Rapid Vienna exiting the European Cup. Rangers had won the first leg at Ibrox, with Wilson again on target and Baxter, as usual, the provider.

The Light Blues had arrived in the Austrian capital on the Sunday, with the tie scheduled for two days later. As the Rangers flight touched down, Vienna was amid a whiteout of snow and few in the travelling party believed the game would go ahead, despite the fact that 50,000 tickets had already been sold.

Rapid had other ideas, however. It was left until the day of the game to clear the pitch of snow, with hundreds of soldiers wielding shovels to do as much as necessary to make sure the game took place.

By Tuesday, ticket sales had increased to 70,000, which may have influenced matters, and efforts were made to make sure the game got the green light. Rain was now falling, leaving underfoot conditions soft and dangerous, which made the match a bit of a lottery. The Hungarian referee decided it was playable and Rangers took to the field, Jim Baxter as skipper leading his side out.

It was Wullie 'Bud' Johnston's first big game in Europe, and his lightning pace was causing problems for the home side and their particular game plan for the evening, of playing a very well-drilled offside trap.

Twenty minutes in and Baxter took the initiative, skipping away from three Rapid defenders before playing a delightful and well-timed pass to allow Jim Forrest to run beyond the square defence to open the scoring.

Many say this was Rangers' finest hour on their European travels, and guess who was pulling the strings? Before the full-time whistle, the home fans were cheering Rangers and jeering their own, going so far as to launch snowballs at the home side to convey their displeasure.

Davie Wilson recalls: 'Stanley was sensational. He wasn't bothered about the mud and mush below his feet. His confidence was higher than ever and, believe me, that was no mean feat, but he turned on all his tricks and enjoyed every minute of the match until *crack*. It was like a gun had been fired. Jimmy went down as if he had been hit directly with a bullet.'

Vienna defender Walter Skocik had been led a merry dance by the Rangers captain on the night and had not been able to get near him for eighty-nine and a half minutes, with Baxter nutmegging him on numerous occasions throughout the match. The big home defender had been chasing the Rangers genius like a man demented and with the final whistle only moments away the red mist came down and he claimed his revenge.

Davie Wilson saw it coming. 'The big guy was hunting Stanley down and charging about in a rage,' he recalls. 'I shouted for the ball to take it into the corner and kill some time, but Jim was either not listening or he wasn't finished making a fool out of most of the Rapid team. Thirty seconds to go of a great team performance, with a great team result, then a shocking challenge that brought us all back to reality with a bump. It was a nightmare.'

Rangers trainers Davie Kinnear and Joe Craven came racing across the Prater mud heap, but Baxter himself told the medics his leg was broken – they didn't need an X-ray.

The referee blew for full time, with Baxter still spread out on what was passed off as turf that fateful night.

The Rangers party were to travel by coach to Salzburg to get a flight back to Glasgow, as Vienna airport had been closed because of the appalling weather conditions, which by now included a pea-souper. It was not a road trip that appealed to Slim Jim, especially aboard a bumpy ambulance, with fresh plaster encasing his right leg. Forty miles into the journey, after consultation with manager Scot Symon, who was on the official team bus that was travelling in front of the ambulance, it was agreed that they could about-turn and head back to the team hotel in Vienna.

Despite his obvious pain and discomfort, it wasn't long before the injured superstar was consoling himself back at the team digs, sipping the finest champagne, brandy and Black Label scotch, with beers to wash down some fine fillet steak for a select crowd who had now joined Baxter for a party in his room.

It was like Austria's answer to the St Enoch Hotel – and just as it would have been back in Glasgow, the bill would be heading in Rangers' direction.

The day after the game Walter Skocik visited Jim, offering his apologies for the challenge. He was almost in tears, and full of remorse, while the Austrian press highlighted Baxter's influence on the game, which had ended on such a sour note. The Austrian international manager, Franz 'Bimbo' Binder, said Baxter was world class, while a Vienna TV commentator suggested he was up there with Pelé. Faint praise it wasn't, and many years later Slim Jim admitted he was a bit special that night.

The impact of the Skocik challenge would have deep and lasting consequences, however, and not just in a physical sense for Baxter and Rangers Football Club. James Curran Baxter's time at Ibrox was coming to an end.

Baxter would not wear a Rangers jersey again from that night in Vienna until March the following year; in fact, he played only eight more league games, with one Scottish Cup appearance, during his time with the club.

In the next round of European Cup, Rangers minus Baxter lost out to eventual winners Inter Milan, and the fans were left to wonder what might have been. Likewise, on the home front it was a major anti-climax, with Rangers finishing fifth in the table and failing to secure a European place. They were then dumped out of the Scottish Cup by Hibernian at the third-round stage.

Were Rangers a one-man team? Certainly not, but Baxter's vision and ability to make things happen for his teammates left a void that the peripheral players at Ibrox just could not fill.

Teammate Davie Wilson suffered a similar injury. He recalled: 'I had a clean fracture previously and was back quickly, but I was fit and I worked hard to be back as quickly as possible. But there again I was disciplined and a non-drinker. Stanley lacked that discipline and although he was naturally fit, but maybe not quick, he didn't handle the lay-off well and, to be fair, I think we as a team missed him and our confidence dipped without him.'

The Rangers directors already had an inkling of what might come to pass. It had been evident before the leg break that the relationship between Baxter and the Rangers board was strained. The directors' patience was being tested, as stories were becoming more and more regular about indiscipline and escapades involving their star player that even Scot Symon could not hide or smooth over. From Baxter's view, medals were welcome, but he felt his wages did not reflect his contribution to the team; plus, chasing the holy grail of Europe saw Rangers continually coming up short.

The directors would not allow the reputation of the establishment club to be compromised and behind the scenes they were plotting to sell on their prize asset.

There is an interesting postscript to that night in Vienna. More than twenty years after Baxter broke his leg against Rapid, former Ranger Gordon Smith, who was a sensational Jock Wallace signing in 1977 and scored twenty-seven goals from midfield in his treble-winning debut season, was playing for another Vienna team, Admira Wacker, where his manager was Gustl Starek, who had been part of the Rapid squad in 1964.

Smith remembers a surreal conversation going back to 1986. 'I had been in Austria for a few months, playing for Vienna team Admira Wacker, and could now speak a degree of German. My manager, Gustl Starek, didn't speak any English, so we had not been communicating. However, one the first conversations we did have was when Starek asked me if I remembered a player called Jim Baxter! I couldn't believe it and said he was my favourite player as a kid and my inspiration, as I always wanted to play just like him.

'Starek then told me that he had been a young player at Rapid when Rangers had played there in the European Cup [Starek did not play in the match] and that Baxter's performance was probably the best he could ever remember from his time in the game. It has to be remembered, too, that Starek was a midfielder himself of some note, who was capped twenty-two times by his native Austria, and after Rapid and F.C. Nurenberg, he later played in the great Bayern Munich team with Beckenbauer, Muller and co.

'I reminded him that Baxter broke his leg that night and he said yes, he knew that, as his Rapid teammates had been trying to injure him all night because he was totally running the match. He went on to say Rapid just couldn't handle him in the normal sense and they saw this as their only way of dealing with him!'

Smith continued: 'It was a very interesting conversation to have in German and in Vienna regarding my hero, but I will never forget how complimentary he was about Baxter, even if his teammates that night had left a mark on one of Europe's best players that undoubtably shortened his playing career.'

Denis Law also reflected on that night in Austria. 'If Wembley 1963 was the day that Jimmy Baxter truly arrived on the world stage and made people sit up and take note that this was a special talent, that night in Vienna with Jim at the peak of his career was a disaster and the night his decline started.

'The timing was just awful. He had the world at his feet and had admirers at every big club, including in Italy. He had asked me how I had coped during my time at Turin, as Inter Milan were close to making an offer for him. It was a prospect that Jim was interested in. I have no doubt he would have got a big move, to a club much bigger than Sunderland, had he not left the field that night in Vienna on a stretcher.'

Gordon Smith returned to Rangers as a player, and then again as a director of the club. He is steeped in football, and his grandfather, Matta Smith, remains the only man to have won the Scottish Cup twice with Kilmarnock. Gordon originally grew up a Kilmarnock fan, but when he saw Baxter for the first team he switched allegiances. Indeed as a kid, Gordon would only kick the ball with his left foot rather than his natural right, and it was only to emulate Jim Baxter.

It was a practice that paid dividends, as during Gordon's own professional career no one was ever sure if he was naturally left- or right-footed.

11

CHANGE AND HOW

'Never the same after Vienna'

The disappointment of Baxter's leg break was obvious, and it soon became apparent that the Rangers directors had no appetite for another summer pantomime in their endeavours to establish a wage their prize asset considered acceptable.

Jim Baxter was to be married in the summer of 1965, and with a new wife came responsibilities and an even stronger desire for a higher income.

Mixing with his international colleagues while on Scotland duty had also highlighted to Baxter the gulf in wages between footballers in Scotland and England. He was especially frustrated to hear that many players, vastly inferior to himself, were earning twice or sometimes nearly three times his Ibrox income. This was something Baxter could not comprehend.

The question being asked was: was Baxter the same effervescent – and to a degree innocent – character who had arrived in Glasgow only five years previously? Was Slim Jim quite as slim as he once was? Did that swagger signifying the same level of self confidence that was obvious before the trauma of Vienna and the awful leg break?

There was also a distraction, perhaps an off-field issue that had accelerated the crash-course lifestyle that influenced Scotland's finest footballer's character on and off the park. Changes were pending and they would be far from minor.

Many believe the broken leg left Baxter doubting his own ability. Was he fallible after all? Jim Baxter never thought for a minute he could be caught by the type of sucker punch he suffered that night in Austria. Baxter thought he was better than that. He was streetwise and savvy. He had spent his life evading such tackles with ease.

Baxter's former international teammate Billy McNeill believes his good friend and former Old Firm opponent was never the same player again. 'Jimmy just didn't think that could ever happen to him. Lesser players got caught like that – not him. He used to skip out of tackles and laugh at those that tried to "do" him! In fact, he often made them look foolish by going back and doing the same thing again. He had a sixth sense for it, but that cold December night in Austria it deserted him. I honestly think it was a massive, massive blow, not just to Jim physically but psychologically.'

Jim Baxter had been gifted with natural fitness. It was a great attribute to have, but he had a real aversion to training. After the leg break, where rehabilitation was essential, it's fair to say that hard work was not on his radar, even if it meant his return would be delayed and his level of fitness in his prime days at Rangers would perhaps never return. Baxter's international teammate Dave MacKay was constantly encouraging Jim to spend time on the training ground, but Jim was of the belief that he didn't need to. He was Jim Baxter, naturally fit, fleet of foot, with a quicker football brain than most.

Like Baxter, MacKay too had injury issues. And while he was a top performer with Tottenham Hotspur, he likewise enjoyed a social life of pubs, clubs and fine dining in London's West End.

As has been said many times, Baxter just wanted the ball. He wanted to play the game the way he wanted, which was to get it on the 'carpet' and not give possession away. Scot Symon was his biggest supporter in that regard, but young centre-forward Jim

Forrest, who was on target with the opener that night against Rapid in Vienna, felt it was the beginning of the end for his teammate.

Forrest confirmed: 'Jim was never the same after Vienna. When he returned from three months out, he really was struggling and a lot of that was down to neglecting how he should have been recuperating. He was also getting a little bit older, and maybe his party lifestyle and his persistent ducking and diving at training were starting to catch up with him. Knowing Stanley, though, he had no intention of changing his attitude or his lifestyle.'

Baxter had been placed on the transfer list by the Rangers directors once before, in December 1962, but the rift had been healed. Now in 1965, there was no likelihood of an amicable agreement to keep him on Edmiston Drive. Baxter had a house to buy and if Rangers wouldn't fund it, he was absolutely determined that somebody else would.

Those funds eventually came from Sunderland, with the Roker Park club paying Rangers £72,500 for Baxter's talents, but this was only after a succession of much bigger clubs failed to follow up their original interest with a firm offer.

It was widely expected that the next stop in Baxter's career would have been London, with Chelsea under Tommy Docherty mentioned as a suitor. That was a move that appealed to Baxter, but it never progressed after the initial tentative enquiry. Also from London, and a move that would have got Baxter's approval, was a potential switch to Tottenham Hotspur, who at one time were favourites for his services.

White Hart Lane boss Bill Nicholson was a fan of Baxter's qualities on the field, but despite the prompting and referencing from his skipper Dave MacKay, Nicholson had concerns about Baxter's off-field activities. This concern was also shared by Leeds United legendary manager Don Revie, who was reported at the time to have said, 'I would love to have Jim Baxter in my team, but I like to be able to sleep at night!' Docherty had been quoted as summing up the situation in three words: 'Leopards and spots.'

The stampede that was expected for the services of James Curran Baxter just never materialised. Chelsea, Tottenham and Leeds were all off the pot.

Danny Blanchflower was at the end of a glorious Spurs career and Baxter was being lined up as his replacement. Dave MacKay and Slim Jim were great friends away from the game and enjoyed each other's company socially; on the park, they were on the same wavelength and formed a formidable partnership when paired together in the dark blue of Scotland. The Wembley win of 1963 was a prime example of how Baxter and MacKay complemented each other, but they were not destined to play together at club level.

Arsenal, under Billy Wright, flirted with a move, as did Italian giants Inter Milan, but again nothing concrete was on offer. Perhaps the rumours of Jim's lifestyle were the reason.

Jim's preference was still a move south of the border. Having played against England three times, and been on the successful side on each occasion, it was a surprise that his bad boy reputation appeared to outweigh his match-winning qualities.

One by one, the big guns of the English game distanced themselves from the Rangers' star despite Tottenham boss Nicholson supposedly meeting Baxter and going on to discuss a proposed move with his opposite number at Rangers, Scot Symon.

The path was left clear for Sunderland to make their move.

Former Scotland boss Ian McColl was in charge at Sunderland and from their time together with the national team he had first-hand experience managing Jim.

Baxter may have been favoured with a sizeable signing-on fee, and even double his basic weekly wage, but did it make up for the step down to a club without the prestige, stature and history of Glasgow Rangers?

It was a move that was doomed to failure, according to his international teammate Ian Ure, who had left Dundee for Arsenal less than a year before. 'Wrong club at the wrong time,' Ure claims. 'Jim was used to playing with better players than Sunderland had, and the way he led his life lacked professionalism. The pace of the game was different in England and travelling was part and parcel of your working week. It took quite a level of discipline to make it in England. Jim was just not cut out for it. I remember predicting at the time it would be a disaster.'

If Ure had doubts, their former boss Ian McColl was convinced he had signed the missing link for his side and he was confident the wayward genius would prove the doubters wrong.

A summer of change indeed, but would the maverick in Baxter change with the responsibilities that came with marriage and a new footballing challenge?

Was Wearside ready for Jim Baxter?

12

RATED AT ROKER

'Wearsiders have a hero'

Sunderland sealed the deal to make Jim Baxter a Black Cat in the summer of 1965. The contract was signed in the North British Hotel in Edinburgh, but it was clear that Scot Symon was far from happy about losing his prodigal son.

This was a transfer driven by the financial demands of Baxter and the wish of the Rangers directors to detach themselves from a man who many thought was trying to prove he was bigger than the club.

Baxter's former international boss, Ian McColl, was the man who put his head on the block to take the mercurial midfielder to Wearside. McColl himself had only just taken over the Roker reins from caretaker manager George Hardwick, who had done well to ensure top-flight survival for Sunderland in their first season back after relegation in 1958. Hardwick superseded Alan Brown, who had moved on after seven years in charge, much of which had been spent reinventing the football club after suggestions of illegal payments to players prior to his appointment. Sunderland weren't found guilty of any wrongdoing, but the club were stigmatised for a long time thereafter.

Strangely, after fifteen years at Ibrox, McColl had played his last game for Rangers in the 1960 Scottish Cup final against Kilmarnock, the very day that Symon had gone public about the transfer of Baxter from Raith Rovers. McColl was a Rangers icon and was part of the famed 'Iron Curtain' defence comprising Sammy Cox, Willie Woodburn and George Young. He played 526 times for the club before moving into management with the national side almost immediately after hanging up his boots.

McColl had delivered back-to-back Home International Championships in 1962 and 1963, with Baxter a key component in his sides. He knew what he was getting when he signed Slim Jim.

In his first season at Roker Park, Baxter made thirty-eight appearances and scored five goals, including a home debut double in a 4–1 win over Sheffield United. He was also on target in wins against Chelsea and Aston Villa. Perhaps the prophets of doom had called it wrong. Maybe a leopard could change its spots.

Deep down, Jim was frustrated by the lack of quality in the team and he knew that he would be fighting battles at the wrong end of the table compared to his five years of success with Rangers. Baxter was later quoted as saying he 'could hardly have made a worse move'.

However, the extra income was a welcome boost, with his Rangers weekly wage almost doubled to a basic £80, plus £40 per point. This could be further enhanced by appearance money in cup competitions and a handsome additional financial incentive for a healthy league position.

There was also the small matter of a cheque to the value of £11,000 as a signing-on fee lodged in the Baxter bank account. The 'cut' of the fee would have been more than enough to buy a new marital home had Sunderland not provided one, which in context would have been equal to around £200,000 in today's terms.

Meanwhile, back in Glasgow, Davie Wilson recalls his thoughts on the departure of his teammate: 'We had a great team, but with Stanley going it was getting broken up too soon. The directors made the decision and, for me, it was a terrible mistake.'

Ian McMillan had already returned to his roots in Airdrie after six years at Ibrox, four of which were spent partnering Jim in the

Rangers engine room. His was another voice that, when the transfer was confirmed, questioned Baxter's choice of club. 'Sunderland?' he says. 'Why Sunderland? Jimmy Baxter deserved a bigger stage for his talents.'

Sunderland needed a hero, but one man did not make a team ... or did it?

Back across the border, one newspaper ran the headline: 'The King Is Gone'. The English edition of *The Sun* heralded Baxter's arrival at Sunderland in print:

> Wearsiders have a hero who will add a new dimension to their enjoyment of football. He's different! On the field, no matter the company, Jim Baxter is different. Even the way he dresses, with the briefest of shorts hitched up to make them briefer still ... he's as brash and modern as tomorrow. His dress is as mod as his play, though ... flashy and up-to-date.

Fifth Beatle anyone? Though this title may have been later bestowed on George Best, Baxter was the sporting icon closest to the style of the Fab Four before he came a long.

Baxter had headed south with his new bride Jean by his side. The couple had tied the knot in Garturk Church, Coatbridge, on 16 June 1965. They were like the Beckhams of their day. Roads were closed all round the area of Whifflet near the church, with old and young, football fans and the general public, travelling from far and wide to catch a sighting of the happy couple.

In the evening Baxter's favourite haunt, the St Enoch Hotel, hosted a reception for the wedding party and their guests. This time the bill was not to Rangers Football Club's account.

With his new-found responsibility, and the distractions and bright lights of Glasgow left behind, Baxter viewed his transfer as a new start. But was settling down really on Baxter's agenda?

As he was leaving Glasgow, a revolution had begun on the other side of the city. Jock Stein had taken the reins at Celtic and delivered the Scottish Cup within three months of his appointment. Now in pre-season, by a quirk of fate Celtic were in town to take on Sunderland. They would face their old tormentor-in-chief, now installed as the new lynchpin in the Roker Park side.

Celtic legend Billy McNeill takes up the story: 'We got some revenge that day by beating Jim's new team 5–0 and we wasted no time in giving Jim some stick because, believe me, he had never been shy on dishing it out to Celtic over the years, when he held the upper hand. There was no malice in it, though, just the usual stuff between players – between mates.

'Perhaps that day we got the first confirmation that Baxter was not going to be the success in English football that he should have been. Perhaps even the first confirmation that Jimmy had gone to the wrong club.'

Ian Ure was at Arsenal at the time and despite having great respect for Baxter's qualities, he also suspected Roker Park was the wrong choice. 'Jim was just not equipped for the English game. The first pre-requisite is you need to be an athlete and you had to be disciplined with training schedules that had to be built round many miles of travel for the most insignificant league match, and of course the game was played at a higher pace, with midfielders not given time on the ball like they got back up the road.'

Jim was chasing the cash but didn't have the work ethic that was needed to support the unquestionable skill he had. Ure continues: 'Sunderland, a bottom to mid-table club, were more Dundee than Rangers, and he didn't have the quality of teammates around him to make any kind of impact.'

Baxter's old friend and former Celtic half-back Pat Crerand had moved south two years earlier and had been an instant hit with Manchester United, a club that was not prepared to take a chance on Baxter, though Crerand wishes they had.

'Old Trafford would have been perfect for Jimmy,' he says. 'He would have been playing with better players and enjoying being part of a real big club; it may have prolonged his career.'

Someone who agrees with Crerand is ex-Sunderland teammate Neil Martin, who, like Baxter, moved to Roker Park in 1965 and, again like Baxter, had fallen out with his Scottish club over his desire for an extra £10 per week. Hibernian refused to budge and so Martin signed for Sunderland in the autumn, although he went for a slightly more modest fee of £45,000.

Neil says, 'If Jimmy had signed for Liverpool or a big club like that, it would have made such a difference to him. Playing in a better team, he may have kept his focus and revelled in a team with better players who were on the same wavelength as him. He was some player, even allowing for the fact he just didn't train.'

Sunderland were in a mess and, before moving south, Martin had played in a League Cup semi-final against Celtic at Ibrox. Before the game Celtic legend Billy McNeill had a word with the Hibs centre-forward. Neil remembers the conversation: 'Billy said, "I hear you are going to Sunderland. Are you sure it's a good move? We played them pre-season and thumped them 5–0. They were hopeless. Only Stanley looked any use!"'

With hindsight, Martin wishes he had heeded the warning.

He continues: 'Ian McColl was the boss and he was still just a novice. He had a wee Scots colony built at Roker, but it worked more against him than for him. Jimmy Baxter was the ring leader-in-chief and with loads of Scots for company, including myself, Bobby Kerr, George Mulhall and George Herd, he was never stuck for someone to go for a pint with. Although with Jim it was never just a pint!

'When Jim's cousin and fellow Fifer George Kinnell was signed from Stoke City, it was double trouble, as the two of them loved a drink, loved a party and were pretty much inseparable. And both didn't much fancy training!'

The revelations continued: 'It was George who invented a bar-room drinking game when we were stuck in hotels, which was often the case, as we travelled the length of England to and from matches. It involved working your way from one end of the gantry, one drink after another, and the winner was the last man standing.

88

'Jimmy saw no harm in this at all. He saw it as a way to relieve boredom, and Jimmy was easily bored.'

Martin couldn't wait to get started after his move from Edinburgh. 'I remember my first game after signing. It was Sheffield Wednesday away and I had yet to train with the team, having only travelled down to sign on the day before. The bus stopped to pick Jimmy up and I couldn't believe what I saw. Slim Jim it wasn't!

'Jim was well overweight and looked anything but fit, and when I said, "Big Man, what's happened to you?", he winked and said "That's the way it goes, Neilly boy. I really didn't give a monkeys."

'Jim did give a monkeys, though, of that I have no fear, and while he never lived up to his Rangers form south of the border, that broken leg in Vienna was the real reason, to me. He just wasn't the same player, but there were exceptions.

'At Hampden in 1965 against Italy, John Grieg scored the only goal of the game and I partnered Alan Gilzean up top, but it was Jimmy Baxter who controlled the game in the company of some Italian superstars.'

Neil also recalled an old Inter League game when England entertained Scotland at Roker Park while Jim was still at Rangers. 'That night Jim was unplayable. He showed all his tricks and teased and tormented his English opponents so much that they were frightened to go near him, as he was determined to showboat and take the micky. That performance may have been the reason Jim thought it would work for him at Roker Park. The Sunderland fans loved it, but when he eventually signed for them that brilliance was very rarely seen.'

In Jim Baxter's first season south of the border, Sunderland struggled. There were moments of promise, with Baxter in sparkling form as Sheffield United were beaten 4–1 in August, but the team couldn't gain any consistency, the most they could offer fans a run of three consecutive wins throughout the whole season.

Blackburn Rovers and Aston Villa saw the Black Cats enjoy the rarity of back-to-back wins at Roker Park, and they followed that up with a 2-1 win on their travels at Blackpool, but results were at best patchy. Baxter was showing his brilliance, but with the same inconsistency as the team in general.

On 1 January 1966, it all went wrong, with Sunderland humiliated at home in a 5–1 thrashing handed out by West Bromwich Albion. The fans were less than pleased that their inspirational summer signing wasn't able to lift the team to better things. However, two days later, in the North-east derby that followed the West Brom game, there was some relief, with Sunderland beating local rivals Newcastle United 2–0, with Baxter the star of the show. But again inconsistency was the issue, and Sunderland didn't win a game in the month of February.

Sunderland just could not put a run of victories together and Baxter struggled to come to terms with it – it was in total contrast to his days as a Ranger, when winning was habit-forming. Sunderland brought the curtain down in their league programme with a 2–0 home win against Everton, but over the season it really wasn't good enough. It's not what the fans expected when Baxter swapped Glasgow for Wearside.

Liverpool were crowned champions for the seventh time in their history. The Roker Park club finished a lowly 19th, with thirty-six points secured from forty-two league games played. Northampton Town took the drop into the Second Division, with thirty-three points, only three less than Sunderland.

In the FA Cup, Sunderland were eliminated in the third round, going down 3–0 to eventual winners Everton.

A new season started in August 1966, but Sunderland's problems were just the same. A lack of depth and quality in the squad saw them again struggle to build any momentum and they recorded only four wins in the first three months of the championship. On 5 November, Sheffield United were again dismantled in a 4–1 win and the Black Cats followed that up with another four-goal display in their next home game against Burnley, but any joy was short-lived. A trip to Old Trafford found Manchester United in top form and Sunderland were trounced 5–0.

It took until January before Sunderland recorded back-to-back league wins, which were then followed up with three successive 2–2 draws against Liverpool, West Ham and West Bromwich. They started to climb the table, however the season petered out with only two wins claimed in their final ten games. Sunderland and Baxter were not a good fit. Wrong club at the wrong time, and Baxter regularly commented to anyone who would listen that he had left far better players behind at Ibrox.

At the end of 1966–67, Sunderland had moved up two places in the final league table to 17th but still only finished with thirty-six points, the same as in the previous campaign.

In the FA Cup, things started well, Sunderland beating Brentford 5–2, then Peterbrough United 7–1, before being paired with an emerging Leeds United side under Don Revie. In the first game at Elland Road, Sunderland drew 1–1, but they went down 2–1 at home in the replay. The Baxter influence McColl was after never materialised.

Into season 1967–68 and despite a good pre-season Sunderland were nearer the bottom of the table than the top as Christmas approached. Eight games were lost, four drawn, and with only six league wins on the board Sunderland decided it was time to cut Baxter loose. Baxter himself wanted a bigger stage and had become increasingly frustrated that perhaps the club's ambitions didn't match his own.

13

WEMBLEY RETURN, 1967

'We've got better players'

To say Jim Baxter had enjoyed his first trip to Wembley is more than an understatement. Baxter scored both goals in the 2–1 win over England in 1963, despite Scotland playing the bulk of the game with only ten men. When the Tartan Army again invaded Wembley again two years later, Baxter wasn't available, as he was recovering from his leg break, but the Scots left with a creditable 2–2 draw. Roll on just over a year and that England side under Alf Ramsey were crowned world champions.

Did Baxter need any further motivation when he returned to the squad for the 1966–67 British Home Championship? I doubt it. In fact, when Baxter had first gone to Wembley in 1963 for that epic 2–1 win, he was quoted at the time as saying, 'Wembley … this is the London Palladium. If I don't turn it on here, you can kick me up the backside after the game.'

So a return in 1967 was a prospect that appealed to Baxter. Perhaps he viewed it as a welcome departure from his stress and frustration at the time of playing in a very ordinary Sunderland team.

Scotland had started that year's championship in a pretty flat fashion, drawing with Wales at Ninian Park and beating Northern Ireland by the odd goal in three at Hampden. Baxter missed the game against Northern Ireland but was in the engine room for the draw in Wales. In those days, the home nations tournament was played over the season and the final game saw Scotland travel to take on England at Wembley on 15 April 1967.

England started the game with only one change in the side from the team who had lifted the Jules Rimet trophy at the same venue nine months before, with Jimmy Greaves replacing Roger Hunt, while new boss Bobby Brown surprised many with his team selection for Scotland.

Brown handed a first cap to thirty-six-year-old goalkeeper Ronnie Simpson, despite memories of the last Celtic keeper to play for Scotland at that venue, and the disaster that was Frank Haffey, who had conceded nine goals that unforgettable day in 1961.

However, these were halcyon days for the Scottish game. Apart from Simpson, three other Celtic players – Gemmell, Wallace and Lennox – took the field. Little did anyone know they would be European Cup winners only a month later.

Ronnie McKinnon and John Greig were part of the Rangers side that narrowly lost the European Cup-Winners' Cup final to Bayern Munich within days of Celtic's famous win in Lisbon.

Add into the mix three players who would walk into any Greatest Scotland Ever XI: Billy Bremner, Denis Law and Baxter himself. Baxter's good friend Jimmy Johnstone was missing through injury. Jinky was considered a huge loss, as he had been on target twice when the teams had last met at Hampden the previous year. Despite Jock Stein being in charge at that time, England had headed south with a 4–3 win under their belt.

But now Bobby Brown was in charge, and Scotland had a full-time manager for the first time. The culture of a committee picking the side under the direction of then SFA secretary Willie Allan was no longer in use; Allan used to hand each committee member a list of four players for each position, from goalkeeper to outside left, and by chosing their preferred players members would to pick the Scottish international XI.

Completing the Scots' line-up in 1967 was Chelsea full-back Eddie McCreadie, along with relatively unknown and untried centre-forward Jim McCalliog from Sheffield Wednesday. At the time, it was reported all in the Scotland camp were up for this game, with Denis Law in particular keen to get a result. He is famously recorded as exclaiming 'Bastards!' when it was confirmed to him coming up the final fairway during a game of golf that England had won against West Germany in the Wembley final in 1966. Law had chosen to golf that day rather than watch the game on television.

Now, it was Scotland's time. Baxter and Law were plotting the tactics, with manager Brown almost content to let them get on with it. In the dressing-room, with only ten minutes remaining until kick-off, Slim Jim had his head in the *Racing Post*. When it was suggested that he should perhaps be getting warmed up, Baxter first stretched out his left leg and then his right, and quipped, 'That's me warmed up!' His eyes never left the form guide.

When the game got started, Baxter did look quite out of shape, but he strolled through the game nonetheless.

Joining the Scotland camp for only the second time was Celtic's flying machine Bobby 'Lemon' Lennox. Lennox had made his debut against Northern Ireland five months earlier, with his Parkhead teammate Bobby Murdoch deputising for the injured Baxter, so this, the occasion of his second cap, was his first opportunity he had to hook up with Jim. On the first day in the hotel, Bobby was the new kid in the squad, but he was immediately waived over by Baxter to join him and Law over breakfast. He remembers it well.

'Jimmy just called across the dining room in that quiet Fife lilt, "Over here, wee man ... sit doon an gee's yer patter!" Bobby recalls. 'Jim just exuded confidence and he really was one of the boys, but he was so laid-back. Nothing seemed to get to him, and in the dressing-room ahead of that Wembley match Jim's demeanour rubbed off on all of us. As he said, why should we be scared of them? They may have won the World Cup, but we've got better players.'

As the game was about to start, Lennox got the message from

Baxter, who was playing in behind him, 'Keep moving, wee man, wi' your pace you'll terrorise them, and don't worry, I'll find ye!'

Bobby remembers: 'Jim just kept repeating to anyone who would listen, just give the ball to me, that's all I want.'

With twelve minutes of the match remaining, Baxter did indeed find him with an inch-perfect delivery inside the English penalty box. Bobby dispatched the ball into the net beyond Gordon Banks, giving him the honour of being the first Celtic player to score at Wembley.

But the day belonged to Baxter and Scotland.

England's skipper for the match was Bobby Moore, who had lifted the World Cup just a year before. He and Baxter were similar in as much as they both enjoyed nights out and were known for their incredible capacity to consume alcohol. Both sadly also lost their lives to cancer at a fairly young age. Moore was eighteen months younger than Baxter; he was only fifty-one when he died in February 1993. Moore suffered cancer of the colon, which then spread to his bowel and liver. It has also been revealed that he had testicular cancer eighteen months before that famous World Cup victory, but at the time this was kept quiet by Moore and his club, West Ham United.

It was pancreatic cancer that finally brought Baxter's life to a premature end.

Though similar, both players had different outlooks on life during their careers. While both loved to party, Baxter worked on the assumption that his heavy drinking made no difference to his on-field performance. In contrast, Moore worked hard on the training ground to burn off his excesses. It was well documented that Moore was known to be out on the town every Saturday after a game – often after drinking the buffet car dry of beer on his way back to London, if he was travelling by train with his West Ham teammates from a fixture in the north. Moore would head to the toilet when the train approached Euston to shave, change his shirt and freshen up before heading into town to make a night of it. 'Win or lose, we're on the booze' was Moore's motto, but he always made amends for his indulgence by heading into Upton Park or at the Hammers' training ground at Chadwell Heath the morning after and putting a shift in. The tracksuit would be on and Moore would have the bin liners under it to get a sweat going, then it was lap after lap on the track until he felt the previous evening's intake of lager, with gin and tonic chasers, had been worked off. Not a strategy that Baxter ever adopted, until perhaps very late on in his Rangers career second time round, but by then it was impossible to resurrect the gift of fitness that he'd enjoyed in his teens and early twenties.

But in 1967 it didn't matter. Booby Moore et al. had been put to the sword with a Slim Jim masterclass. The celebrations after the match lasted into the following morning, with it being more than unlikely that Scotland's man of the match hit the training ground the next day. We have no record of Bobby Moore getting it out his system the next day either!

There were the usual after-match formalities to go through before Jim and Denis Law decided it was time to move on and perhaps enjoy some of the delights London had to offer. They had pre-arranged to meet up with their good pal Dave MacKay in one of the bars in the Café Royal just as soon as they could slip away from the banquet. When they met up with Dave and a few of his pals from Edinburgh, the party was in full swing and under a mountain of glasses the table was decorated with a very special 'tablecloth'. It was huge chunks of the unmistakeable green turf of Wembley, which had been uprooted as souvenirs, as thousands invaded the pitch at full time. Jim, Denis and Dave then moved on, as they had an invitation to party at the Savoy with pop star Cilla Black, who at the time had her own television show, *Cilla*.

From the taxi, Jim spotted his 'Wee Dad' and his uncle John walking through central London hours after the game. Jim stopped the car and invited them to join him at Cilla's for a bevvy. His dad Rab replied, 'It's OK, son. Enjoy your night, we're fine. We're going to the pictures.'

Amid all the celebrations there was one man who wasn't quite so convinced by Slim Jim's performance that day. Bobby Brown may have been a rookie international manager, but he had concerns. 'Baxter paid no attention to me – or anyone else, for that matter. He wasn't interested in instructions. It was as if he had his own game plan and nothing was going to change it,' he remembers.

'We actually should have won the game by a bigger margin. Looking at the record book, a 3–2 win doesn't truly reflect the superiority we displayed that day. Jim Baxter controlled the entire ninety minutes and we could have scored five or even six goals, but Gordon Banks had made a couple of incredible saves to deny Denis Law and because of that I wanted to rub it in, so to speak, because there was only one team on the park.

'To use a Scottish term, Baxter was "doing my head in"! Denis Law, too, wanted Scotland to turn the screw. Jimmy and wee Billy Bremner just wanted to take the mickey, but I was still carrying the scars of 1961 and wanted goals.'

In the build-up to the game, the omens weren't good for Scotland, as they set up camp at their regular Wembley base at the Hendon Hall hotel. The bookmakers made England outrageous favourites, with a £1 wager on Scotland offering a generous £4 return. For a visiting winning scoreline at half-time or full time, as the Scottish team managed, that £4 return increased to £8 for each £1 wagered. Injuries and call-offs made it difficult for Bobby Brown to put out the side he wanted, and so he had to settle for a makeshift eleven that he hoped would get the job done.

'I didn't underestimate the task, and indeed it was a pretty daunting introduction to international football management for me. After all, it was the world champions we were facing in their own backyard.'

Scotland had failed to qualify for the 1966 World Cup finals; in fact, Billy Bremner had taken over Bobby Brown's team talk, rousing the players, and none more so than the Anglos, who earned their living south of the border and had been listening to teammates harp on about England's World Cup success the previous summer. The squad was also in transition, though Brown had good players available to him. In fact he had exceptional players in Law, Baxter, Greig, Bremner and Gemmell.

McCalliog was the surprise inclusion and one not many back in Scotland new much about, as he had gone south as a teenager and progressed through the ranks at Leeds, Chelsea and then Sheffield Wednesday.

Brown knew the youngster was ready. 'I had watched McCalliog in an Under-21 game with his club and just felt he was what we needed against England. I wanted to play him in central midfield to complement Bremner and Baxter, and give him licence to get forward to support Denis, as I wanted him right on top of Bobby Moore and Big Jack Charlton, not giving them a minute's peace.

'It worked! Jim Baxter pulled the strings and tormented England, but McCalliog, for me, ran him close for man of the match. He covered every blade of grass, defending when we didn't have the ball and supporting the attack when we did. Of course, he popped up with the crucial winning goal.'

Denis Law agrees with his former boss: 'I was surprised that young McCalliog started. It was a big decision from Bobby Brown. He told me that Jim would do the running, but I had to stop Bobby Moore passing it out from the back. Now, that wasn't the role I had been operating in at United at the time, but that was the game plan, although I doubt if Jimmy Baxter had been listening. Jim just wanted the ball at his feet and then he proceeded to prompt and probe with passes that little Bobby Lennox, young McCalliog and I lived on.

'It was a memorable day, that's for sure, but looking back all these years later, did we just settle for a 3–2 win over the world champions? Of course we did, but maybe, if we had wanted it, we could have won by a record margin and I could have forgotten the events of two years before.'

It's incredible that after this Wembley triumph Baxter would pull on a Scotland shirt only two more times before his career was over. His last appearance for his country was on 22 November 1967 in a 3–2 win over Wales, exactly 221 days after he had been hailed a superstar after his virtuoso performance at Wembley.

However, that was for the future. Baxter's performance that day immortalised him in Scottish football folklore.

It also captured the imagination of teenage Londoner Kevin Raymond. A child of Irish immigrants who had gone along to the game, he was mesmerised by the display of Slim Jim and was compelled to put pen to paper to remind himself that Baxter was on the field doing what thousands of kids were doing in working-class streets all over the world. The poem he wrote captures his memories of the day and portrays his magical times growing up a football fanatic.

A Working Class Hero? Is Jim Baxter to me!

'Go on Grand-Dad tell us,
Tell us of that day,
When Scotland wi' Jim Baxter at his best
Beat the England team away.'

'Well, if memory serves me right,
My bonnie wee lad, the story go's like this:
Scotland made the trip to Wemberly in '67
To play the Champs of '66.'

'Were England unbeatable Grand-Dad?
'Unbeatable? Tis hard to say,
But Scotland led by Baxter
Sure made them pay that day.'

With Jules Rimet stood watching,
Jim Baxter was our conductor in dark blue
Sending pinpoint passes like greased lightning
Almost thirty, forty yards, it's true.'

SLIM JIM

'What did England do, Grand-Dad
Did they try to stop him playing?'
'Aye, my bonnie wee lad, they did try that
But Baxter? He outplayed them.

Grown men were seen to cry tears
For a nation once more proud
As Baxter and his Scottish peers
Brought cheers that echoed loud.

Jim Baxter sat upon the ball
In the middle of the park
Then he'd start the England nightmare off again
With a taunt, a feign, a pass.

They tried hard to get the ball off him
My, how those English boys did try
But Baxter tantalised and sucked them in
Then nonchalantly knocked it wide.

That game you boys play in the street
Keepie-uppie … is it called?
Jim Baxter played that in front of ninety thousand fans
Right along the Wemberly touchline
The England team were overawed.

A young man in his prime he was
Possessed with ball at feet
When England saw him gliding o'er the green
Yon blond cap'n called 'Retreat'.

Baxter walked about the pitch
A God amongst mere men
He'd beat one man, then turn around
And beat that man again.'

'The scoreline! Tell us, Grand-Dad,
How did it end up?'
'Son, the result? It didnae mean a thing
When you drank the heavenly elixir
From Jim Baxter's dark blue cup.

When this game is often talked about
You'll hear praise as old ones sing it
What a match! A terrific victory
But how the hell did Scotland win it?
The other twenty-one? Are sadly part of history, son
'Twas Jim Baxter in a dark blue shirt
Finest ninety minutes!'

I can visualise growing up in London, when you could go to a game, any game, travel by the underground and perhaps be squashed up next to a guy who that day might have been playing centre-forward for Chelsea or centre-half with Arsenal, or was even an inside-forward for Spurs. These were the days of genuine working-class heroes.

Despite his lavish lifestyle, Jim Baxter too was a working-class hero, of that there is no doubt.

14

DOWN IN THE FOREST

'Those were the days'

Sunderland had underachieved and Baxter knew he needed a bigger and better stage for his talents. By December 1967, it was time to move on. Sunderland had been canvassing interest for the services of Baxter, as they needed cash. After his stunning performance with Scotland at Wembley in that historic 3–2 win over the world champions, Baxter's stock was high, but still the big clubs felt Jim was just too hot to handle.

Manchester City, under Joe Mercer and Malcolm Allison, were reported to be interested, but just like a few years previously it was not followed up. Sunderland manager Ian McColl was rebuffed when he offered Baxter to Matt Busby at United, while Bill Nicholson of Tottenham again distanced himself from suggestions that Jim was tailor-made for White Hart Lane.

Baxter wanted to play with better players and was missing big games and winning medals. It was part of the fabric at Rangers that they contested cup finals every year and were expected to win the league title from day one of every campaign. A winning mentality was installed in all the players at Rangers, but this key component was not evident in the Sunderland dressing-room.

Jim Baxter's confidence didn't wane. Baxter still believed he was the best, although he was less than inspired by his teammates. He had secretly hoped a big London club or perhaps Manchester United would take a chance on his wayward genius, but it wasn't to be and again Baxter found himself struggling to play with guys who just weren't on his wavelength.

The Wearside club sold on their prize asset for £100,000, giving them a £20,000-plus profit on the fee they had paid Rangers only three seasons previously.

The campaign of 1968–69 had started badly for Nottingham Forest's title ambitions after crashing out of the Fair Cities Cup to a team of Swiss part-timers, having held so much promise following 5-0 on aggregate in the previous round. Forest then lost three games in a row in November against Fulham, Leeds and Everton, without scoring a goal. It was time for Forest to improve their squad.

The committee-led Nottingham Forest hierarchy needed drastic action, and Rolls-Royce-driving chairman Tony Wood decided that James Curran Baxter was the man to redress the decline; he was the kind of marquee signing that the fans would relate to, even if manager Johnny Carey was less than convinced.

Such a move met no objection from Baxter, particularly when it was confirmed that his share of the transfer was £12,000 and his weekly wage would be enhanced by an additional £20 over his basic pay at Sunderland. Baxter also believed the Forest decline was only temporary, especially with players of the calibre of Terry Hennessey, Frank Wignall and Ian Moore on board.

The Nottingham Forest move, however, proved to be a disaster. The twenty-eight-year-old Baxter who reported for duty was not the same player who had lit up Wembley, and Jim himself knew it.

Baxter did hit the headlines while a Forest player, but more often than not it was front-page news rather than the back pages. Getting involved in scrapes and fights, and being thrown out of pubs and clubs were the sorts of things that grabbed the headlines and Baxter found himself in the Sunday tabloids for all the wrong reasons. Years of indulgence had now seriously caught up with him and the moniker 'Slim' Jim was not nearly as fitting as it had once been.

Months after Baxter joined up at the City Ground, Forest recruited Liam O'Kane, a young defender from Northern Ireland. O'Kane went on to serve Nottingham Forest for thirty-eight years as a player, coach and scout, but when he arrived in 1968 he was eager to play in the same team as Baxter, having witnessed the wayward genius tear Northern Ireland apart on more than one occasion while playing for the national team.

Liam remembers: 'Jim was special, but I was amazed when I turned up for my first day. Everyone was on the training field, but not Jim; he was relaxing in the bath. He wasn't injured, he just didn't train, and I soon discovered this was a regular occurance.'

O'Kane, like Baxter, also suffered a leg break, and knows the mental toughness required to fully recover from such an injury. He believes, like many others, that that night in Vienna went a long way to scarring Baxter mentally. Psychologically, it introduced the realisation of Baxter's own vulnerability. It may also have triggered an increase in his partying – he was suddenly aware that his time at the top was limited.

Jim still exhibited flashes of genius, however. His touch and vision could light up a game. Liam again recalls: 'My first involvement with the first team at Forest was an away game at Old Trafford. In those days it was only one substitute, so I found myself in the stand as the travelling reserve. We kicked off and the ball was passed back to Baxter. His international teammate Denis Law was quick to close him down. Jim dropped a shoulder before pushing the ball through Law's legs, then skipped round him as if he wasn't there.

'Paddy Crerand was next to offer a challenge, but Baxter didn't break stride and nutmegged the former Celtic man, too.

'It was a full house Old Trafford against the European Cup winners and Baxter was in his element.

'He was up there with the best – and I include my former Northern

Ireland teammate George Best in that. The sad fact is that they were both geniuses – but flawed geniuses. Why?'

The 'why' for Baxter might well have been something to do with his upbringing in Fife. Was the change too dramatic, from having very little to having it all?

O'Kane later worked under Brian Clough, who had his own demons.

'Could Cloughie have sorted Baxter out?' he ponders. 'Well, they would probably have been kindred spirits, both a bit tormented, and both took some solace in drink. But it would either have been a match made in heaven or a car crash waiting to happen. I suspect it would have been the latter, unfortunately.'

Ian Storey-Moore was a first-team regular at the City Ground and looked forward to welcoming Baxter to the club, with fresh and fond memories of some of Jim's performances in the dark blue of Scotland, even if he had been less than consistent at Sunderland. The Forest fans and Storey-Moore wanted to go one better than their second place finish in 1966–67, but it was immediately apparent that Jim was no longer 'Slim' and, despite his recent stunning Wembley performance, he was not what fans and teammates had expected.

'Jim was badly out of condition and appeared to have no interest in addressing his fitness,' Storey-Moore claimed. 'Jim was great company, but his wit was much quicker than his feet. He would go missing for days on end, and when he returned it was clear he had been off on a bender. It wasn't unusual for Jim to come in with black eyes, or cuts and bruises from where he had fallen foul of bouncers and stewards from the clubs and pubs of Nottingham city centre. When he had too much to drink, Jim could be a pest, a nuisance, but the problem was Jim didn't know when he'd had enough. Jim was fun to be with until it went too far and he became a different person.

'Bacardi was Jim's tipple and I never saw him with a single, it was always a double. One bottle of Coke was enough for four spirits. It hardly went cloudy!

'Don't get me wrong, I enjoyed his company and we used to go along to Trent Bridge for the cricket. We were friends with the West Indian cricket captain, the great Garfield Sobers, the first man to hit six sixes in a first-class match. Gary was just like Jim. They were kindred spirits. And when they got together it was days and days on the sauce. They became known locally as Drunk and Sobers! It was a nickname for the twosome that was well deserved.'

On the field, Forest manager Matt Gillies, who took over from Carey in 1969, kept hoping for a miracle from Baxter. Carey was an old-fashioned manager and the progressive committee, who had visions of Forest becoming a genuine big club in England, were never comfortable with what they perceived to be his dated methods. Matt Gillies had worked wonders at nearby Leicester and had a wonderful eye for young talent. So it was Scotsman Gillies that the Forest board turned to when they lost confidence in Carey.

'Jim was in self-destruct mode,' said Storey-Moore. 'There were the odd flashes of genius but, being candid, his best days were long behind him by the time he came to Forest. However, you still couldn't fail to like him; in fact, I actually loved him to bits.'

Jim also continued his betting habit. Ian Storey-Moore recalls: 'Jim went to the races at Nottingham with a few of the boys one day and he lost £6,000 in one afternoon. He just shrugged his shoulders and said, "Ah well, boys, it's no' ma day."

'Two dressing-room incidents will live with me forever. Both involved Jim. We were almost ready to take the field when Johnny Carey went over to Jim as he was tying his laces and said, "Big one today, Jim, Manchester United, the top team in the land. Give me a big performance today, Jim. It's a perfect surface, right up your street, the fans are in and are in fine voice. Listen to them! It's your kind of game today, Jim, it's your stage, you can win us the game today, show us what you can do."

'Without any expression whatsoever, Jim gave the manager a glance and broke into song. The song was Mary Hopkins hit of the day, 'Those Were the Days'. He wasn't a bad singer either. Carey just walked away, knowing it was not an argument he could win.

'Jim didn't mean to demean Carey, it was just his way of responding, perhaps admitting that he was no longer capable of running a game from midfield the way he used to.

'Next was an away game at Newcastle, and we were hopeless. One of the worst team performances I can ever remember being involved in. We were back in the dressing-room when the manager came in and was looking for a target for his venom. He could have picked any one of us eleven. We were all shocking that day. As Carey scanned the room, everyone was looking down, looking away or had their head in their hands. Anything to avoid catching his stare or being the centre of attention. Not Jim. Jim just started heading to the bath. The manager confronted him and said, "Jim, you were off it today. Not just off it, you were dire. Just awful." Jim tapped him on the head and said, "Don't worry, Boss. There's plenty more where that came from."

'Typical Jim. Not a care in the world. He was probably already planning his Saturday night out.

'Jim was a genius, of that there is no doubt. When I left Forest for Manchester United in 1972, I saw everything I had witnessed in Jim Baxter repeated in my new Old Trafford teammate, George Best.

'I also remember Jim getting a few of the boys together and heading to York for the races. It was a day when things went well for Jim and by the last race he was up over £5,000. It was a two-day event and Jim was feeling lucky, so he decided to stay over for the second day of racing and made a feeble excuse for missing training. Although there was nothing strange in that, when Jim came in the day after he had lost the lot – not just the £5,000 he had been in front, but a bit on top as well.

'Like Jim, my career was finished at twenty-nine. I couldn't recover from a long-term knee injury. Jim just couldn't handle or cope with his choice of life on the edge, the non-stop partying. Again, like George, his body eventually packed up on him.'

Storey-Moore picked up a solitary cap for England and was actually paraded by Brian Clough as a Derby County player, although he never actually played for them. Derby were committed to making Storey-Moore their record signing in 1972, but the Nottingham Forest board refused to sanction the deal for their star winger, despite County being willing to pay £225,000 for his signature.

Storey-Moore confirms: 'Clough lied to me. He told me a bare-faced lie that Forest had accepted his bid. They had not and the deal never went through.'

Two days later Matt Busby made Storey-Moore a Manchester United player. Brian Clough claimed Forest, who were Derby's biggest rivals, 'deprived the game of dignity'. An interesting comment from a man who had his own demons to deal with. It would have been interesting to get Clough's thoughts on Jim Baxter – how, and indeed if, he would have managed the wayward Fife maverick.

The move to the East Midlands didn't reignite Baxter's desire nor was he willing to show his virtuoso skills, as showcased in that 3–2 win over World Cup winners England in 1967. In fact, analysis shows that the decline of Nottingham Forest runs almost in parallel with Baxter's time at the club.

While back in his early career he could turn on the magic whenever he wanted, in this respect he could not turn back the clock. But when the chance came to return to Rangers, he was willing to try.

In season 1966–67, before Baxter made the move from Sunderland, Forest had finished runners-up to champions Manchester United in the league; only four points separated them from the Old Trafford giants. Forest had won twenty-three games and lost only nine in that campaign, scoring sixty-four goals, conceding less than a goal a game on average.

If for Manchester United the following season it was onwards and upwards – they went on to win the European Cup – for Nottingham Forest it was the opposite. Their fortunes were a million miles removed from those of the Old Trafford side. In season 1967–68, with Baxter on board, of the forty-two league games played, Forest won only fourteen, drew eleven and lost seventeen. They scored fifty-two goals and conceded sixty-four. Forest finished in 11th place, midtable, as Manchester City claimed the title. It was the Sky Blues' first league-winning season since 1937.

In 1968–69, it got even worse. Forest narrowly escaped relegation. Scot Matt Gillies had replaced Johnny Carey in the manager's office, but over the course of the another campaign, the club yielded only ten wins, with thirteen draws and nineteen defeats. The goals tally was a meagre forty-five, while they shipped fifty-seven. Leeds United won the title for the first time in their history, but it was near neighbours Leicester City who were relegated with thirty points, as Forest finished 18th on thirty-three.

Leicester took slight consolation from reaching the FA Cup final, though they lost by the narrowest of margins, 1–0 to Manchester City. Forest had been dumped out of the cup in the third round, going down 3–0 to Preston North End, who were in Division Two at the time.

While Baxter was at Nottingham Forest, manager Carey had been relieved of his duties, as was his former boss Ian McColl at Sunderland. What did fate have in store for his next manager, Davie White, when Jim packed his boots and headed north for his second spell at Rangers?

15

RETURN TO IBROX

Rangers were in turmoil

In 1969, Rangers were in turmoil and Celtic were dominating the Scottish game.

Since Jim Baxter's departure, Rangers had lifted only one trophy, the Scottish Cup in 1966, after a dramatic replay that saw Kai Johansen's goal separate holders Celtic from the cup.

Johansen was one of the early Vikings who sailed into the Scottish game, joining Greenock Morton in 1964 from Odense in his native Denmark. In 1965, Scot Symon made him a Ranger after he had impressed the Ibrox manager during the Stanley Matthews testimonial match. Johansen had been part of the Matthews select side that took on the All Stars, which included a certain Jimmy Baxter and a youthful Willie Henderson.

Rangers had again come close in Europe, losing the 1967 Cup-Winners' Cup final after extra time in Nuremberg to emerging giants Bayern Munich. It was a questionable goal from Franz Roth that won the tie for the Germans at home. With a team struggling with injuries, Symon gambled by playing defender Roger Hynd as a striker and he scorned more than one gilt-edged chance to put Rangers in front. They paid the penalty for missed chances.

In competitive terms, the European arena was still fairly new, but

Scottish clubs were revelling in the challenges it offered. It's incredible to think that Rangers contested that final only a week after Jock Stein delivered the European Cup in Lisbon, making history with Celtic, as the first British club to win it. It was, of course, in that same spring of 1967 that Jim Baxter put on another Wembley masterclass.

Rangers needed to find a way to wrestle back supremacy from their great rivals, who had feasted on the Ibrox club's inadequacies, with domestic trebles in seasons 1966–67 and again in 1968–69. Celtic fell one short of a hat-trick of trebles, with only a league and League Cup double in the season in between. Dunfermline, under George Farm, claimed the Scottish Cup in 1968 to deny Celtic that record. The Pars beat Hearts in the final, though it was the Tynecastle side that had eliminated Rangers at the quarter-final stage. Winners Dunfermline had caused a huge upset when they won 3–0 at Celtic Park in the first round of the competition.

Legendary Rangers manager Scot Symon had been ousted from his position in 1967 and replaced by rookie boss David White. He become only the fourth manager in Rangers' history.

It was a bold appointment.

David White had been a wing-half with Clyde for his whole playing career, then went on to manage the Bully Wee for a season before he got the invitation to join Rangers as assistant to Scot Symon.

Within five weeks of White taking up his post at Ibrox, Symon resigned and White was elevated to the top job. He was only thirty-four years of age and appointed manager of one of the UK's biggest football clubs.

White was up against it from day one, as Celtic were at the peak of their success, and despite losing only one game in his first season in charge – against Aberdeen – Rangers finished the campaign runners-up to champions Celtic. The following season the young tracksuited manager made good headway in Europe, with memorable wins against FK Vojvodina, Dundalk, DWS of Amsterdam and Athletico Bilbao, before losing out at the semi-final stage of the Inter-Cities Fairs Cup to Newcastle United. The teams were tied at

0–0 after ninety minutes at Ibrox, but the Magpies were comfortable 2–0 victors at home at St James's Park.

On the domestic front, it didn't get any better. Rangers were demolished 4–0 by a rampant Celtic side in the Scottish Cup final in front of a crowd of 132,870. Rangers were missing star striker Colin Stein, who was suspended, and without his fire power Rangers never really threatened. It was a day that the tactics deployed by Jock Stein were perfect for the occasion; in the Rangers dugout, David White had nothing to come back with. It was a brutal game, with tackles flying, but Rangers had no match for the pace of Willie Wallace, Stevie Chalmers or Bobby Lennox. In midfield, Bobby Murdoch and Bertie Auld got the better of John Greig and Andy Penman.

Rangers needed inspiration, a talisman, an icon … Rangers needed a player to spark the revival, to bring a lift to the dressing-room and raise morale among the support.

South of the border James Curran Baxter had just been released by Nottingham Forest.

Davie White ignored the advice of many. He thought it would be a gamble worth taking, allowing the now not-so-Slim Jim to recapture past glories and be the catalyst at Rangers to stop the Celtic juggernaught. The fans were delighted at the prospect.

Rangers had competition from Hearts, who made Jim a very favourable and financially attractive offer, but Baxter held out for Rangers in the hope that an offer to return would materialise.

Materialise it did, and Baxter signed on the dotted line in the summer of 1969, captivating the imagination of a long-suffering Rangers support.

T-shirts were quickly printed and offered for sale down Edmiston Drive and the Copland Road. They were emblazoned with the slogan: 'The King Is Back'.

It was only two years since Baxter had run the show as World Cup holders England were humiliated at Wembley. Surely, a return to Ibrox would get the career of the wayward genius back on track. He was moving back to Ibrox, where he had blossomed and become one

It could have been me: 'My adulation with Jim Baxter started in the early sixties in Coatbridge. Almost every night, I would have an anxious stand at the corner of North Bute Street, where his girlfriend Jean Ferguson lived. I would be waiting for the great man's MG to come around the corner. When it did, I would be there with my autograph book in hand and we struck up rapport when Jim would say to me: "No you again, wee man!"'

National
Service
beckons.

The Cup
final that saw
Baxter gift
the ball to Ian
McMillan.

© PA IMAGES

Slim Jim gives a young Pat Stanton of Hibs the slip as Willie Johnston waits on a pass.

Happy times – Mr and Mrs Baxter in 1965.

COURTESY OF TOM PURDIE

Returning from Vienna with a broken leg.

Ralph Brand douses his teammates with a bucketful of water as captain Bobby Shearer holds on to the Cup following Rangers' third successive Scottish Cup final win, which completed the domestic treble. Left to right: Ralph Brand, Billy Ritchie, Davie Provan, Bobby Shearer (holding cup), Ron McKinnon, George McLean, Jimmy Millar, John Greig, Jim Baxter, Willie Henderson (front, seated), Davie Wilson (front, wearing hat).

Treble Season: Rangers players show off trophy haul. Left to right: George Mclean, Willie Henderson, Ron McKinnon, Billy Ritchie, Jim Baxter, Bobby Shearer, John Greig and Davie Provan.

Baxter is raised shoulder high by his team mates as Rangers celebrate another League Cup win.

Scot Symon's face says it all as Baxter signs for Sunderland with his new boss Ian McColl looking on.

1969 at the Albion training ground and less-than-Slim Jim and Alex Ferguson knuckle down to 'skip training'.

Jim Baxter with Rangers Chairman and building magnate John Lawrence, who organised the Bearsden house when Jim came back to Rangers in 1969.

Scotland squad ahead of Wembley 1963. Back row left to right: Alex Hamilton, Eric Caldow, Bobby Brown, Dave McKay, Ian Ure, Jim Baxter. Front row left to right: Willie Henderson, John White, Ian St John, Denis Law, Davie Wilson.

A rarity. A Baxter header at Wembley in 1967 as Nobby Stiles and Billy Bremner look on.

Denis Law celebrating Jim Baxter's goal against England, April 1963.

Jim with Norma, presenting a cheque to Professor James Garden and his team at the Renal Unit.

The Jim and Jinky Roadshow in full swing. Ringmaster Bob Smith had his work cut out for him keeping the boys on the straight and narrow.

The famous Dukla Pumpherston charity football team of 1994, featuring Diamond Dave McKinnon. Other former Rangers in the line-up include Alex McDonald and Johnny Hamilton. Andy Ritchie, John McCormack and John Blackley are also there, as is former World Champion boxer Pat Clinton. Baxter is in the back row, third in from the right. Chick Young is in the front row, fourth from the left.

Jim with Agg and Rab.

Heading for a day
at York Races.

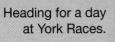

Jim with sons Alan
(left) and Steven.

Jim Baxter with Norma – one month before he died.

Slim Jim. Simply the Best.

of the finest players in Europe. What could be wrong about a return to Rangers? After all, Baxter was not yet thirty years old.

As it was to prove, Baxter was damaged goods. His reputation was in tatters and his confidence had been shot to pieces by his experiences south of the border. Jim being Jim, he hid that lack of confidence well, but he knew he wasn't the same player who had left just four years earlier.

Prior to being given a free transfer by Forest, they had hawked the man they had paid £100,000 for only two years previously round every senior club in the country, with a nominal £15,000 fee on his head. They would have probably settled for less.There were no takers.

The suggestion of Rangers' interest was just the tonic, and although that offer from Heart of Midlothian, under John Harvey, was better than excellent and would have made him the highest-paid player at Tynecastle, and one of the highest paid in Scotland, Baxter favoured a deal to make him a Rangers player for a second time.

By 1969, the Rangers directors realised that they had to match salaries on offer elsewhere, and south of the border in particular, but even then, securing the services of Baxter without a transfer fee was a contentious decision. The board was split before chairman John Lawrence gave manager White final approval to complete the deal.

Initial discussions were for a two-year contract, but Jim elected to settle for a twelve-month arrangement, with the belief that he could negotiate an enhanced financial package after year one. Baxter was intent on proving himself all over again in his first season back. White wasn't the only one taking a gamble. Baxter could have taken the comfort of a two-year deal, but backed himself to succeed.

His strategy looked to be a sound one, as he buckled down to training and was positive in his comments, reinforcing the view he was worth the risk his manager was taking. White was after the 'feel good' factor. Jim, even when not so slim, was his chance to provide it. The new signing certainly captured the imagination of the supporters, who agonised at being second to Celtic during the years of Baxter's absence.

Pulling on that blue shirt again, Baxter's confidence soared and he couldn't wait for the season to start. However, the matter of his signing-on fee had still to be finalised, despite a figure in the region of £12,000 having been agreed. David White knew he had a heavy gambler to deal with, and feared the worst if the payment was made to his new signing in hard cash.

White took the initiative to encourage chairman John Lawrence to provide a house for Baxter and his family as payment in kind. It was the inducement for signing. Lawrence had a massive building empire and immediately made a property available in the leafy Glasgow suburb of Bearsden. The last thing the board or manager wanted was Baxter setting up base camp again in the St Enoch Hotel!

Baxter didn't envisage his reward for signing materialising in the form of a house, but after consultation with his lawyer, and after only twenty-four hours elapsing, Baxter agreed to the plan and the contract was finalised.

It was, with hindsight, quite ironic that the Rangers board delivered a house to Jim Baxter on his second signing, when it was all he had wanted to be able to afford four years previously when he was looking to enhance his original Rangers income. He walked away then with his star in the ascendancy, but was only earning £45 per week. Now he was back, his skills on the wane, his basic weekly wage was more than he had ever earned in his career and he had been gifted a house in a very desirable area. Rangers had also broken new ground by relaxing their rigid wage structure to get their man. White had put his neck on the line.

Deep down, however, everyone probably knew Slim Jim had arrived at the last chance saloon. This was confirmed only six months later when, in January 1970, the word on the street was that Baxter would be leaving Rangers in the summer.

On the park there were still some golden moments, but the Rangers side of 1969–70 was nowhere near a match for the Ritchie-Shearer-Caldow days.

Off the park, it didn't take long for things to start to fall apart either. The day after signing, Baxter headed back to Fife to share his good news and celebrate with his chosen few. The next morning the Rangers manager took a 'heads up' call from a senior police officer alerting him to the fact that, the night before, James Curran Baxter had been apprehended in Fife for drink-driving.

Only twenty-four hours earlier Baxter had promised the assembled media pack inside Ibrox, as he was paraded as a Ranger for the second time in his career, that he had turned over a new leaf and they could be assured of his dedication to restoring Rangers to their former glory.

White couldn't believe it when the call came through, but almost everyone else involved in the Scottish game could.

Colin Jackson, who had a twenty-year playing career with Rangers, was a member of the ground staff when Baxter first left for Sunderland; he had progressed to the first-team dressing-room on Baxter's return. He remembers the return of the 'King' very well.

'I was a huge Baxter fan from his first spell at the club. He had time for everyone, including all the young apprentices. He always craved company and, in fact, when I was in digs at Canniesburn, Jim lived just up the road at Bearsden. It was the kind of house we all would have loved and sometimes, if I was lucky, he would even give me a lift to or from training.

'But when he came back he was barely recognisable on or off the park. He was still the same Stanley, full of fun and not a bad bone in his body, but he was overweight, bloated in fact, while everyone could see in training that his legs had gone. It was tragic.'

When Baxter signed up again at Ibrox for that second stint, it also meant meeting up again with his old adversary, Harry Davis.

Davis was now on the coaching staff under White, with responsibility for the Reserves and the job of physically conditioning the first team. In the case of Baxter that was a lost cause, even for a determined and disciplined character like Davis.

He recaps: 'I put all our history behind me and, to be fair, so did Jim, but it was an impossible task to try and turn the clock back. This wasn't the Jimmy Baxter that I had played with. His self-destruct lifestyle had caught up with him and I wasn't overly surprised. My memory could still vividly recall years previously Jim with the smell of drink on his breath as we changed next to each other. This was not just at training but on the day of games too. It was something I will never forget. He also smoked and didn't care who saw him with a cigarette in his hand. Jim had it all and blew it all.'

Before White had made Baxter a Ranger second time round, Davis urged his boss not to do it. Harold again remembers: 'Davie was determined. He saw Jim as the jewel in the crown of the side he was rebuilding, and he put great faith in him on the false promises and assurances of his intent. Baxter threw it all back in his face. I was certainly not surprised and Davie White shouldn't have been either. In my opinion Baxter's return was wrong for Rangers, very wrong.'

While the parties continued off the field, on the field there was the odd cameo. Things started well, including a win against rivals Celtic, but it was destined to end in tears.

Baxter left Rangers within months of White being discharged of his duties. White was the only Rangers manager never to win a major honour during his tenure, until Paul Le Guen joined him after his short time in charge, between July 2006 and January 2007.

White did get some revenge for all of those difficult days when he was playing second fiddle to Celtic by beating them in the final of the Scottish League Cup in 1973–74 when he was manager of Dundee FC, but at Ibrox it was destined not to be.

16

BAXTER'S BOSSES

'Just give the ball to Jim'

Jim Baxter was never one for authority and he gave a succession of managers a headache they could have done without. Even the best of them took flight when offered the great man as an 'asset'. Leeds United boss Don Revie refused to take Baxter to Elland Road at the peak of his powers because he 'liked to sleep at night'. But when Baxter was focused and delivering what he was capable of on the park, most managers were prepared to put up with his indiscretions, which were at times outrageous. As he matured, whether it was in Glasgow, Wearside or Nottingham, they definitely grew more regular.

During his time in the game, Jim worked under a total of twelve managers, at both club and international level. Willie Butchart was the first, and as manager at Crossgates Primrose he was the man who gave sixteen-year-old Jim Baxter the platform to play football and be paid for it. Butchart had an association with Primrose that stretched for a period of sixty-six years, starting from his involvement at the Fife junior club as a mascot, aged twelve. Butchart also took Jim's second cousin George Kinnell to Humbug Park, named after a pit that was part of Cuttlehill Colliery, which operated on that same site in the mid- to late nineteenth century. Butchart was secretary–manager of the club and prided himself on the fact that he had signed a player who had played in a Rest of the World team. Every visitor to the neat little ground was shown the framed picture of Baxter and the global legends from Wembley 1963. Crossgates Primrose actually closed down in 1960 after Baxter had left, but Butchart started them again in 1983. It's fair to say Jim had a special affection for Butchart and Primrose, and was quoted as saying, 'Willie Butchart did a lot for me and when I go back to Fife I always look him up.' When Baxter left Crossgates for the seniors and joined Raith Rovers, he bought his mother Agg a new washing machine with his signing-on fee.

It was Bert Herdman who next took a gamble on Baxter, signing the skinny miner from Crossgates. Herdman immediately sent him back to Primrose on loan to continue to toughen up. Herdman was Raith boss from 1945 to 1961 and consistently had the Stark's Park side punching above their weight, despite having to sell his best player almost every year just to balance the books. Herdman was old school. A suit, shirt and tie topped with a bowler hat was his normal working attire. He saw something in the young Baxter that others might not have noticed and was hugely influential in allowing his team to play to their strengths; he was one of the first managers to deploy the tactic of 'Just give the ball to Jim'.

Baxter valued the faith Herdman had shown in him and was actually originally reluctant to leave Raith for Rangers, as he felt he still owed the manager for giving him his chance. Jim Kerray was a Raith teammate of Jim's and recalls how he got his chance: 'Jim had been playing well in the reserves, and he was still lightweight, but when we got a couple of injuries Mr Herdman had no problems in selecting him because he knew he had a great football brain. His only instruction to Jim in those early days was "Don't dally on the ball, move it quickly and always show to get it back again!" It wasn't bad advice and Jim was a quick learner. When he got into the team, he never really looked back.'

Scot Symon had spent a lot of man hours cajoling the stuffy

board of directors at Rangers to loosen the purse strings to take Jim Baxter to Ibrox. He saw Baxter as the missing link, the keystone in the side he wanted to build for the assault on Europe, but success on the domestic stage was essential too. Symon had been a wing-half himself in a successful Rangers side, so he knew what he was looking for when he was in the market for a left-half.

Jim Baxter must have been Symon's best-ever signing. Apart from the haul of silverware in his five years at Ibrox, Rangers made a huge profit on the transfer fee received from Sunderland when he left in 1965. Symon managed Rangers from 1954 to 1967, succeeding the legendary Bill Struth.

Symon was sacked in 1967, but by then had taken Rangers to two European finals and had delivered six league titles, five Scottish Cups and four League Cups in his ten years in the hot seat. Consider Baxter's contribution to those trophy success: three titles, three Scottish Cups and four League Cups. Baxter's influence was enormous. It maybe explains why he was given such latitude by management in his time with Rangers.

Eric Caldow thought the manager was too lax with Baxter: 'Symon was too soft with him, no doubt about that ... whatever Jim did, Symon turned a blind eye. Symon wasn't a nice man but Bill Struth was. Struth was different class.'

Centre-half Ronnie McKinnon was a Symon fan, but he too thought Baxter operated by his own rules. 'You just couldn't tell Jim and while Scot Symon was great with me, I wouldn't have got away with half the things that Jim did.'

Symon was a traditional football manager. Rarely seen on the training ground and never seen wearing anything other than a three-piece suit and shirt and tie, he continued the strict Struth disciplinary principles but occasionally allowed Baxter to operate beyond the established code others had to follow.

When Symon left, his assistant David White was elevated to the main job. By then, Baxter was long gone from Rangers, but White and Baxter were to team up later.

119

Ian McColl was the manager of Sunderland, or the Bank of England club, as they were known, because of their dealings in the transfer market. Sunderland had returned to the top flight in 1964–65 and did well. McColl believed Baxter was the player to take them to the next level and he was prepared to maintain their Sunderland 'Bank of England' tag to do so.

McColl had, of course, worked at close quarters with Baxter in the Scottish national squad and the pair had achieved a fair degree of success together.

McColl was the man in charge at Wembley in 1963 for that famous 2–1 win, despite Scotland playing the bulk of the match with only ten men. It was McColl who gave Jim Baxter his first cap in his own first game in charge in 1960, the 5–2 win against Northern Ireland. McColl gave Baxter twenty-seven of his thirty-four caps.

Neil Martin was with Baxter at Roker Park and he saw McColl's desire to get more from his new signing. 'They'd had a good season before Jim arrived and, although I joined after Jim, Ian McColl still had Jim on a pedestal. I think underneath it all Jim respected McColl, but they were both equally frustrated that the team just didn't have enough good players.' Ian McColl had won the Home Championship with Scotland in 1962 and again in 1963. He took up his position at Sunderland after five years with the national team. With Scotland, he won seventeen matches, drew three and lost only eight in his twenty-eight games in charge. At Sunderland, his only club appointment, he managed only thirty-nine wins in 124 games before being sacked in 1968. McColl never worked in football again.

Jock Stein took temporary charge of Scotland during 1965–66 to try and rescue a place at the World Cup finals, scheduled for England in 1966. It was a part-time appointment, as Stein combined the role with his job as manager of Celtic. Stein had been a miner like Baxter before turning full time as a footballer and would have many stories to share with Slim Jim about days at the pit, but Baxter only played under Stein for Scotland on one occasion. It was a special game, mind you. On 9 November 1965 Scotland beat Italy 1–0 in front of a full house at Hampden. John Greig got the winner and Baxter was the provider. It gave Scotland real hope, but it was a decimated squad ravaged by injury that travelled to Naples for the second leg and Scotland were turned over, their World Cup dreams shattered.

Jock Stein won the European Cup with Celtic in 1967, a feat that prompted the famous line from Liverpool boss Bill Shankley: 'John, you are immortal!'

Stein later managed Scotland on a full-time basis, but first-time round his record reflects of seven games, three wins, one draw and three defeats. Stein was awarded a CBE in 1970. Many observers thought he should have been knighted, being the first man to win the European Cup for a British club side.

John Prentice was next in the Hampden manager's office. He was another former Rangers player and had management experience with Arbroath and Clyde. Prentice was Scotland boss for only four games, all of which were at Hampden. Three of the four were lost, the other, his last game in charge, was an unexpected 1–1 draw against Brazil, with Steve Chalmers of Celtic on target for Scotland. It was the only game Baxter played under Prentice.

The Brazil match has memories for Rangers' elegant centre-half of that period Ronnie McKinnon: 'We were training down at Largs ahead of the Brazil game and Jim was his usual confident self the day before the game. I said, "Jimmy, we are playing against Pelé tomorrow. Pelé!" Jimmy said, "Pelé? Pelé? Who's he?" He was half serious. That was Jimmy. He had supreme confidence, was a fantastic player and he genuinely believed he was the best player in the world. Prentice's tenure as Scotland boss was indeed short; he lost his job when the Hampden hierarchy got wind that he was in Canada looking for another job.

Prentice's replacement was Malky McDonald, who was given the job of caretaker manager. McDonald was a Celtic centre-forward of the 1930s. He lasted two games only, and his record is one win, one draw. Baxter was selected by McDonald for only one game, the 1966 1–1 draw with Wales. Interestingly, Malky McDonald managed

Kilmarnock either side of Willie Waddell's spell as manager at Rugby Park.

Baxter then packed his kit at Roker Park and moved on to Nottingham Forest, where his first boss was Johnny Carey. It's fair to say Carey had Baxter foisted upon him. The Dublin-born manager had no influence over Baxter's £100,000 move to the City Ground. Carey was known as 'Gentleman John' and that maybe tells its own story.

Carey was ten years a player at Manchester United and spent seven of them as club captain. He had won promotion while in charge of Blackburn Rovers in 1958 and subsequently managed Everton and Leyton Orient. In his time at Forest, he doubled his duties, being in charge of the Republic of Ireland national side as well.

Carey's coaching was limited, as Forest legend Liam O'Kane remembers: 'Johnny would shout, "Just fizz the ball around and it will come good." He used to smoke a pipe and when we looked over during a game if the smoke was coming out constantly we were not doing well and he wasn't happy. When he was less frantic, drawing on his pipe, you knew he was quite content on the way things were going.'

It's fair to say Baxter had too many distractions in Nottingham and chairman Tony Wood, who was the man that championed Baxter's signing and went a long way to financing it himself, was left disappointed that the new signing wasn't in fact the 'last piece of the jigsaw' as he had been hoping. Carey was relieved of his duties in December 1968, with Baxter still on the books.

Next to take charge at Nottingham Forest was Scot Matt Gillies. Gillies was born in West Lothian but had played almost all his football south of the border. He came with a good pedigree after ten years managing Leicester and had a fantastic record for developing young talent, including legendary English goalkeeper Gordon Banks and Scotland's Frank McLintock. It was Gillies who signed John Robertson and Martin O'Neill for Forest; both later enjoyed incredible success under Brian Clough. Gillies was tactically astute, and was a pioneer of practising set pieces and simulating match action on the training ground. It's recorded that Matt Gillies wanted to cut Baxter loose as soon as he took the job at Forest, but it took him just less than six months to end Jim's time in Nottingham. Gillies left Forest himself in 1972, by which time Baxter's boots were long hung up.

In between Carey and Gillies at Forest, Jim Baxter was still pulling on the dark blue of Scotland, including, of course, for the 1967 epic 3–2 win at Wembley. Bobby Brown was the new full-time Scotland manager and his first game in charge was Baxter's Wembley. Incredibly, Brown never got to field that same team ever again as Scotland manager. Brown capped Baxter three times, including Jim's last appearance for his country. It was a game that brought the curtain down on Baxter's international career. Though he went out on quite a high, with a 3–2 win against Wales in November 1967, it's unlikely Jim Baxter knew at that time that he was finished as far as representing his country went.

Bobby Brown enjoyed working with Baxter: 'Jim was a maverick. It didn't matter what I told him, as he went out and played off the cuff in whichever way he fancied playing at the time. It was frustrating, but you had to balance the brilliance with the bampottery!'

Brown was a distinguished goalkeeper who served Rangers for ten years and managed St Johnstone before taking the Scotland job. Brown took control of Scotland twenty-eight times and can point to a reasonable record of nine wins, eight draws and eleven defeats. He left the international scene in 1971 and turned his back on the game to focus on his family catering business.

By 1969, Baxter was back at Ibrox. This time it wasn't Symon who put his neck on the line to bag Baxter but his thirty-four-year-old successor, David White. Like Symon and Baxter, White was a wing-half, but of no great pedigree. White went against the advice of many and gave Baxter a contract that was worth more than he had ever earned in the game before. Baxter promised to work hard and repay the faith White had shown in him, but it was destined to end in tears.

Ronnie McKinnon recalls: 'White was ahead of his time and radically different to Scot Symon. He had his own methods and styles, but, like Scot Symon, he maybe cut Jim too much slack.'

White was sacked in 1969 but left a legacy of a very good squad that was the nucleus of the team that won the European Cup-Winners' Cup three years later. There had been a high-profile media campaign fronted by former Rangers player and Kilmarnock manager Willie Waddell that David White had lost the principles of Rangers Football Club with a lack of dignity, and results like the European exit at the hands of Górnik Zabrze didn't help. Baxter's on-field influence was nominal and his form little better than patchy. When White was sacked after two years in charge, the Rangers board turned to a journalist to replace him.

White out, Willie Waddell in.

Waddell had won the league with Kilmarnock in 1965 but had been more recently earning his living as a sports writer with the *Daily Express* and the *Evening Citizen*. It could have been construed that Waddell had his own agenda and had orchestrated a campaign to undermine White at Ibrox.

Waddell had made his Rangers debut as a seventeen-year-old and had played for the Ibrox club until he retired, aged thirty-four. When he returned as manager in 1969, he was on a mission to restore the Struth values to the club. Ronnie McKinnon felt his presence immediately: 'Mr Waddell wasted no time in letting the dressing-room know what was expected. Discipline was his first objective and we were all told about the responsibilities we had just representing Glasgow Rangers. It was clear Jim and Waddell were on a collision course from day one. It was never going to work. Waddell took no nonsense and nobody was surprised when Jim's time was up.'

Waddell was indeed the last man to manage Jim Baxter the footballer. It was a sad and acrimonious way to end a fantastic but frustrating career.

Baxter worked under a total of twelve managers in that career. Every one of them would have killed to have had Jim's ball skills and footballing qualities during their own playing careers. Most wanted to 'kill' Jim for the torture he occasionally put them through. A final observation would be that Jim gave far more to all the managers listed than he ever got back, with the probable exception of Carey and Gillies at Forest, who had the misfortune to work with the genius Jim Baxter when he was at his most wayward.

Willie Waddell just wasn't prepared to take the risk.

THE PARTY IS OVER

'Sorry news for you, Jim'

Not only was Jim Baxter's football career at a crossroads, his life was too.

Jim was no longer required in the new Waddell regime at Ibrox and had been given the dreaded free transfer amid strong suggestions that his legs had gone. Deep down, Slim Jim himself probably knew his many years of failing to train had caught up with him and his body was no longer able to match the demands of a still very active and inventive football brain.

James Curran Baxter, Wembley Wizard on two occasions, the second of which was just over two years before, was only thirty years of age, but his days as a top-flight footballer were over. In fact, his days as a footballer full stop were over.

Former teammate Jimmy Millar, then in charge of Baxter's first club, Raith Rovers, thought about offering Jim a return to Stark's Park, but on the advice of others Millar was persuaded that his friend and one-time genius on the pitch was not worth the hassle.

As early as January 1970, the grapevine was buzzing that Baxter would not be given a new contract when his one-year deal expired. The rumours were accurate and in April, when the call came to climb the marble staircase to meet manager Willie Waddell, who had replaced Davie White, Jim was aware of the fate that lay ahead for him.

On his way up to the manager's office Jim met Davie Provan heading in the opposite direction. Provan had tears in his eyes. He had been given the same treatment Baxter was about to face.

Waddell was the new broom, sweeping clean through Rangers. Along with Baxter and Provan, back-room men Harold Davis, Lawrie Smith and Davie Kinnear were also jettisoned, as were goalkeepers Norrie Martin and Erik Sørensen, while Swedish international winger Örjan Persson was placed on the transfer list. Waddell recruited Jock Wallace from Hearts as his right-hand man.

Waiting for Baxter in that familiar room were Waddell and his assistant Willie Thornton, and while he had received many disciplines within those walls, most were from Scot Symon when he had been sitting behind the desk now occupied by Waddell – and more often than not he had been called to this office as a favourite son.

It was Waddell who broke the ice with the comment, 'Well, Jim, this is sorry news I have for you, but I have to tell you that the Rangers Football Club no longer requires your services. I want to thank you now for all you have done for the club.' There was no explosion from Baxter, no bad language, no emotion, no obvious resentment and no resistance; the hurt and frustration were hidden well.

Baxter had returned to Rangers and committed himself to training, shown a willingness to work hard and attempted to rebuild a reputation that was in tatters after his experience with Nottingham Forest. He was determined not to let Davie White down and actually played some good stuff at times in that second spell, but he was not the same Slim Jim. He was not the returning King that many expected and, of course, the Rangers team of 1969–70 was nowhere near as capable as the one he had left just over four years earlier.

Baxter's good friend and one-time international teammate Dave MacKay, who had enjoyed incredible success with Tottenham and Derby County despite sharing Jim's passion for a night out and a refreshment or two, had continually cautioned Jim about the need to train. MacKay preached at his friend, saying his lack of commitment on the training ground would catch up with him. But that was perhaps now a hollow memory for Baxter: he had lost his natural fitness, which had stood him in good stead, and despite his best efforts – he was known to train with bin bags wrapped round his now not-so-slim frame to aid weight loss – it really was too little too late.

There were a couple of incidents that perhaps also influenced Waddell's decision to cut Baxter loose. There was the well-documented drink-driving conviction that coincided with his return to Ibrox and there was an unsavoury punch-up in Romania after a match against Steaua Bucharest, when alcohol had been removed from the after-match banquet but consumed by Jim and some other Rangers players in a local nightclub.

The club's management had taken exception to the players bringing in their own refreshments, while the reaction of the bouncers was hostile in the extreme, with a few blows exchanged with the Rangers players. Willie Waddell was on this trip in his capacity as a journalist and the exploits of the ring leader were not a particularly well-guarded secret. Baxter saw it as a bit of a laugh!

Consider, too, that Davie White's downfall came after Rangers had crashed out of the European Cup-Winners' Cup within six months of Baxter's return, having fallen to Górnik Zabrze of Poland at the second-round stage. On the eve of the second leg an incident involving Jim and his good friend Willie Henderson, which may well have been blown out of proportion, saw the long knives out for manager White, and Baxter again in the news for all the wrong reasons.

Rangers had gone to Largs on the Ayrshire coast to prepare for the match against Górnik Zabrze, with a 3–1 deficit to chase from the first leg in Poland. Twenty-four hours ahead of the game, Rangers planned a light morning training session at the Inverclyde Centre, a short coach journey from the team's base at the Marine and Curling Hall Hotel in Largs. Neither Henderson nor Baxter made the coach journey that day and the fallout was huge.

Willie Henderson and Slim Jim had buckled down in training and had indeed lost weight since returning. They were sharing a room in the hotel and the night before the training session took a sleeping pill each to help them relax. This practice is pretty commonplace when players are stuck in hotel rooms with little by way of recreation or distraction. Basically, both players slept in the next morning. As simple as that.

However, the fact the bus to the training ground departed without them left the story wide open for exaggeration, and the press pack lapped it up amid reports of both players going AWOL and being back in Glasgow partying and gambling heavily in the casinos of the city rather than preparing properly with a massive European tie on the agenda.

Many suggested Waddell had his own agenda to oust White – through his newspaper column he regularly referred to the Rangers manager as 'the Boy David' – but the Górnik Zabrze affair and the reporting of events leading up to the match, which saw Rangers again lose 3–1, going down 6–2 on aggregate, was the last straw.

Despite Baxter opening the scoring in the Ibrox tie, White was sacked and Waddell was appointed as his successor. It was almost immediately obvious the writing was on the wall for Baxter and his second spell at Rangers.

Under Waddell, Baxter made only three appearances, but he never rocked the boat or caused dressing-room disharmony; he just knuckled down and tried to play his way back into the new manager's plans.

Henderson, too, was under fire, although he did last a further two years before eventually being moved on, despite a European final being just around the corner. In May 1972, Henderson took a call from South Africa, with an invitation to join Durban United. Wee Willie still carries disappointment when he recalls the events leading up to his departure from Rangers.

'I took the call from Durban and told them, while it appealed, I had a European Cup final to prepare for and the boss wouldn't

129

be too happy if he knew. The caller confirmed Willie Waddell had already granted his permission for me to join them! The only thing was, he hadn't told me.'

This maybe explains a bit about the way Waddell operated.

Wee Willie also recalls the Górnik Zabrze incident: 'We were given a bawling out by the manager and we deserved it, but the reaction to a minor misdemeanour was out of proportion. We were never out of the hotel.'

As it worked out, Rangers' best performers on that night against Górnik Zabrze were Henderson and Baxter.

The next day White arrived at Ibrox at around 9 a.m. to prepare for training unaware that a meeting of the directors after the game the night before had already sealed his fate. His desk was emptied and he left the stadium within twenty minutes of arriving, no longer the manager of Rangers FC. It was swift and sudden, but perhaps not unexpected.

Immediately, White's assistant Willie Thornton was named interim boss until a new manager was appointed. Within the week, the vacancy had been filled by Waddell, a former front-line team-mate of Thornton in the Rangers side of the postwar years, who, after steering Kilmarnock to the First Division title in 1965, had traded the football field for the Fourth Estate, becoming a sports journalist with the *Evening Citizen*.

Latterly with the *Scottish Daily Express*, where his recent work included a highly critical report on Rangers' internal discipline, or indeed the lack of it, with the Largs escapade in particular highlighted as a bad example of what was going on at Ibrox under White's management, it's easy to see where some felt 'Deedle' was going.

Despite the lack of silverware, Waddell had inherited quality from White, as would be confirmed when Rangers won the Cup-Winners' Cup in Barcelona in 1972, with no less than fifteen players involved in that successful campaign, all of whom worked under White. Sadly, there was no place for the genius of Jim Baxter.

Baxter himself was quoted after his second spell at Rangers saying: 'Never go back, somebody once said. He could have been right.'

As for White, he went on to manage Dundee and guided them to a League Cup win over Celtic four years later.

After Rangers, management was something Baxter considered. When his phone didn't immediately ring with demands for his services, he quietly sounded out some old friends in the press to see if perhaps a manager's job could be secured. Queen of the South declined his interest. His first club, Raith Rovers, needed to replace his former teammate Jimmy Millar, who had chosen not to give his close friend a playing contract only months earlier, and indeed a Baxter was given the job as new manager at Stark's Park – unfortunately, it was not Jim but Bill Baxter (no relation) who joined from rivals East Fife.

When finally lowly East Stirling showed no appetite for the services of the former Rangers and Scotland star, Baxter knew that football had turned its back on him.

The party was over.

18

NO HALF MEASURES

Drinks and laughs galore

Baxter had made a lot of money over the years, especially on his most recent transfers to Sunderland, then on to Nottingham Forest, but he had lost a lot along the way as well. He needed to work. He needed an income.

Like so many other ex-footballers struggling with life outside of the game, a position as mine host in the public house trade looked a good fit and an obvious option. Glasgow was the only real location for Jim Baxter to move into the pub game. After all, he had a fair bit of experience of pubs in that part of the world.

James Curran Baxter took over the licence of the New Regano Pub on the corner of Paisley Road and Admiral Street, not much more than a goalkeeper's kick-out from Ibrox.

What could possibly go wrong? An assured ready-made clientele of a blue persuasion would surely frequent a hostelry with Jim Baxter's name above the door, especially as the former Rangers star promised to play an active part in the day-to-day running of the bar.

Well, it almost went wrong before it got started.

The bar had first been granted a certificate to sell liquor around 1910, but when Baxter lodged his application sixty years later, it was a split decision on whether Jim was to be given the green light to become its landlord. The licence was granted by eight votes to five, but the court was divided after hearing objections to Baxter's application from Glasgow's chief constable. Sir James Robertson recalled the incident when Baxter was convicted for the road offence in August of the previous year, when he was fined £25 and disqualified from holding a driving licence for twelve months. These, of course, were the consequences of his evening celebrating his return to Rangers as a player.

It was reported in the *Glasgow Herald* of 21 October 1970, 'An agent for Baxter said that Mr Baxter was a personality not unknown in football circles and was a member of a famous Glasgow club for a time.'

The agent is quoted as saying: 'At the time of this offence, Baxter had been engaged in an exhibition match in Dunfermline. Persons of his standing suffer from adulation and hospitality which they do not want but is often forced upon them. It was very much a border-line case and he has learned a short sharp severe lesson which he will never forget.'

It was a blinding, match-winning performance from the agent – almost like Baxter himself, controlling a match from midfield and playing to the galleries.

The licence to sell strong drink was granted, and the bar immediately had its name changed simply to Jim Baxter's.

Baxter said afterwards: 'I am delighted. I will be working full time in the public house. We hope to have alterations made by Christmas.'

Interestingly, on the same day, supermarket giant Tesco were refused a licence to sell alcohol from their first store about to be opened in Scotland on the south side of Glasgow. During this period in Scotland, James Curran Baxter's brand of fame on the worldwide football stage was obviously greater than that of Tesco's.

Was a new career in the licensed trade for someone with Baxter's party lifestyle a good move? Well, it should have been. Baxter was an incredible host and on matchdays at Ibrox, which was only a ten-minute walk from the bar, it was always wall to wall with fans and Jim had time for them all. The downside was he was just as happy sharing rounds of drinks as telling tales and reciting his football stories with the punters. Jim still enjoyed the adulation of the Rangers faithful, which was good for perhaps five of the thirteen years Baxyer's name was over the door.

When Rangers struggled on the field, the fans voted with their feet by not attending matches and that affected the numbers who came through the door of Jim's Paisley Road hostelry. If fans were not drinking, it has to be said, Baxter was. At the time, Jim admitted himself, he was putting away the best part of three bottles of Bacardi a day.

Meanwhile, sadly, his marriage to Jean became a casualty of Baxter's lifestyle and errant ways. The couple divorced in 1981.

Former Rangers teammate and Manchester United manager Alex Ferguson once also had a pub almost straight across the road from Jim Baxter's, but while Ferguson kept an eye on his investment in the Burns Cottage, or Fergie's, as he renamed it, with a lounge bar named Elbow Room (how apt, as anyone can recall Alex Ferguson's style of play will agree!), he limited his time with customers and certainly didn't socialise or drink to excess on his own premises. To be fair, Ferguson played until 1974 and took his first steps on the management ladder that same year with East Stirling – the same East Stirling who had rejected Jim Baxter for the same role. Ferguson, therefore, did have other distractions, as he combined his football and business interests, while Baxter was just one of the boys.

Other than family, Baxter was at his happiest enjoying good company, with drinks and laughs galore.

Perhaps football punditry is something Baxter would have taken to, but the opportunity never arose. When you think back to his newspaper columns years before, albeit they were mostly ghost written, the content was usually insightful – enlightening even – and he was never afraid to offer his opinion, even if it did challenge or upset those in authority. Baxter would have excelled in such a role, but in those days TV and radio coverage didn't carry the same level of analysis and a call from the recognised broadcasters never came.

The pub was his only income, but the area around Paisley Road was changing, with old tenements being demolished. Residents who were regulars in the bar moved on, as they were relocated to other parts of the city or to new towns such as East Kilbride or Cumbernauld. As Rangers' on-field slump continued, only the hard-core fans looked in either before or after home games. Many fans were often back in the bar – and even on their second pint – before the final whistle had blown, so poorly were Rangers playing. The level of apathy from the support for the Light Blues was obvious.

Baxter kept the bar going as long as he could before selling up, when fate again played its hand fairly quickly thereafter. Rangers were revitalised during the Souness revolution and crowds were soon flocking up the Paisley Road to see Rangers back in the ascendancy.

It may also be considered fateful that as the pub was sold, Jim met Norma Morton, who became his partner, confidante and soulmate for the remainder of his life.

In those days, licensing laws saw pubs closed in the afternoons, but Jim Baxter's was always good for a lock-in.

Public houses and betting go hand in hand, so it was no surprise that during his time as landlord Baxter's gambling also spiralled out of control. Horses, dogs and card games in the pub saw huge sums of money changing hands. Even side stakes over a game of pool often ran into four figures.

Jim had been introduced to gambling as a ten-year-old boy back in Fife. He would collect lemonade bottles and cash them in for a few pennies, and then they would get a 'tossing' school together. Two coins were tossed in the air and bets were placed on whether they would come down both heads or both tails. It wasn't long before the stakes were raised and the value of the coins was only symbolic, with hundreds of pounds being won and lost. Pontoon was also commonplace and played in every mining community from Fife to Yorkshire. If it involved gambling, Jim Baxter had probably experienced it.

135

Gambling was a way of life for him and while running his own pub, things were no different. Regularly, the bar takings were lost on bets laid at local bookmakers, with the selection of bet too often influenced and fuelled by Bacardi.

It was a lethal combination.

Baxter himself could not put a figure on what he had gambled away over the years, but suggestions of values in excess of £250,000 are unlikely to have been exaggerated.

It wasn't just pool that was the side bet attraction in Jim Baxter's bar. With a few regulars, Jim would cover customers bets on as simple a chance as what colour or style of shoe would be worn by the next punter coming through the door.

One visitor to the pub who got caught up in the closed shop afternoon activity was Jim's former Ibrox teammate Willie Henderson. He had popped in one afternoon 'after hours' for a bottle of lager.

Now, Willie fancied himself as a pool player and when he took on one of Baxter's regulars and potted five balls after his opponent broke but sunk nothing, Willie was playing to the galleries. 'Get some cold water,' said Willie, 'this cue is red hot.'

Bets were being struck all around the room, with not a lot of money for the former Rangers winger. Despite the good start, by 5 p.m. Willie was down around £600.

Just another afternoon in Baxter's bar.

To this day, Willie still says it was the most expensive beer he's ever had in his life.

Willie may have got off lightly. Around the same time, another customer got caught up in an afternoon card school and, feeling confident, threw his Mercedes keys into the pot as collateral against what he thought was a good hand in a game of Three Card Brag. The mug punter was lucky to leave with enough to cover his taxi fare home, while the winner headed off in style in his newly acquired luxury car.

Never a dull moment.

Typical Jim Baxter: no half measures.

19

JIM AND JINKY

'An amazing friendship'

With Jim Baxter's public house now firmly consigned to history, the one-time Ibrox idol needed an income and opportunity knocked from an unusual source.

Paul Cooney was head of sport at Radio Clyde, passionate broadcasters and champions of Scottish football since their first transmission. Paul had the idea to pair Old Firm legends Jim Baxter and Jimmy Johnstone as a dream team on the clubs and pubs circuit. Both men had tales to tell and were real characters in their own right. The pair got on well together and, with the balance of Rangers and Celtic in equal proportions, the formula of the Jimmy and Jinky Roadshow, he thought, was undoubtedly a recipe for a sell-out tour.

Cooney recruited well-known football broadcaster Bob Smith to host the shows. Bob was a veteran of Radio Clyde, Sky Scottish and iconic STV show *Scotsport*, but I doubt if anything he previously experienced would have come close to or prepared him for the escapades on the road with not one but two of Scotland's greatest-ever players.

Baxter had found favour back at Rangers and revelled in his role as a matchday host with the prawn sandwich brigade on corporate visits to Ibrox. Slim Jim was at his happiest in company, especially when football was the topic of conversation.

Rangers historian David Mason worked closely with Jim and got to know him quite well when they were regularly paired together on hospitality duty.

David recalls with fondness: 'Jim was gold dust. He was not just a really nice chap, he was always approachable for the fans. Not what you would expect from a genuine superstar. He had time for everyone, and I never saw any sign of the on-field arrogance being transferred to his hosting duties, but he still had that devilment in his eye and loved a wind-up. Jim Baxter was a special person and a real gentleman.'

David also highlights how Baxter was adopted by Rangers fans; he was taken to the hearts of the Gers supporters from the day he arrived in 1960. Even after he left, many still saw him as number one. There was a degree of reticence, too, from the fans: although they were disappointed when he left, they stayed connected with him, even when he failed to look after himself. Jim allowed his weight to balloon and saw his career go downhill at an incredible pace.

'He was one of them. One of the Rangers family,' says Mason, which sums things up nicely. 'When I ask any of Jim's contemporaries at Ibrox who was the best player they ever played with, without hesitation they say, to a man, Jimmy Baxter.'

The Jim and Jinky show was ready to roll. The plan was to take the show as a 'Questions and Answers' event all across Scotland and into selected venues in England, places where a high proportion of Scots were living.

Bob Smith takes up the story: 'My role was to compère the show and my initial feelings when I met Jim for the first time were and are still very clear. Jim told me in no uncertain terms, he said, "I am the boss." He had an aura and I was pretty much in awe of this Wembley legend.'

Smith then had to use all his powers of psychology to keep Jim in check; Baxter laughed like a drain when Bob retorted in a Bruce Forsyth voice, 'I'm in charge!'

However, Jim had pride in his performance and showed an unexpected level of professionalism. He took responsibility for all promotions and publicity for the shows, while he rehearsed the content with Jinky every night before they took to the stage.

Very quickly, Jim had a DVD launched to support the roadshows and you could see and feel the pride he was gaining, as he realised he was wanted and had worth again, as both Rangers and Celtic fans flocked to see two of the finest players each club had ever had on their books.

Bob continues: 'Jim and Jimmy Johnstone had an amazing friendship and an incredible respect for each other. Rivals on the park, but now they looked after each other and really established a bond that was amazing to witness. Jim, too, was always analytical after a show and critical of his own performance, saying, "I wish I had said this or I wish I had said that" and he would build that in for the next show. Jim wanted to get it right, but he still took a bit of managing.'

One of the first shows was in Corby, Northamptonshire, where the steel industry had seen a huge influx of Scots in the 1960s. It was Thursday night and the stage was set for the Jim and Jinky show in the Corby Celtic Supporters' Club. In attendance were members of the Corby Rangers Supporters' Club, ahead of them hosting a gig the following night.

The show went well and both Jims were in fine form, sharp-witted, full of stories, and the pair bounced off each other with a real spark. Bob again picks up the tale.

'Night one was a rip-roaring success. We met with the Rangers club committee the day of the show to go over a few points. Jinky kept disappearing during discussions on the pretext that he was playing snooker, but unbeknown to me he was downing quite a considerable amount of alcohol, both beers and shorts. Not being a drinker, I had no idea how this might affect him. Baxter said it was going to be tough to do the show that night when he saw the condition of the Wee Man. He suggested Jinky should take a shower to sober up and Johnstone agreed, on the condition that his pal Stanley took one, too. Can you imagine, two of Scotland's greatest-ever players in a shower together ahead of going on stage with their chat show? Neither could concentrate on the shower for laughing at the other.'

To nobody's great surprise, however, it worked and both went on stage and brought the house down with another great performance. Of course, there was another slight twist from the shower incident. Baxter, who had sunk a few jars himself, had a request of his own. Bob couldn't believe it when Baxter said to him, 'Introduce me as Hector Nicol. I'm not going on unless you tell the punters it's Hector Nicol!'

Baxter dug his heels in and eventually Bob took the mic and, needing to get the show going, said, 'Ladies and gentlemen, it gives me great pleasure to introduce a Glasgow Legend … Ladies and gentlemen, the best of attention please for … Hector Nicol!'

Baxter was in tears! He thought this was hilarious, and Jinky, who wasn't in on the plan, was bent over with laughter. As Bob says: 'You can imagine the reaction of the audience, but they all saw the funny side when the man they had all turned out to see stepped forward. Typical Stanley – he loved a prank!'

The show again hit all the high notes and both former players left the stage to loud applause. But the drama of the evening was not yet over.

The three bold boys had made the journey in Baxter's car, and as Jim and Jinky had enjoyed the hospitality of their Corby hosts, perhaps even a little too much, Bob was given the job of getting the trio back up the road. Smith got the foot down, with the two legends crashed out in the back seat behind him.

Bob continues the story: 'I was in a hurry to get home, as I had another Radio Clyde commitment early the next day, so I put the foot down. Maybe just a wee bit too far down, as we sped up the M1.

'I heard the siren and spotted the dreaded blue light in my rear-view mirror. As the police car got closer, it was obvious it was me they had in their sights. I was duly pulled over. The cops approached the car and went through the usual routine that saw me explain I was teetotal and ferrying this pair of ex-footballers back north. That seemed to lighten the mood. They asked who my passengers were and when I told them, the senior officer's face lit up almost before I had finished getting Baxter's name out!

'The policeman confirmed he was a Sunderland fan, and Jim Baxter was his all-time hero. I had to wake Jim up and explain the situation. Jim immediately switched on the charm, almost as if he had waved a magic wand. After a brief chat we were indeed waved on our way, and as the offending driver I was mightily delighted not to have picked up a ticket. I think, had we pushed it, we might even have got a police escort back to Glasgow.'

One other story from the Jim and Jinky period involved a memorable event at the Penicuik Masonic Club. It was a Sunday afternoon gig arranged by Rangers goalie Andy Goram. Bob recalls the details: 'As we got set to take the stage, the Wee Man insisted that I introduce Stanley first. Jim stepped forward to a very warm welcome. Next up, I introduced Lisbon Lion Jimmy 'Jinky' Johnstone, a man who had inflicted so much agony on Rangers and their fans over the years, but tonight he had lined up a special memory for his big pal Stanley.

'Jinky joined Jim and me on stage, and after the usual introductions and opening chat Jinky said it was very warm in here and would the audience mind if he removed his jacket? Very polite! With no objections to the jacket removal, Jinky stood to reveal a Masonic Apron rolled from his lap, which he had picked up in the committee room when nobody was looking! It was classic and went down a treat. Jim Baxter said it was one of his best laughs ever and he will have had a few!'

Bob did a great job keeping two rascals on track and both loved that brief return to the limelight. I dare say the show fees were welcomed by both.

Smith remembers those days fondly. 'How lucky was I?' he says. 'Working with two absolute legends and being able to call them both friends was just incredible. It's hard to believe that we lost both at a fairly young age. In fact, Jim Baxter almost knew he was destined not to see old age. I recall dropping him off at his Shawlands flat one night and he said, "Bob, I'll be dead in five years." Sadly, he was right, but what a sad loss he remains. It was a privilege to have known him.'

It is fantastic that two legends could work so closely together, despite being from either side of the Old Firm divide. For Baxter, life was for living and he considered it far too short to get involved in bigotry, race or religion fallout. Baxter was a Fifer, a man of the people; he only craved company and a few laughs along the way.

Around the time of the Jim and Jinky roadshows, Baxter would still pull on the boots occasionally to star for the charity football team Dukla Pumpherston. Dukla were a team made up of former footballers, media people and sporting celebrities. They would play almost every Sunday if a good cause needed their coffers boosted.

Dukla still took their football seriously, but they were like a troupe of travelling entertainers who loved to have a laugh along the way. This company was right up Jim's street, even though he wasn't able to play as often as he would have liked. It was camaraderie he craved. It was rolling back the years to when he was the main man, and he was still idolised by his Dukla teammates. The crowds were more than happy to pay their hard earned money and flocked to see him, despite his playing days being more than twenty-five years behind him.

Another former Ranger, Dave MacKinnon, whom Celtic's former player and manager Tommy Burns had nicknamed 'Diamond' because he played for Airdrie and couldn't bring himself to acknowledge the fact he was once a Ger, was also in the Dukla squad.

Diamond, now a director at Hamilton Accies following spells as chief executive with both Kilmarnock and Dundee FC, was in awe of just being in the same team as his boyhood hero. He recalls the Dukla Pumpherston days with relish: 'I was retired from playing, but I would still run about like a madman, while Jim would just patrol the middle of the park, as he was not very mobile by this time.

'But he could still pass the ball. I can remember the first time I played a one-two with him! I was ecstatic to have received a pass from the great Jim Baxter. It was a dream come true. I was chuffed. Actually, I was even more chuffed when I first met him and he said, "I remember you wi' Rangers … Ye'd tackle a brick wall!"'

The Dukla Pumpherston side of that era would regularly feature Chick Young from the BBC, ex-Hibs and Celtic defender Jackie McNamara, Morton legend Andy Ritchie, 'Sloop' John Blackley, boxer Pat Clinton and Alex 'Doddy' McDonald, who was a European Cup-Winners' Cup winner with Rangers in 1972.

MacKinnon remembers the social side of their games as well: 'I am a non-drinker, but Jim loved to sit with the boys after the game and have a few beers or a spirit or two. He'd captivate us with stories of his playing days. When Jim spoke, everyone listened, and he revelled in the company. I guess he was never happier than when it was the lads together, a couple of bevvies, football talk on the agenda. That was why the Jim and Jinky show was the success it was. Jim Baxter was a natural. He had no agenda other than to have a good time and he could easily mix in any company at all.'

The Dukla days and the roadshows were almost a throwback, and one has to just think back to those afternoons in Ferrari's restaurant in Glasgow with Jim, the Rangers star, in the ascendancy. The company included a host of Celtic players: Billy McNeill, the Celtic legend known as Caesar, Paddy Crerand, former Celtic and Manchester United player turned TV pundit (as he has an opinion on everyone and everything) Mike Jackson, and Tommy Gemmell. Hardly a shy bunch and all dyed-in-the-wool Celtic men.

But not for a minute did Baxter give that consideration. He was with his pals.

An unusual alliance between Jim and Jinky it may have been. Double trouble it certainly was. But they carried huge respect for each other. A respect that didn't deteriorate even as the health of both men sadly went into decline.

20

BAXTER AND THE MEDIA

'He had great elan in his play'

In 1991, well-known journalist and broadcaster Chick Young decided Jim Baxter should have a testimonial dinner. Like Jim, Chick was a 'Southsider'. He was also captain of the charity team Dukla Pumpherston, for whom Jim still occasionally turned out.

Chick knew that if Jim wasn't at home, he would find him in his 'office', as he liked to call it. It was the Georgic Bar on Pollockshaws Road. Salubrious it wasn't, but again, it was an environment that Jim was comfortable in and he was accepted there as a local and regular, and not just another former footballer living on past glories.

A gala dinner was arranged in the Thistle Hotel in Glasgow, with more than 1,000 in attendance. Everyone stood and cheered as Jim walked to his place at the top table as guest of honour, with the spotlight on him. Chick, chairing the event, introduced him: 'Ladies and gentlemen, the finest left-half the world has ever seen!' As Baxter took his seat, he took the mic from Chick and retorted, 'I've never left a half in my life!'

The highlight of the night might have been the auction, where the main prize was the original shirt Slim Jim had worn for that infamous Wembley win of 1967.

Chick tells the story: 'We wanted to make this a special night and a good earner for Jim. The Wembley shirt was the absolute real deal and we put together a letter of authenticity to add value for any bidders.

'There were a few big hitters in the audience, but I had rigged up a landline on the top table and invented a telephone bidder, a memorabilia fanatic from Zurich in Switzerland. I knew this would get the stakes raised. We went to £10,000, £11,000, £12,000 … Others got off the pot, but it left three bidders only. The "mystery" collector from Switzerland, a Glasgow businessman and David Murray, then chairman of Rangers. When the bid got to a remarkable £16,000, I decided that it was time for the telephone bidder to leave David and the other chap to fight it out. Next bid was £17,500 – the exact figure that Rangers had paid for Jim's services back in 1960. Now here we were about to see someone pay that same value for a momento from arguably Jim's best-ever game.

'The hammer fell and the new owner of the shirt wasn't David Murray but Ronnie Wishart, who was the managing director of Archer Motor Group in Glasgow.

'That shirt still enjoys pride of place and can be seen in the Falkirk showroom to this day.'

To put that value into context, £17,500 in 1991 was just about £1,000 less than the annual UK average salary and would have bought you three brand-new top-of-the-range Ford Escorts.

Chick and Jim bonded from their first meeting, when Chick was a cub reporter with the *Daily Record*. Chick also reckons he was present when Jim pulled on his football boots for the last time. 'It was around the time of his testimonial dinner and Dukla Pumpherston had been invited to Mull to play a match to open new playing fields on the island. Jim was first to have his name down for the trip and when we set off in our minibus, it's fair to say we had quite a "cargo" in hand for the journey. Or so we thought … With Jim in fine form, it was all but finished before we got to the Erskine Bridge! We also had another problem: the last ferry would not get us in on time before last orders. So we fixed that by arranging a local fishing boat to deliver us to Tobermory long before the bell rang.

'We had a good night, and the whole town was out to welcome our team, but Jim was the only show in town. He was the man who everyone wanted to see, and he was never allowed to put his hand in his pocket to buy a drink. This was actually one of Jim's problems. He was such a sociable guy when he got a refreshment or two, and although he was in good company he just didn't know when to stop.'

Dukla took on a local select the next day and Jim was determined to play. Chick won the toss and decided to kick off.

'I touched the ball to "Dingy" Hamilton, who was another ex-Ranger, and he slipped it back to Jim in the left-half area. Now, by this time Jim was big. And I mean *big*. We had struggled to get a shirt to fit him. He had insisted on wearing his favourite number 6. As the ball came on to him, Jim stubbed it with his "glove", or left peg, as he called it, and the ball popped forward around three feet before bouncing and spinning straight back to him. It might have been more than twenty years since Jim had last played profession-ally, but he still had such a magnificent touch that he could control the ball and put enough backspin on it to come straight back to him. Everyone just looked on in astonishment.

'But Jim wasn't content with that. He then replicated his Wembley showboat, with a few keep-ups and then went to sit on the ball.

'Disaster!

'As Jim crouched to sit, it moved and he fell over, pulled a muscle in his back and was stretchered off. The game was less than forty seconds old, but he went off the field to a hero's welcome. Jim retired to the bar and comforted himself with a couple of large Bacardis.'

Another television and radio presenter who also built a bit of a bond with Jim Baxter was Jim Delahunt, who used to present the iconic *Scotsport*. Delahunt is now the main man on Radio Clyde's *Superscoreboard*, but when he and Baxter's paths first crossed it wasn't football that was the topic of conversation, it was the gee-gees!

Jim had been a useful footballer in the Ayrshire Junior ranks, but he was also a trainee jockey. It's easy to see how the two Jims were comfortable in each other's company.

146

Delahunt rolls back the years: 'I met Jim for the first time in July 1984. He was a regular visitor to Tarbert, Loch Fyne, where my girlfriend came from, and I had seen him in the bar of the Tarbert Hotel on the quayside on several occasions with his pal, John Morton. On the Saturday of the King George VI and Queen Elizabeth Diamond Stakes at Ascot, we both found ourselves in the front bar, lacking a TV screen to watch the race. Jim sensed I was in the same boat as him and we got talking about horses and racing and who we thought would win the big one at Ascot.

'It wasn't long before we both realised we were on the same horse, Teenoso, ridden by Lester Piggott, and the winner of the previous year's Derby at Epsom at 9/2.

'I had a column in a weekly paper at the time and there was no way Jim would have known me from Adam, but I had grown up in Saltcoats with a kid who would shout, "I'm Jim Baxter" when we were playing shooty-in, so I was more than well aware of who he was.

'Over a few pints we worked out that, one way or another, we were going to see this race and eventually a barmaid said we could get a room upstairs with a TV to watch it in private.

'She proceeded to send up two pints of lager at twenty-minute intervals and we watched and cheered as Piggott and Teenoso took the lead three furlongs out and were never headed by the great Sadler's Wells, which finished second. Tolomeo finished third, and the favourite, Time Charter, trailed in fourth.

'The time of 2 mins 27.95 seconds was the second-fastest ever in the great race. Baxter and I must have spent every penny we had won on celebratory drinks.

'I met him a few times after that and we never stopped giggling about that memorable day in Tarbert when we got completely sloshed, thanks to Piggott and Teenoso. A great footballer, in my book. I could not say I knew him as a man, just as a companion whose company was pretty special indeed.'

As a commentator on all things Scottish football for forty years

147

with the BBC before retiring in 2005, Alastair Alexander held Jim Baxter in the highest esteem. Alastair has a special memory of Wembley 1963, saying: 'I was not with the BBC in 1963, but I was commentating mostly for the visually impaired at various football grounds rather than on radio, and it was as a fan that I travelled to Wembley in 1963.

'Now, most people remember Jim Baxter and his keepie-uppie antics at Wembley 1967, but few recall that he had actually done the same thing four years before. It was 1963 and as the teams took to the red carpet for the pre-match pomp, Scotland were first to be introduced to Lord Derby, who was head of the Football Association at the time and first in the line of dignitaries. Scotland captain Eric Caldow, whose match lasted only a matter of minutes that day, following the leg-breaking challenge from Bobby Smith, introduced his ten teammates.

'As the officials moved on to meet the home side, Jim Baxter had already tired of the ceremony and had started to amuse himself with some ball juggling and an impromptu game of keepie-uppie that had the visiting fans in raptures. It was an act of supreme confidence from a man who was a supreme footballer. Maybe the fans saw it as a sign; Baxter just took the game by the scruff of the neck. He almost won the match single-handedly. It was a tragedy that Baxter's career ended prematurely. I did have pleasure in commentating on Baxter with Scotland a few times after that 1963 experience, but it's the one thing I will never forget when anyone raises the subject of Jim Baxter.'

Alastair goes on: 'I attended Jim's funeral in Glasgow Cathedral when he died in 2001 and it was such a tragic loss. I had total respect for him and I consider myself very lucky to have enjoyed his company on a couple of occasions.'

Another doyen of broadcasting in Scotland is Archie Macpherson, who has covered football for more than four decades on both radio and television, and indeed had his contribution to the Scottish game recognised with a BAFTA in 2005. Archie recalls Jim the player and

Jim the man, saying: 'On the field, Jim was quite imperious, particularly in his first spell at Rangers, in those heady days of the '60s when Scotland claimed we were world champions, being the first to beat England after they had won the World Cup. He could be a bit of a rascal too, and that devilment came through in his play.

'We should cherish those memories, as he was quite unique in his style and swagger. He had great elan in his play and was, to use a great Glasgow word, "gallus" in the extreme. I loved watching him play, and he played the game the way it should be. A beautiful game.'

Archie was in Jim's company not long before he died. 'It was the Variety Club Ball in Glasgow and with my wife I shared a table with Jim and his partner, Norma. As it was, it was only weeks before his sad death, but we didn't know that at the time. I was saddened by his condition that night. The end was nigh and his decline had been rapid. He was shrunken. Effectively, he was finished, we could all sense that, yet he still tried to put on a brave face, but he was a hollow imitation of the Jim Baxter of old, who had majestically strolled about football pitches, controlling top games against the finest opponents in the world. Here he was, not quite on his death bed, but we knew, as he struggled for breath and could hardly talk, that Jim's time was just about up. A great man and a great loss. So sad.'

Derek Johnstone set a postwar Rangers record, scoring 132 of his 210 goals in league matches, until it was broken by a certain Alistair McCoist. Johnstone exploded on the scene with the only goal of the 1970 Scottish League Cup final to beat Celtic, a win that saw Rangers claim their first silverware in four years. Derek was sixteen years and 355 days old when he climbed above Celtic captain Billy McNeill to head home that winner.

Johnstone carved out a very successful career in the media after his playing days were finished, featuring regularly on both radio and television, and remains the match analyser on the Rangers official television channel.

But back to those early days, and Dundee-born Derek could easily have passed Jim Baxter on his way out of Ibrox, as he made his way in. Baxter left in the spring of 1970 and Derek joined in the summer of the same year. Before becoming a full-time professional with Rangers, Derek had trained with the first team on a few occasions in the preceding season. He laughs when he recalls the first time he saw Baxter on the training ground.

'It was at the Albion. I was just a kid, but I was big for my age and could hold my own, playing with bigger lads, so I was asked to join in with training with the first-team boys. I looked over as we were lapping the park and Jim Baxter was lying flat out behind the goals. I asked one of the other lads if he was all right or was he injured, and he said, "Don't be daft, Jimmy doesn't train!" He was having a kip.

'Jim Baxter was sound asleep while the rest of us had to put a shift in. Do you know this, though? I still rate Baxter as the best player ever in Rangers' history. Alan Morton would be a candidate, and Davie Cooper, who I played with too, but for me Jim Baxter just shades it as the best ever, the top man!'

Another self-confessed Rangers fan, from a slightly later era to Baxter's heyday, is writer and broadcaster Graham Spiers. Graham is regularly heard on the BBC and is a columnist for the *Herald* newspaper. Graham conducted what was probably Jim Baxter's final interview only a few months before he died. He remembers: 'I belong to a certain age of Scottish football fan who is too young to remember Jim Baxter in his prime – though plenty people told me all about Slim Jim. So when the point came, many years after his career had ended, for me to meet him and interview him, I seized the moment with relish.

'Baxter was quite often seen around the south side of Glasgow, which became his lair in later life, and there was often a minor stir as he walked into a restaurant somewhere along Pollokshaws Road. You'd see older men nodding and whispering to their (bored) wives something to the effect: "That's the great Jim Baxter just walked in …" I was in one restaurant myself in the mid-1990s and witnessed just such a moment.

'The time for me to go interview Slim Jim finally came in November 1999, just two years before he died. The hook for my interview were the forthcoming Scotland–England play-offs for Euro 2000: it provided the excuse to wander back thirty-two years in Baxter's company to that afternoon in 1967 when, in the dark blue of Scotland at Wembley, he personally toyed and taunted England in Scotland's famous 3–2 win.

'When I caught up with him, Baxter was just Baxter: chirpy, garru- lous and endlessly piss-taking, even after all these years, about the supposedly great England players. I remember in particular his mirth over Alan Ball and his "wee squeaky voice", which Baxter likened to Jimmy Clitheroe, a popular radio and TV comic of the time. "Wee Alan Ball sounded just like Jimmy Clitheroe," he said, "so I went up to him and said, 'Is it true that your dad is wee Jimmy Clitheroe, cos you sound just like him.' Well, he went f*****g spare and chased after me the whole game, trying to kick me. It was a great day, that, in 1967."

'He continued: "I did a bit of keepie-uppie and I remember Denis Law back-heeling the ball to me at one point. It was great fun. I went to the pub to celebrate for four days after that win. I didn't return home until the Thursday."'

Baxter in later life – indeed, all through his life – was typical of a certain breed of gifted Scottish footballer back then: he was great fun to meet, and a nice bloke, but you knew that both indiscipline and a certain lack of responsibility were deep-rooted within him. While Jim enjoyed himself, others close to him had to handle all the chaos.

'What I found fascinating about Baxter, to fast-forward to more recent times, were the views of Ian McMillan, the Wee Prime Minister, whom I interviewed in February 2014,' Spiers recalls. 'McMillan was a teammate of Slim Jim's in that great Rangers side of the early 1960s, but he was also totally different from the feckless Baxter. McMillan was sober, responsible, a church-goer, all of which came out pretty sharply in the way he spoke about his old teammate.'

In its midst, there were McMillan and Baxter: the former a clean-spoken, church-going erudite man, the latter a feckless sybarite who just wanted to have a good time. McMillan on Baxter is fascinating.

'Jim Baxter was a silly man in many ways,' McMillan tells me. 'Had it not been for his behaviour, he could have played for an awful lot longer, he was such an inspirational player. He didn't need to think what he was doing on the pitch, it just came naturally. He was absolutely brilliant; Jim went by men as if they weren't there.

'I used to go in to Ibrox on a Saturday morning, only to hear what Jim had been up to on the Friday night. If he hadn't played for Rangers, he'd have been locked up some nights. He was that sort of chap.

'But he had a good streak in him as well. He could be kind and generous. The shame of it is, but for his lifestyle, he could have played for far longer.'

21

THE SECRET

'Devastating'

Cowdenbeath might have been known as the Las Vegas of Scotland, what with the mining community almost to a man prone to a game of pitch and toss. Card schools were evident in every hostelry, while horse racing and 'a punt on the dugs' was just a way of life. One exception to the rule was Rab Baxter.

Rab was strictly teetotal and he was never seen in the bookies – he would have had no idea how to work out doubles, trebles and accumulators. Rab had never got the gambling bug. He had never put on a bet in his life. His wife Agg was the same. Both lived a simple life and enjoyed being at home in front of the telly. Nothing made them happier than when their famous son Jim came to visit from his new home in Glasgow.

And Jim the Rangers star player was just as comfortable joining his parents in front of the telly as he was rubbing shoulders with the rich and famous social set in the best restaurants and clubs of the Empire's Second City.

On visits back to Cowdenbeath Jim was even known to nip out to the local park, where he'd put his expensive and tailored-to-perfection jacket down for a goalpost and have a kickabout with the local kids. There were no airs and graces with James Curran Baxter.

But the truth is, behind the Baxter family idyll lay a devastating secret – one that Jim himself was initially only aware of in part. It was a secret that took more than half a century to fully unfold. The secret divided a family and deeply wounded a number of people who worshipped Baxter – not in terms of his celebrity, but as one of their own.

The Fife community that was far removed from the bright lights of Glasgow and the publicly perceived persona that James Curran Baxter had become also showed an integrity that remains bewildering yet incredibly heartwarming.

And the truth, which Jim Baxter had spent much of his adult life trying to forget, was that he had been adopted by his uncle Rab and his wife Agnes because his real mother – who he had known all his life as his Aunt Betty – had abandoned him as a baby and given him away. But the real truth would take thirty years to unfold and leave Jim Baxter with a wound that would never heal.

The fateful day in November 1990 when he bumped into an old woman in the street who asked, 'Are you not going to say hello to your wee mammy?' had a devastating effect on Baxter the man. How Baxter the professional footballer would have dealt with it is unclear, as his playing days were well over by then, but what we do know is that after the meeting he told his partner, Norma, that he could hardly drive home.

Baxter knew he had not been brought up by his biological parents, and in fact was aware of who his natural mother was, but it was never spoken of. Was it embarrassment or heartbreak that made a young Jim Baxter expunge the truth from his mind? He never encouraged discussion on the thorny topic; instead, he chose to ignore it and hope it would never surface again. What he certainly didn't understand was the reason why he had been, as he saw it, abandoned by his birth mother and handed over to Rab and Agg. The weight of this burden hung heavily around his neck for decades, unresolved in his mind until those words from his birth mother hit him like a physical blow.

How would a heavy drinker such as Jim handle the situation? He had hidden the facts away. Baxter had never told his wife or two boys, but he opened up to Norma after that meeting in Cowdenbeath. Decades of confusion, fear and hurt at being abandoned came rushing back. He wanted to hit the drink, go on a bender to lock it out again, but Norma consoled him, tried to make him see the positives and encouraged him to embrace the truth and make good the relations.

As his mind raced through his memories, he remembered Adam Moffat, whom he had considered his cousin, coming into the pub in Paisley Road to tell Jim that his dad, Robert, had died and to ask him to take a cord at the interment. Jim had refused, as he felt he hadn't really been close to his 'uncle', but now here he was, being reminded that, in reality, Robert Moffat wasn't just Adam's dad but his own, too.

In the early days growing up, Adam and Jim had been close pals, as there was only a few years difference in their ages, but despite looking very alike nobody put two and two together. Jim and Adam both knew in their teens that they were brothers, but by then Agg and Rab did not encourage them to spend any time together. They both just got on with their lives as best they saw fit.

Jim Baxter achieved fame and fortune, and at no time were those family tensions ever allowed to distract him from being simply the best. At no time did immediate family put themselves first. At no time, until much later in his life, did Jim himself know the absolute truth about his upbringing and his formative years in that close knit community of Cowdenbeath and surrounding villages.

In 1939, the world was, of course, a very different place.

In 1939, in the village of Lumphinnans, just a mile away from Cowdenbeath FC's Central Park, Robert Moffat and Elizabeth Curran made a life-changing decision that they themselves could only influence in part. The consequences of that decision would affect the lives of many and shape the character of the man who would go down in history as Scotland's greatest-ever footballer. They reluctantly decided that they could not keep their infant son because they weren't married. It was generally acknowledged that this would be in the boy's best interests and the pressure to have the baby adopted was overwhelming.

Baxter's first real hint of the truth was when he was playing football as a twelve-year-old. The schoolboys all played with a competitive edge, and one over-the-top tackle saw young Baxter react to his predator by calling him a bastard. Young Baxter had no idea of the real meaning of the expletive he had just used to alarm his opponent, but he was even more confused when a youth from the other side replied, 'He's not the bastard, you are!'

Baxter shrugged it off at the time, but the way the slight had been delivered had a strange edge and it most definitely left a mark on him. When he returned home, he was determined to find out what it meant and Agg was forced to tell him that he had been adopted. Baxter was devastated, but Agg refused at this point to tell him any more – he would have to wait a further seven years before Agg and Rab told him his biological mother's name. Agg was determined that the identity of his biological mother would remain a mystery for as long as possible so that she would continue to be excluded from his upbringing. Little did Jim Baxter know that for all these years his birth mother lived less than three miles from his own front door.

Roll on sixteen years and another twelve-year-old had a shock coming. Young Elizabeth Moffat was glued to the television in her friend's house, watching the grainy images *live* in the front room, as Scotland and England went head to head at Wembley, with Slim Jim the star of the show.

'Your brother is having some game today!' her friend's mum said to her.

Brother?

Elizabeth knew, of course, that she was the youngest child of Elizabeth and Robert Moffat, or Betty and Bert, as they were better known. Young Elizabeth had two brothers, but neither of them were footballers. Adam was ten years older than Elizabeth and Bert was two years younger than Adam. So what on earth was this neighbour talking about?

All of a sudden Elizabeth's thoughts turned to conversations many years before when her brother Adam and her cousin Jim had stood shoulder to shoulder and everyone had remarked that they looked so alike.

At this point the penny dropped and the closely guarded secret, with its origins going back to the early days of the Second World War, was well and truly out of the bag.

But how much of the story did the Wembley hero Slim Jim Baxter really know? Had he known all along and suppressed the truth in his own mind, unwilling or unable to come to terms with the reality? And did a family secret that would remain at least partly buried for fifty years have any bearing on Baxter's self-destructive tendencies?

Many years later, following the revelation of his meeting with his 'mammy', Jim Baxter locked himself away for days and refused to come out. As far as he was concerned there was nobody like his mum, Agg, but now he was forced to question his relationship with her. He was in turmoil.

A family meeting was called to clear the air, but there was no warmth or common ground found between the senior members of the Baxter clan and the Moffats. Agg, the matriarch of the Baxter household, ruled with an iron fist, and it is not unlikely that she had used fear to hammer in the wedge that had divided the two families all those years, but now it had worked itself loose.

Agg and Rab Baxter had wanted Jim as their own and always feared potential rejection; in their minds, once Jim knew the whole, truthful story of his adoption he would want to go back and be part of the Moffat family. With this in mind, Agg in particular never encouraged any communication between Jim and his biological parents or their three other children.

Now Jim wanted to make things right, but it was a thin line he had to walk to avoid falling out with either side. He needed to acknowledge the truth, but he knew it would open gaping family wounds. It was finally time to come to terms with his past.

22

THE REAL JIM BAXTER

'A profound psychological effect'

Jim Baxter really was utterly distraught. That chance meeting with his 'Aunt Betty' and her seemingly throwaway comment brought back all the years of pain and anguish that he had buried in the recesses of his mind. He was inconsolable and now faced a dilemma. He had known for years that he would ultimately have to make a decision and now the time had come.

Baxter loved his parents Agg and Rab to bits, but now he could no longer ignore the fact that his biological mother loved him too and wanted him to know it.

Elizabeth Moffat, or 'Aunt Betty', had carried her secret with immense dignity, as had the whole Moffat family, but although many years had passed Elizabeth's hurt had never waned. Jim was her firstborn and she wanted to be acknowledged. She wanted him to see things from her perspective. In Elizabeth Moffat's book, the timing was right.

Time was not on Elizabeth's side, and little did they know it but the sands of time were beginning to run out for James Curran Baxter too.

All those years of ignoring his birthright, all those years of hoping he would never have to face the reality of history, all those years of using his lifestyle and celebrity as a shield exploded in his mind like a bomb. That question outside the bookmaker's shop in Cowdenbeath

– 'Are you not going to say hello to your wee mammy?' – had enormous consequences. Here was the woman Jim Baxter had been indoctrinated into thinking of as his aunt throwing a hand grenade into his secret past.

Norma saw the devastating effect this chance meeting with his biological mother had on her partner. 'Jim was inconsolable,' she said. 'He cried like a baby. He was shaking and in a trance-like state, totally devastated that it had come to this. His mind was in turmoil. He just didn't know how to react to this bombshell. Sure, Jim had known for more than thirty years that his aunt Betty was really his biological mother, but from the day Agg had told him he had vowed to himself that it wouldn't change anything. He wouldn't allow it to, for Agg's sake.

'Now the day had come when Jim had to confront history and Jim was not prepared for it. He was not prepared for it in the slightest!'

Jim still believed that he was just a mistake and that his mother had refused to take responsibility for her actions – this was the story Agg and Rab had told him, aged twenty, and they had never made any effort to explain that really this hadn't been the case. In reality, it had been a combination of the fact that Agg and Rab could not have the children they so desired, while a young unmarried mother, Elizabeth Curran, was hardly equipped for parenthood, especially with the baby's father off the scene, having signed up for the Royal Air Force and by now posted away.

As Jim was only twelve years old and just at high school when he discovered that Wee Agg and Rab were not his natural parents, he didn't feel any urgency to trace his true birth mother; the shock of the revelation was enough, plus Agg and Rab made it clear they did not want him searching for her. But he also knew that one day he might have to acknowledge who his biological mother was.

Jim was twenty and had just completed his move to Rangers when he was sat down and given the full story, although perhaps in a clumsy attempt to make the confused footballer more comfortable with the truth of the story, they carried a spin that his true mother and father hadn't really wanted him.

It is astonishing to think that the truth about Jim Baxter's true origins could have been hushed up so effectively, particularly within such a close family. Never knowing that the boy in question would go on to become one of his country's most famous sons, each of them had agreed to play their part from the beginning. But at what cost? If we step back for a moment to 1904, we find that Slim Jim wasn't the first with the Baxter name to have made an impact in Raith Rovers colours. The team from the Lang Toon were captained by Burntisland-born Bob Baxter, who later took up residence in Lumphinnans outside Cowdenbeath. Bob's career came to a premature end through injury; indeed, in 1915 he laid down his life for his country in the Great War, when he was killed in action.

Bob left a young family, including two sons, Rab and Dave Baxter, and a widow, Elizabeth. James Curran also lived in the village of Lumphinnans and had eyes for the young widow whose husband had been killed in the war. Soon, with their mother Elizabeth, Rab and Dave were taken into the home of James Curran and they lived together as a family.

James Curran became their stepfather when he married Elizabeth. Later the couple were blessed with a daughter, Elizabeth Curran, half-sister to Rab and Dave.

The Baxter boys both showed ability on the football field as they grew up, with Rab starring for a number of local junior sides, while Dave went senior with St Johnstone. Dave later followed in the footsteps of his biological father, playing with Raith Rovers, where he won the 1938 Second Division championship.

In 1934, while still with St Johnstone, in a match against Dunfermline at East End Park, Dave Baxter went off on a darting run down the wing with the ball at his feet. Watching from the sidelines was his stepfather James Curran, who, in the excitement, suddenly collapsed. Curran was taken to the Dunfermline and West Fife Hospital but sadly died from the seizure he had suffered at the match.

Five years later, in Kirkcaldy Maternity Hospital, nineteen-year-old Elizabeth Curran gave birth to a boy. It was 29 September 1939 and the Second World War was becoming a reality. Elizabeth Curran was Rab and Dave Baxter's half-sister and she was not married. The baby boy was named and registered as James Curran in honour of her late father.

By this time, Elizabeth's half-brother Rab Baxter was married to Agnes Denholm. They had no children of their own and were unable to have any, which was a great sadness to the couple. This was a time, of course, when having a child out of wedlock was more than frowned upon, and Elizabeth Curran was forced to give up her son James before he was six months old.

With Rab and Agg childless and desperate to raise a family of their own, it seemed an obvious solution for them to adopt the baby. And so Rab Baxter took James Curran from his half-sister Elizabeth and with his wife Agnes brought the youngster up as their own in their home in Hill of Beath. Later, when the adoption was finalised, James Curran became James Curran Baxter – later to be universally known as Slim Jim Baxter.

Elizabeth Curran was heartbroken at having to give her firstborn child away, even if it was to close family, but she carried her secret with dignity. Secrets, however, are difficult to keep, especially in a small village where everyone knows everyone else's business.

Maybe now we can see how that young lad could call Baxter a 'bastard' at the tender age of twelve, its basis in the knowledge that he was of dubious parentage rather than just a superbly talented footballer who was making him look foolish during their kickabout in the park.

The truth was that while Jim Baxter was growing up as an only child, in reality his three cousins – Adam, Bert and Elizabeth – were in fact his actual siblings.

Baxter's sister Liz remembers that time well, recalling Jim and his relationship with his family. 'Jim didn't spend any time with my parents – his real parents – growing up. He knew them, of course, but only as aunty and uncle. Actually, my mum was asked by Agg to stop giving him birthday and Christmas presents because he wondered why she was the only aunty to do so. Young Jim had no idea of the special bond that existed with his aunt Betty.'

Liz continues: 'Remember, too, that Rab and Dave's mother Elizabeth – my grandmother – had married my grandfather James Curran after their father had died in the Great War. The Baxters and Currans had the same mother – my grandmother – but different fathers. She lived in Lumphinnans until she died, which would be in the 1960s.'

Liz, who was fifteen years younger than Jim, continues: 'Years later Jim would introduce Adam, Bert and me as his brothers and sister, so he never tried to hide that fact from anyone, as it wasn't a secret in our immediate family, nor in our small village. It was something that had happened and was not really spoken about. Obviously my mum had her thoughts but she didn't really express them. Yes, Jim did know eventually who his birth parents were, but he didn't get the true reason for his adoption from Agg and Rab. They confirmed Elizabeth and Robert Moffat were not his aunt Betty and uncle Rab but his true mother and father, and that his young cousins Adam, Robert and me were actually his brothers and sister, and that definitely had an impact on him.'

The circumstances of Jim's adoption and the reasons that Elizabeth and Robert had had to give him up as a baby remained unresolved until Jim's fateful meeting with his birth mother outside the bookmaker's; all along, Jim had assumed that he had just been abandoned, and it seems Rab and Agg did not want to dissuade him from this view.

Liz goes on: 'It wasn't until later in life he found out the true story as to why he went to live with Agg and Rab. I think because of who he was and what he had become, my parents didn't want to be seen as jumping on the bandwagon or accused of wanting to be part of his life because he was famous. My parents could have sold their story to the papers any time but that's not what we were about.'

Psychologist Tom Lucas is well known throughout professional football and has helped many individual star players overcome their problems away from their chosen sport. His advice would have gone down well with Baxter for sure, as long before psychology became such an important factor in the modern game, Slim Jim was adhering to its prophecy. Lucas once told a group of star players: 'All that matters out there is your own performance. Don't worry about what others are doing if you can't help or alter what is happening. If all of you perform to your very best, then the result will be the best one you could achieve.' Baxter as a player always did just that.

Lucas says: 'Although I did not know Jim Baxter, I grew up at the time of his peak as a footballer. Slim Jim was recognised the length and breadth of the land. Therefore my observations about Jim are based on family knowledge and the information provided by Tom Miller of Rangers TV.

'It is clear that when Jim was made fully aware of the true identity of his mother that this would have had a profound psychological affect on him. Indeed, this knowledge may go some way to explaining his attitude to women in general, if, in his eyes, he felt he was abandoned as a baby. The issue of reconciliation will have been a painful and painstaking process that may ultimately never have been resolved. This "pain" Jim would or could have carried with him for many years.

'It was in football that Jim found his "escape". It was on the playing field that he became alive. He was like an artist with a blank canvas ready to produce a masterpiece. This allowed Jim to freely express himself. It also gave Jim the opportunity to move away from the sometimes claustrophobic life of a small mining village.

'Jim was dapper, good-looking and had a swagger that did not belittle his undoubted talent. Indeed, he was the forerunner to the late George Best. Their lifestyles have a similarity in how they dealt with, or didn't deal with, the fame, adulation and money.

'To move from a small mining village to a big city gave Jim a sense of freedom unimaginable in his hometown. The shackles came off. Jim discovered just how good a footballer he was. This allowed him to mask the perceived "pain" of rejection by his maternal mother.'

Although Jim Baxter found out that he was adopted when he was twelve years of age, though he may have had suspicions for some time, he did not know who his biological parents were. Rab and Agg loved him as their own son, brought him up well and helped him along the path that would set him apart from other men for all time. And Rab, Agg and Jim had a close, loving relationship and bonds that could not be broken.

So when Jim Baxter found out the truth of his adoption, that his cousins were in fact his siblings and that the people he had thought of as his biological parents had adopted him, it was a bombshell that he could not handle. He was happy to publicly recognise his brothers and sister, but he found it impossible to reconcile how his mother could have given him away. How could she have done that, then marry and have more children, but still leave Jim out of their happy new family? Was the shame of an illegitimate child so bad? He also felt strongly that he could not betray the people who had actually brought him up and had done it so well. The sands of time had run and there could be no going back.

That said, within the family everyone continued to play their part, working their way around a secret that they knew about but never properly acknowledged. Jim Baxter was, of course, at the centre of it all, and it affected him deeply throughout his life. He was adored and worshipped by many, famous beyond what anyone could ever have imagined for him, and yet at his core there was a deep unhappiness that came from his inability to understand or come to terms with the unarguable fact that, for whatever reasons, his birth mother had abandoned him as a baby.

It was not until that chance meeting with his 'wee mammy', when she made it clear that she wanted to make proper contact, that he was finally able to confront the demons he had within him. But, by then, the demons had begun to take their full toll on his health. His hard partying, hard-drinking lifestyle was a reaction to his fame, adulation and star status, but it was also a way to deal with the pain he had suffered from suppressing the family secret that haunted him throughout his life.

23

FAMILY VALUES

'Football in the blood'

Liz Dair, as she is now known, married as a teenager and it is no surprise her first son was a footballer. In fact, Liz had two sons, Jason and Lee, both of whom were very capable on the pitch.

The father of the boys was also a very useful player. Ian Dair had been a midfielder with Stirling Albion and Cowdenbeath in the '70s, and had played for Glenrothes when they won the 1975 Scottish Junior Cup. Ian's brother, Tom, was also a star performer, in his case with Hibernian FC.

Jason and Lee had football in their blood.

And not only was there a real football heritage on their dad's side; the boys' mum, before her marriage, was Liz Moffat, youngest of a family of four children to Elizabeth and Robert Moffat. Liz had three brothers: Adam, Robert and the eldest, James. Liz, Adam and Robert all shared the Moffat surname, while James had been renamed Baxter at an early age.

Lee Dair started his football career at Rangers before moving on to play with Raith Rovers, East Fife and Cowdenbeath, while his older brother Jason had three spells at Raith and also played in the colours of Millwall, Dunfermline and Motherwell.

From an early age, both boys knew that the legendary Jim Baxter was part of the wider family, but it was only as they matured to adulthood that they discovered just how close a relative he was.

Liz has some regrets that her boys and her brother James weren't closer: 'Both Jason and Lee would have loved to have spent more time with Jim and perhaps involved him in their own football careers, but you don't miss what you've never had and the boys made their way in the game on their own merits rather than by any suggestion about influence from a famous uncle.'

Liz regrets more that as a family they didn't all bond earlier: 'It is only when you get older that you realise – when you are younger, you get so involved in other things, and of course any relationship with Jim wasn't encouraged by Rab and Agg. But I did bond with Jim, although it was much later than I think we would all have liked.

'Jim and Adam were like two peas in a pod and shared all the same interests, including the bad habits – a bet or two and a few refreshments. They would meet fairly often and my other brother, Bert, would be there too, as they tried to make up for lost time.

'I remember going to visit Jim and his partner Norma in their home in Glasgow with my mum. After we got there, within half an hour Jim and my mum went away and had a right old chat. It was very emotional. I think they straightened out a few truths that night.

'Agg and Rab were still a huge influence on Jim's life back then, even with Jim not in the best of health, but he loved them both dearly. He didn't want to hurt them, although against their wishes he welcomed us and accepted us as his family. In fact, Jim always made a point of introducing Adam, Bert and myself as his brothers and sister when we were in company.'

Unfortunately, Liz's dad, known as 'Puff', never got to enjoy that bond. He died in February 1980, long before any reconciliation had been possible.

Elizabeth Moffat (née Curran) died in April 1994, seven years before her firstborn passed away, but she was content that she had established a relationship with Jim, however brief it had been. It was something they both wanted and cherished for the rest of their lives.

The Moffat and Dair families were proud as punch to have been connected to Jim Baxter and would have been delighted to have played a bigger part in the life of not just Jim but also Jim's own two sons, Alan and Steven.

When Liz Dair was clearing out her mother's things after she had passed away, she found a hoard of pictures and newspaper cuttings that charted the career of James Curran Baxter. They covered every era of Baxter's football life, from Crossgates to his second spell at Rangers, when he ultimately hung up his boots. A mother on a mission, with heartbreak behind her smile. Elizabeth will have taken some comfort from her collection, but she must also have thought often about what might have been.

Many years later and back in Hill of Beath, a statue of Jim Baxter and a memorial garden in his name were being unveiled outside the ex-serviceman's club in front of a galaxy of stars from the football world, including Jim's former Rangers teammates Sandy Jardine, Ralph Brand and John Greig, alongside Alex Ferguson and lifelong Raith Rovers fan Gordon Brown.

Sadly, Jim's siblings were mere bystanders at the ceremony, excluded by decision. Despite all the time spent together before Jim's death, they were still kept at arm's length by others. Agg in particular seemed to be calling all the shots. The dignity displayed by his brothers and sister was incredible. But it wasn't something new. This dignity had been present for sixty-three years. Later, in the club, where drinks and a buffet were being offered to guests, there was no sign of the Moffats; they had not been invited. Instead, they sat in the adjoining bar.

Jim's partner Norma did spend time with Liz and her brothers that afternoon and offered her apologies, explaining that Agg, even at the age of eighty-eight, could not bring herself to acknowledge the family connection. She had rejected out of hand any suggestion that they should be part of the event, which shows how determined she was that Jim's biological parents should never be publicly acknowledged. By this stage Jim had been gone for two years, but still she kept up the pretence.

Was it spite or vindictiveness? Possibly not. Was it fuelled by insecurity and fear that the boy they had brought up as their own would disconnect and reunite with his natural family?

It may just have been based on that unwritten rule of no contact, the same one that had forced the families up to this point to not acknowledge one another. It had been this way from the day James Curran had become part of the Baxter household.

Anyone who knew Jim knew that he worshipped Rab and Agg, but he recognised the difficulties that his biological mother and father had faced all those years ago. In his later life, when he was fully aware of the facts, and understood finally that he had not been given away as unwanted, as he had always previously believed, but was a casualty of cruel circumstance, he wasted no time in letting his birth mother know that he loved her and valued her, but remained deeply frustrated by the years they had lost when they should have been in contact.

Psychologist Tom Lucas has this to say of Jim's predicament: 'He was a genius. As is often in the case with geniuses, they are hugely complex characters. He could play and he came alive on the football field. Nothing else mattered to him when that whistle blew. But when not playing football, his extremely sharp and active mind probably analysed his upbringing over and over again. "Why was I given away?" This could easily have haunted him and he blanked it away from football by living on the edge. Alcohol, parties, woman-ising and gambling.'

It was all part of his laissez-faire attitude, that live for today nonchalance, although those traits were also evident during matches, when he played the game off the cuff, or so it appeared, though it was probably more a case of just how he himself wanted it to be.

'Looking back to Jim's birth, a child being born out of wedlock wasn't that uncommon in those days, but families closed ranks and made the most of things. If there were family disputes, few were resolved amicably and relationships were often permanently damaged. Just think back to the mid-'80s and the miners' strikes. Coalmining in Fife, and indeed throughout Scotland, was in decline in those days. In England, things had gone into meltdown, with the strikes against pit closures. The Scottish pit workers had sympathy for them, while some broke rank and split the community. In fact, breaking the strike often split families, and those wounds remain just as deep today. Families remain divided.

'That family rift between the Currans, Moffats and Baxters is something Jim was probably extremely aware of and it was not something he wanted to be held responsible for, but he probably felt he was. He craved love, and while he clearly had it at home, he also found it in an adoring public. That probably shaped his character, but as much as he harboured his confusions it was clear he was a genuine, warm and caring person who made friends easily and valued friendship more than any possessions he may have picked up in an amazing career.

'A fascinating and sensational character, I wish I had got the chance to have a cup of tea with him to get inside that head, but I have to settle for having watched him play as a football fan and that itself makes me feel privileged.'

Another who knew Jim from his upbringing in Cowdenbeath is Forfar Athletic FC manager Dick Campbell. Dick's uncle Willie Menzies, who had been a footballer himself with Sligo Rovers and others, lived next door to the Baxter family and Dick, with his twin brother Ian, were always visiting in the hope of catching a glimpse of the football hero who lived next door. It was the days when nobody ever thought of locking their doors, not in a mining community where they looked after their own. If one house made a huge pot of soup, it was shared with half the street. Dick remembers Jim Baxter preparing to head to Wembley.

'We were playing football in the yard. My uncle Willie, or "Big Ming" as he was known locally, was playing too, when out came Jim from next door. He was about to catch the bus to Glasgow and meet up with the Scotland squad before travelling by train to London ahead of that game at Wembley in 1963. Jim took his jacket off and joined in with all the laddies. Unbelievable! About to play in the biggest game of his life, but still had time for his young neighbours.'

Dick was very close friends with the Moffat side of the clan and was regularly in the company of Adam, Bert and Elizabeth, and was best man when Elizabeth married Ian Dair.

Dick remembers the head of the family, Robert 'Puff' Moffat, who of course was Jim Baxter's biological father, being a real character, too.

'Puff loved to laugh, loved to party and knew how to enjoy himself. I can see him yet at a typical New Year 'after the Bells' get-together, taking his teeth out and singing, "Tie a yellow ribbon round the old oak tree" ... a funny, funny man and great company. Maybe now, knowing what we do, Jim Baxter had the Moffat genes, that's for sure.'

Dick also worked with Jim on after-dinner work and, as a rookie on the circuit, remembers that Jim was the main attraction more often than not.

'Hold an audience with stories? Jim Baxter had every audience in the palm of his hands as soon as he came through the door of the club or pub, wherever we were working. He very rarely took a drink when we were at a dinner, the odd glass of red wine and that was about it, but he was on a high just being in company and talking football. I remember one night with Billy Bremner at Lochore Institute, neither of them had notes and Bremner with his fag hanging from his lip told of the two of them winding up Alan Ball in the Wembley tunnel as the teams waited to take the field. The place was in awe of both Scottish legends, especially when Jim said, "England? Wembley? What a party that was!" I loved the man to pieces.

'When I was trying to make my way in the game, he gave me great encouragement. I was playing with Dunfermline again, with my brother Ian, and I broke my ankle in a match against Partick

Thistle. It was 1974. After I was put in plaster, Ian and I went for a pint in the Institute and we were summoned over to a quiet corner, where Jim was sitting having a Bacardi.

'He said, "I was at your game today, you both did great. Work hard, stick in and don't let that broken ankle distract you. You need to train hard and come back stronger. You are both right good players!" Well, I didn't think about it at the time, but when you think of his experiences when he broke his leg ten years before and the effect it had on his career, it was some advice. Ian and I left the club that night floating on air.'

Dick has managed Dunfermline, Ross County, Partick Thistle and Brechin City after a playing career that saw him serve Dundee United, Cowdenbeath and Dunfermline. Another Fifer steeped in football. A family man, with his brother Ian also a former player and his sons, Ian and Ross, likewise playing professionally. Family values in Fife when Dick was growing up as a neighbour of Jim Baxter were what that particular community was all about.

Jim Baxter's journey from finding out as a youngster that he was adopted, to then finding out that he had been abandoned as a baby by the woman he knew as 'Aunt Betty' to finally discovering the truth, thirty years later, that his birth mother had not wanted to give him away and profoundly regretted what had happened, was incredibly difficult for him. These decisions, made all those years ago, had a deep and long-lasting effect on him. While his adoptive parents, Rab and Agg, were still alive, Jim Baxter did not feel he could publicly acknowledge the truth, even though he wanted to. His premature death meant that he had to leave this to others – his partner Norma and sister Liz – to fulfil that wish and to finally tell the true story of his upbringing and how it had affected the life of the man widely regarded as Scotland's greatest ever footballer.

In the meantime, as Jim Baxter struggled to come to terms with his past, his own health was becoming a very serious issue.

24

LIVER FOR THE DAY

'Given a second chance'

By 1994, Jim Baxter was desperately ill. He had been in poor health for quite a while but had made no effort to check out the full scale of the problem or to determine his actual condition. Jim's weight had ballooned: anyone who didn't know him would have been of the belief that he had been given his legendary nickname as a sarcastic reflection on his current build. When Jim eventually bowed to pressure from partner Norma and others to visit the doctor, the damage was already deep-rooted. It was confirmed that his liver was no longer functioning effectively, and it was all down to his lifestyle. His many years of hard drinking had caught up with him.

The doctor immediately advised Jim to stop drinking, but it was not something that came easily to a man who had lived for social interaction, with long days and longer nights in pubs or clubs spending time with his pals; it was a habit that would not be easy to change.

When the medics advised that he could die if he didn't change his ways and stop drinking, Jim was said to have replied, 'I'll give it a year and see how it goes.' Jim never really did heed the warning; despite occasional spells of abstinence, he thought he could simply miss the odd round and everything would be fine. Baxter was the leopard that couldn't, or wouldn't, change its spots.

At that time, he used to frequent a few pubs on Glasgow's south side, including a hostelry on Victoria Road owned and managed by his former Old Firm foe but long-standing friend Billy McNeill.

Billy remembers those days: 'Jimmy would come in and mix comfortably with all the regulars and, remember, this was predominately a bar frequented by Celtic supporters. But it was all just boys together, as far as Jim was concerned.

'He used to idle away the days and ask me to send him home if he started to become a pest. He might have been a pest to Celtic on the field, and had a bit of devilment in him even in later years, when he had sunk a few, but Jim was Jim and if you were a pal of Jimmy Baxter's, you were a pal for life.'

Baxter was now regularly being hospitalised, as his health continued to fade, but as soon as he felt well enough Jim always signed himself out. He also knew his condition was totally self-inflicted and he never asked for or courted sympathy.

The sparkling eyes that could previously light up a room were by now sticking out like organ stops and his colour had turned a jaundiced yellow.

Glasgow's Victoria Infirmary had now replaced the St Enoch Hotel as a second home for this Rangers legend. It was the consultants of the Victoria who identified the need for urgent surgery if Baxter's life was to be saved, as his body had refused to respond to every medication that was tried.

Baxter was referred to the Edinburgh Royal Infirmary, where the liver transplant unit was based. Almost immediately, Regius Professor of Clinical Surgery James Garden knew only one course of action was open to him if his patient was to survive. A liver transplant. There really was no other option.

Jim Baxter never pushed for priority or used his celebrity to gain favour. In fact, it was almost the opposite. At the time, had his liver transplant been refused, Jim's demeanour was such that he would have accepted matters and respected the fact that he had been responsible for his own condition; he would have lived, or more likely died, with the consequences.

The first transplant failed, but a second that was effected twenty-four hours later gave Jim Baxter a seven-year life extension.

Professor Garden tells the true and full story of what happened next.

'I first met Jim Baxter when he was admitted to the Scottish Liver Tranplantation Unit in 1994, for consideration of a liver transplant. Jim was obviously a well-known celebrity, but I have to say that when I met him it was clear that he was just another patient who needed to be managed appropriately. His past was well documented in the press, but, as it became apparent over the next few years, it was sometimes difficult to separate out the legend from the fact.

'Jim had been in trouble over the year prior to being referred to SLTU, having been in and out of hospital with complications of liver failure. He had been diagnosed previously as having cirrhosis and the cause of this had been attributed to alcohol. He had actually been in and out of hospital in Glasgow with ill health and the main complications of severe liver disease, fluid retention, poor nutrition and bleeding oesophageal varices (veins). It was not apparent that the question of a liver transplant had been considered when he had been in hospital in Glasgow in the past, although the decline in his health had occurred despite his having been abstinent from alcohol for a period of some nine months. It was his general practitioner who contacted SLTU, raising the question of a liver transplant.

'On the basis of the information available, it did seem appropriate for Jim Baxter to be assessed. He was admitted for a period of about a week to SLTU for intensive tests and assessment to determine if there were not other treatment options available to improve his health. It became clear that his liver failure had progressed to a stage where his liver would not recover, and that he would not survive without a transplant. In our unit, the assessment for transplant was rigorous and involved meeting with surgeons, physicians, transplant coordinators and other staff that provided information to him, and determined what the risks of a transplant might be for him if this was considered appropriate. Our unit, at that time, was unusual in that it had a psychiatrist with designated sessions to assess patients where there were issues such as dependence or other psychological problems that might mitigate against transplantation. It would be crucial to establish that any patient undergoing transplantation would take responsibility for the new organ that had been donated and become available through someone else's misfortune. Jim Baxter's case was then thoroughly discussed at the Liver Transplant Multidisciplinary Meeting.

'The outcome was that it was felt that alcohol had contributed to but might not necessarily have been the sole cause of his liver disease. It was clear that he had managed to maintain a period of total abstinence from alcohol, that his psychological assessment indicated that he would take responsibility for any transplanted liver and that he had good support at home in the form of his partner Norma Morton and his two sons close by. All these factors pointed to a favourable outcome, with a low risk of return to alcohol abuse.

'He was kept in the unit for quite a while to optimise treatment for his liver failure, but was released for a time and placed on the transplant waiting list in the anticipation that a suitable match based on blood group and liver size would materialise.

'We anticipated that his being placed on the transplant waiting list would generate publicity and divide opinion. It was always a challenge to keep the press in check, but we tried to have him maintain a low profile until a suitable liver became available. Jim Baxter was always grateful for being considered for transplant and for being "given a second chance". He felt humbled by the fact that he would have to rely on someone else's misfortune, and was determined to show that he could take responsibility for his health.

'I recall the day that a suitable offer was made. Jim was contacted and came over late evening for admission. I took him through the consenting process again and made sure that any last minute issues were dealt with. He was looking forward to the operation

175

since his quality of life had become so poor. The donated liver was retrieved through the night and was deemed suitable for the operation on Jim to proceed. The surgery could not have really gone any better. Blood loss was minimal during removal of the diseased liver and he was stable throughout the operation. The new liver looked perfect when it was implanted and its circulation restored. After he was transferred to the intensive care unit, it became apparent that his blood tests were not recovering as well as would have been expected, despite the apparently successful transplant. Overnight, it became apparent that the liver was not functioning as would have been expected and a decision was taken very quickly that he would need to be placed on the "super-urgent" list because of this so-called primary non-function.

'He was maintained in the intensive care unit on a ventilator in an unconscious state.

'The fact that we could list a patient in this way was an advantage, because it meant that Edinburgh had priority for any liver that became available. It did, however, mean that we could not be too choosy and that any marginal donor had to be considered. Within forty-eight hours or so, a second liver did become available. At that second operation, I recall being dismayed that we had to remove what looked like a very healthy, albeit non-functioning, liver and replace it by a second donated liver that did not look very healthy at all. I was dismayed at the prospect that Jim had started off before the transplant in a poor condition, had been in intensive care with no liver function for several days, and now had a further liver that did not look perfect! One good sign, however, at the end of the operation was that I could see that the donor liver was producing bile, which was passing from the donor bile duct before this was joined to Jim's own bile duct.

'There was a considerable amount of stress at this time. The second operation was undertaken through the night. After surgery and by the time of his return to the intensive care unit, the blood tests started to improve and it was apparent that this second liver was working. His recovery thereafter was satisfactory. He came off the ventilator within twenty-four hours and was transferred back to the ward area after a few days.

'This whole episode was particularly stressful for me and the team but, of course, Jim had been oblivious to most of the unfolding drama surrounding his two transplants. This whole event provided opportunity for some to make fun of the whole situation. It is said that Jimmy Johnstone made the joke that Jim was transplanted on a Friday but needed a retransplant by the end of the weekend. He made the observation that "it must have been a hell of a Saturday night".

'Jim was an excellent patient during his recovery. There were issues with rejection of the new liver that required manipulation of drug doses to keep this rejection process suppressed. He complied well with treatment, and there was almost a daily improvement in his overall demeanour and outlook.

'The unit did, however, have a challenging time managing his celebrity status. We made the announcement of his transplant and had to deal with all of the issues, as he was seen to be "fighting for his life". There were several attempts by members of the media to try to obtain information about him and his condition. Someone did manage to get a picture of him at his bedside, but in general his presence on the unit was not too disruptive. There was criticism of the decision to undertake a transplant on someone who had clearly brought about his own decline in health. There was, in fact, a dip in organ donation offers at that time, and I recall even having to turn down a possible offer of a donation because the family wished to make this conditional that it would not be offered to someone whose liver disease was due to alcohol consumption. It was always difficult to defend our position and not breach patient confidentiality, but it was not a great surprise that when the final pathology report came back on Jim Baxter's removed liver that it was clear that there was a cause other than excessive alcohol consumption to his liver disease.

'I did see Jim on several occasions after his discharge. He did have to come back into the RIE on a few occasions because of ongoing problems with rejection of his liver. He "surprised" me by presenting me with a trophy at a "Scot of the Year" awards ceremony in Glasgow at the end of 1994. He had actually been an inpatient at the time, being treated for a rejection episode. On another occasion, I was called into the hospital because he had developed an obstructed hernia when he had been putting away his suitcase in the ward. I had been at a black tie dinner and recall sitting at his bedside, gently persuading his groin hernia to reduce. I always thought that it would have looked a bit strange to anyone entering the room at that time as to what I was doing under Jim's bedclothes.

'He had a generous nature and was determined to raise money for the Transplant Unit. I was invited to attend a fundraising event on 9 June 1996 at Victoria's Nightspot in Glasgow. I was a bit anxious about this and my fears were raised further when Jim suggested that I meet him in the bar at the hotel at which I was housed for the evening. It did give me quite a bit of insight into the glare of publicity that someone like Jim had lived under. I remember having a beer while he had an orange juice. All the eyes were on him and his "drink". He drove me to the event venue and I was somewhat surprised that he could park on a double yellow line in central Glasgow. The evening was a meeting of the stars of football. There were players of past Rangers European teams, of the Lisbon Lions and the Scotland Wembley 1967 side. It was incredible to see how much support Jim received from those attending that night. Most ended up on the wrong side of the legal limit for alcohol consumption, but Jim was absolutely sober and drove me back to my hotel. I am still not clear how it was that his car was not towed away that night. Jim raised the most amount of money (£12,000) that the Transplant Unit had ever received from a single donation.

'After his first year, Jim had very little in the way of problems with rejection of his new liver. It came as a bit of a surprise when we picked up abnormalities in his liver function tests towards the end of 2000. Investigations revealed little in the way of problems with

178

his liver, but it became evident that he had developed a pancreatic cancer. Although the tumour looked initially localised and we did consider surgery, further investigation revealed that it had already spread beyond the pancreas and was not curable by surgery.

'I recall discussing with him this devastating news. Again, Jim was always the pragmatist. He felt that he had already had his second chance with his liver transplant and had enjoyed an extended life as a result. He opted not to consider chemotherapy and to focus on his quality of life.

'I attended his funeral at Glasgow Cathedral and was astonished at the number who not only attended the service but also lined the streets of Glasgow that day.

'I attended a couple of other fundraising events towards his statue at Hill of Beath, as well as the unveiling of the statue. I had the opportunity to speak on these occasions to a number of his former football playing contemporaries, all of whom had clearly enjoyed Jim's company and were very fond of him. There were always lots of stories to be told.'

When the pancreatic cancer developed, it remained one of the very few opponents that ever got the better of Slim Jim Baxter.

25

DEATH OF A LEGEND

'Simply the Best'

On Saturday, 14 April 2001, Scotland lost a legend.

James Curran Baxter lost his battle with cancer and died at home in Glasgow with his partner Norma and his sons, Alan and Steven, at his bedside.

Baxter had had more than his fair share of health problems, and while two liver transplants had most certainly extended his life, when he was diagnosed with cancer of the pancreas in February 2001 it was a match that he just couldn't win. His life was over within two short months of receiving the news that this time his illness was terminal.

Baxter probably crammed more into his sixty-one years on this earth than the aggregate of the other ten men in any team at any club in his brilliant but chequered playing career. Yes, drinking to excess was a regular issue from an early age, and he himself suggested he gambled away around a quarter of a million pounds, going back all the way to the 'pitch and toss' schools in the Fife mining community. His lifestyle had taken its toll and damaged him severely, but even in the worst of times he had no regrets.

It was a short playing career for one of Britain's finest football talents, but his life, being over at the age of sixty-one, was also far too short for the man who had tortured the Auld Enemy England at Wembley not once but twice. Perhaps even more importantly, Baxter will be remembered as a Rangers player who transcended the Old Firm divide, having no religious interest of any shape or form. If you were friends with Jimmy Baxter, race, creed or colour meant nothing at all.

Jim had a host of tremendous friendships; even when he was in the company of other '60s superstars such as Puskas and Di Stefano, whose command of English was nominal – and it's fair to say Jim was not well versed in Spanish – they had the common language of football.

Willie Henderson remembers a visit to Jim's flat in the area of Shawlands in Glasgow. 'It was only a few weeks after the dreadful diagnosis of Jim's terminal illness,' remembers Wee Willie. 'We chatted and laughed as usual, and despite knowing he wasn't long for this life, Stanley never looked for sympathy or went into a depression. It was almost the reverse.

'He was clearly in decline, but what a brave face he put on for me that day. As I left, he said, 'That's it, Wee Man. Look after yourself, take care.'

'I knew exactly what he meant and he knew I knew.

'We knew we would never be in each other's company again. We knew all the years of laughs together were coming to a premature end. It was tragic, but what dignity he displayed in the circumstance. It was both humbling and heart-breaking.'

One week later, Willie's phone rang and it was Jim. Willie was hoping for good news, but that wasn't the reason for the call.

'Jim just asked in a matter-of-fact kind of way, would I do him a favour and be a pall-bearer at his funeral? A favour? It meant the world to me to be asked by Jimmy Baxter to carry out his wishes on the day he was to be laid to rest. It's not a job I would ever have wanted, but I was privileged and deeply honoured to be asked. That was a difficult phone call.'

When the end came, Scotland, and Glasgow in particular, was

united in grief. This was never more evident than twenty-four hours after Baxter's death and only two miles from his south side home, where Celtic were facing Dundee United in a Scottish Cup semi-final tie at the recently refurbished Hampden Park. In the area of the national stadium that housed the Celtic fans, a huge banner was held high that imparted a quite fantastic message. It read: 'SLIM JIM – SIMPLY THE BEST'.

Such a show of emotion from the supporters of Rangers' biggest rivals was unprecedented and once again it highlighted how Jim Baxter had no time for the sectarian divide in his adopted home of Glasgow. It was also an indication of how well he was respected in the wider football community. Were Jim Baxter looking down on that cup tie, seeing that banner at the match that Celtic won 3–1, he would have enjoyed the moment and afforded himself a smile. The banner said it all, using the recognised nickname of James Curran Baxter. It encapsulated, too, the unofficial Rangers anthem originally made famous as a recording by Tina Turner.

Baxter's football skills opened doors for him and transcended boundaries. He was unique. A one-off who never forgot his Fife roots. He was as controversial as he was full of devilment, but he had no malice, and while he displayed arrogance in droves on the football field it was not a trait that he carried off it. Of course he was guilty of pressing the self-destruct button, but his 'live for today' policy made him the character he was. When you think back to the confusion and hurt he carried from his childhood, perhaps now, all these years later, we understand better what made Jim the person he was.

A flawed genius, at times tortured by his uncertainty regarding his background, but all the issues and baggage of his early life – even the gambling, womanising, relationships and drinking during his playing career – were parked and locked away when he pulled on his football boots. Then only the game mattered.

After time was called on Jim Baxter's public house venture, Jim and Norma Morton became inseparable. They set up home together

182

and she became his rock. Norma was good for Jim Baxter. They were good together, and without doubt Norma gave Jim stability; she was his soulmate and confidante, kept him in check (as best she could) and most definitely extended his life, allowing them to enjoy eighteen years together. It was indeed in Norma that he confided all his family troubles and, before his death, urged Norma to have the true story of his mum and dad, and his mother and father, told. Jim was determined not to hurt Rab and Agg Baxter, however, so while they were alive he planned to take the secret to his grave.

Apart from Norma, in the final months of his life former Rangers pals John Greig and Sandy Jardine were almost daily visitors to the flat, and the Rangers family were determined to ensure that Jim Baxter would be afforded all the dignity a genuine superstar in distress deserved.

Another former Rangers teammate who was close to Baxter in his final months was Alex Willoughby. Alex, who was renowned for his teetotal lifestyle, was a great comfort to Jim and Norma at that difficult time. Sadly, only three years after Jim died, Willoughby was also struck down with cancer and died in July 2004.

Norma remembers: 'When Jim knew Alex, John or Sandy was visiting, it didn't matter how poorly he was feeling, he defied the odds and insisted on being out of bed, washed, shaved and dressed in shirt and tie to greet his great friends.'

Sandy Jardine and Jim were more than friends. It was Jim who had taken the sixteen-year-old Sandy Jardine under his wing when he had joined Rangers in the final months of the Sunderland-bound midfielder's time there.

Sandy recalled: 'In those days of the '60s, your dad usually got you a job and as I was getting set to leave school at Easter, I thought I would be like my brother and become a joiner or maybe join the police. Dad came in one Sunday night with a couple of drinks in him and announced he had fixed it for me to join the Rangers ground staff.

'I was gobsmacked! I had never even been to Ibrox, but when I got

183

to the stadium and saw that imposing staircase that sometimes we take for granted, and remember, 99 per cent of the Rangers support have never had the opportunity to set foot on it, it was an incredible experience.

'After I signed on, I was sent downstairs to collect my training gear, then it was over to the Albion [the training ground opposite Ibrox] for my first training session. We were getting paired off in twos and on that first day I was paired with Jim Baxter! We would have been about fifteen yards apart and you worked yourself out, then worked yourself in with a wee pass. I was keeping it simple, but Jimmy was pinging it about all over the place, first-timing it, and I was running everywhere to retrieve the ball! It was my initiation and Jimmy was laughing his head off with every "bad ball" I had to chase.

'Stanley was brilliant, but he was never really bothered about being serious in training.'

Forty-six years on from that first day when Sandy Jardine was paired with Baxter and the flame-haired youth from Edinburgh was looked after by the biggest star in the Rangers first team, the roles were now reversed, with Jim grateful for the friendship and support that Sandy showed him in his time of need.

Rangers, and Sandy in particular, helped Norma, Alan and Steven with all the funeral arrangements and in his final weeks Jim was quite explicit to Sandy on how he wanted the service to be conducted. His wishes were carried out to a tee.

Another huge support to the family was Reverend Stuart MacQuarrie BD BSc MBA, chaplain to the University of Glasgow and a long-standing Rangers supporter. Stuart considered it a privilege to spend time with Jim as the end was getting closer, and they shared great stories and memories of good days at Rangers.

Stuart recalls: 'I remember going into Jim Baxter's bar in Paisley Road and being served by the great man himself. His playing days were not long behind him, but he was a great bartender. Now, years later, despite knowing he was terminally ill and only had a matter of weeks left, he still loved to laugh and chat as if he was back in the pub.

'I remember when Jim came back to join Rangers from Nottingham. His best days were clearly behind him, but there were occasional flashes of brilliance, although his fitness had gone. It was changing days in football, with the party lifestyles of the '60s making way for a more professional approach to the game, as was characterised by younger players coming through such as Kenny Dalglish and Sandy Jardine, and of course Sandy just couldn't do enough for his great friend Jim in those months leading up to his death.'

As weeks moved on, Jim Baxter knew his life was ebbing away and, with incredible dignity and determination, the man who had a devil-may-care attitude and had lived for the day in life was now making plans for his death and his funeral.

Top of the list was a piper, and his close friend Alex Willoughby promised to make it happen. But in typical Jim Baxter fashion, he didn't want just any piper – it had to be the best. He was adamant that he shouldn't change, even when facing his maker. Nothing was to change.

Jim passed away in April 2001, only eleven weeks after he had been told his cancer could not be cured. As the news spread, Glasgow became a city united in mourning that a genuine Scottish icon, a legend, had left us. Football fans and non-football fans alike shared universal sadness. Jim had tasted glory and brought pride to a nation, and what a legacy he had left behind: two major Wembley successes, stories of life in the fast lane that saw him fast-tracked from the coalfields of Fife to superstardom.

James Curran Baxter was a diamond in that coalfield and his legend lives on, whether it's in print or old black-and-white video or on DVD; moving pictures of Baxter show him with that trademark shirt hanging out of his shorts, playing the game his way.

Willie Henderson thinks back to a conversation deep in the heart of Ibrox Park, an arena that he had graced so well, when he and Jim took time out from their hospitality duties to chat. Willie's reply to

Jim's question was 'No, I wouldn't change a thing.' Jim meanwhile replied, 'Yes, Wee Man, I would!'

We are left to reflect and speculate on what those changes may have been.

To his lifestyle? Unlikely.

To his football philosophy? Unlikely.

To his attitude to training? Probably.

To his family and relationships? Surely.

The funeral of James Curran Baxter took place at Glasgow Cathedral, with the mourners led by his 'Wee Dad', Rab Baxter, his two sons, Alan and Steven, and his partner, Norma. Rangers players past and present helped fill the cathedral and paid their respects to a working-man's hero. Legends of Scottish football including Denis Law, Sir Alex Ferguson, Walter Smith and Rangers manager at the time Dick Advocaat mixed with politicians, including Scotland's First Minister at the time, Henry McLeish, and Chancellor Gordon Brown.

Fans, too, paid their respects, many turning up in Rangers tops and scarfs. The Reverend Dr William Morris conducted the ceremony and showed his admiration by saying, 'For those of us who were spectators, seeing him from a further distance, his retirement from the game left us and our lives that much poorer.' Reverend Stuart MacQuarrie told the gathering how he had spent a lot of time with Jim in the weeks leading up to his death and how he had been touched by the way he faced up to cancer and his suffering.

'A couple of weeks ago I went to meet Jim Baxter,' he said. 'Instead of me comforting Jim about what would lie ahead, Jim just laughed and joked as only he could. His concern was never for himself, it was for his two sons and for Norma. Jim lifted my spirits and he did the same for those around him.'

Reverend Stuart was not only chaplain to Rangers Football Club, he was a fan and that was confirmed as he continued: 'Jim was one of the greatest football players this country ever produced and also one of the nation's most-loved characters.'

Jim's oldest son Alan and Raith fan and then Chancellor of the Exchequer Gordon Brown covered the Bible readings with passion and emotion. As mourners arrived at the cathedral and were given an Order of Service booklet, discretely positioned inside it was a leaflet urging people to become organ donors. Typical Jim Baxter – still giving on his final journey. It was in recognition of the team whose efforts through two liver transplants had extended Jim's life.

Broadcaster and author William McIlvanney recalled Jim's playing days and said: 'Jim had feet of pure gold and the left was probably inlaid with diamonds.'

When Jim's coffin arrived, the floral tributes were simple. They said 'Dad' and formed the shape of the number 6, which was always Jim's preferred number on his football shirt when he played.

Willie Henderson honoured his promise from the telephone call of three weeks earlier, and the other five with the same duties were former teammates and some of Rangers biggest all-time stars: John Greig, Ralph Brand, Alex Willoughby, Sandy Jardine and Craig Watson. As Jim's coffin was carried from the cathedral to his final resting place and a private service at Linn Crematorium, there was applause from the crowd who had gathered to pay tribute to a football legend and music from the pipes Jim had asked for. The music filled the air and again, just as he had specified, it was to be no ordinary piper. Willoughby had come up trumps, and Jim left to the sounds of his former regiment, the Black Watch Pipe Band.

On leaving the ceremony, Sir Alex Ferguson said: 'I've got a million memories of Jim, far too many to mention. He was the best player Scotland has ever produced, without question. We are never going to see anyone like him again.'

Jim Baxter's legacy may well be summed up by the words of Dick Campbell, who enjoyed that impromptu pre-Wembley kickabout in 1963 back in the streets of Cowdenbeath. 'Jim Baxter? Jim was God's gift to the working classes.'

26

LEGENDS ON A LEGEND

'Jim was special'

John Greig will forever be known as the Greatest Ever Ranger, but he will be eternally grateful to Jim Baxter and Her Majesty the Queen for the part they played in making it all possible.

John picked up that very accolade at a star-studded dinner in Glasgow in March 1999. Rangers legends including Sandy Jardine, Ally McCoist and Graeme Souness all agreed at the time that Greig was the only genuine candidate for the title.

It was 1962 and Rangers had embarked on a tour of Russia. They were, indeed, flag bearers for Scotland as they journeyed behind the Iron Curtain, promoting the development of football throughout Europe, and were undefeated in games played in the Soviet Union. Nineteen-year-old John Greig was part of the Rangers touring party. A twenty-one-year-old Jim Baxter wasn't. Baxter was serving Queen and Country at that stage, as part of his national service, with the Black Watch Regiment, and had been called up for a tour with the army football team instead.

The Russia trip was testing for everyone concerned, with hotels that were more like youth hostels, obvious cultural differences, poor communication and the presence of KGB officers watching their every move. The players had to adapt to spartan conditions and food was also a problem. However, young Greig put all that behind him and stepped up to the plate, as the opportunity presented itself to replace the absent Jim Baxter in the left-half role.

The first match saw Rangers win 3–1 against Lokomotiv Moscow and this was followed by a win against Dinamo Tbilisi in Georgia's ninety degree heat. The final match, which attracted a 60,000-strong crowd, against Dynamo Kiev in the Ukraine, ended 1–1, but Rangers made many new friends on this pioneering trip and Greig grabbed the chance with both hands.

The Greatest Ever Ranger says: 'It was a mystery tour and the facilities were basic, but those who came to our games loved their football. I have a lot to thank Jimmy and the army for because that trip gave me first-team experience, although left-half wasn't my best position. I just wanted to play and would have played anywhere.'

Greig had made his debut the previous September, and adds: 'It was against Airdrie in a League Cup tie and I scored in a 4–1 win, but I was nervous. Really nervous. I was to play inside right that night and Jim Baxter was in his usual left-half position. Jimmy saw I was nervous, as I paced up and down in that old pavilion at Broomfield, and he threw me a ball and said, "Let's play head tennis!" I said we don't have a net, but Jimmy just said imagine the net is there, and as soon as I sent my first header over he grabbed the ball instead of returning it with his own head. I said, "What was that about?" He said, "You hit the net – my point!" He was brilliant, and I saw him calm the nerves of all the younger guys as they came into the team. He didn't have a nerve in his body. He was supremely confident.'

Going back to that Russian trip, John was sharing a room with Willie Henderson, who was only eighteen but already making himself a fixture in Scot Symon's side. Anyway, John remembers: 'Willie decided he was going to phone home to his girlfriend Mary in Caldercruix near Airdrie. We were in Moscow at the time, but the Wee Man wouldn't be dissuaded. He must have been on the phone nearly an hour and had been patched through Paris, London and Glasgow switchboards before the phone finally rang out. A man answered and Willie was all excited, as he asked "Do you know Mary Bell?" By now I'm wondering what was going on, as Willie was raging. I thought he had been cut off after holding for nearly an hour and costing a fortune. It wasn't the case. It transpired Willie had phoned the village phone box and asked the chap who had answered the phone to nip across the road and get Mary Bell for him. The man then asked who was calling and Wee Willie, proud as punch, said, "It's Willie Henderson!" The man replied, "Naw, it's not. Willie Henderson is in Russia with the Rangers." Willie never got to speak to Mary.'

When Rangers returned from Russia, more than 10,000 fans turned out to meet them at Renfrew Airport, but Rangers were soon on their travels again. Greig recalls: 'We were in Germany to play Borussia Mönchengladbach, and again we didn't have Jimmy because of his army duties. Again, I played at left-half and the crowd was full of serving soldiers based in Germany. For the first forty-five minutes of that match, the fans kept shouting for Baxter – they thought I was actually him! I've never kicked the ball as much with my left foot.'

John and Jim Baxter did develop a fine half-back partnership, with Ronnie McKinnon between them. 'We really played 4-2-4,' said Greig, 'before it was really recognised, and Jim and I just complemented each other well. He had such great attacking style and I just went about my business of winning the ball and giving it to Jim. He was a superb footballer, with close control, so that he had the ball no matter how it arrived at him; in fact, he used to demand the ball – it didn't matter if he was in the most ridiculous situation, with players all round about him, he still wanted it and if you didn't give him it, my God, he let you know about it. I would say the closest I've ever seen to Jim's touch and control would perhaps be Gazza or maybe Brian Laudrup, but Jim was special. A real one-off. His confidence was unbelievable. He just never thought about getting beaten. I remember after we were playing together regularly for about six months he said to me, "Hey, Sir, you need to stop all that running aboot, ye'll be burnt oot by the time you are twenty-six!" It's hard to imagine that Jimmy was finished himself at only twenty-nine. It's also hard to imagine that Jimmy, Ralph Brand, Jimmy Millar and myself would walk down Renfield Street to catch the number 54 bus to training. Nowadays, half the players drive Bentleys! There we were, four internationalists waiting on a bus, sometimes in all weathers.

'Mind you, you had to watch how you spoke to Jim, especially on a Monday, as you only got a reply depending what kind of weekend he'd had.'

John Greig remains the only Rangers player to have won three trebles, the first of which came in 1964 under Scot Symon. As a former Rangers manager himself, he recognises the way Symon treated his precious left-half when Jim signed.

Symon was like a father figure to him, but as Jim got older, better and bolder, and almost became a law unto himself, Symon's patience was definitely tested and stretched to the extreme at times. 'Maybe if Jim had been subject to a bit more discipline earlier, his career might have been prolonged and we could all have enjoyed a bit more of the Baxter magic.'

John and Jim remained friendly right up until his death, and Jim's sons went to school with John's boy. As Jim's health deteriorated, John was a regular visitor. 'It was sad to see his health decline. We talked about the good times and replayed that 1967 Wembley game in conversation 1,000 times over. That was an astonishing display. The whole team played well, but that day belonged to Jim.'

If John Greig is the Greatest Ever Ranger, in his time as Rangers manager he signed the club's Greatest Ever Scorer. Ally McCoist was recruited from Baxter's old Wearside club Sunderland in 1983. Sunderland recovered £185,000 of the £400,000 transfer fee they had paid St Johnstone for the then nineteen-year-old two years previously. Like Baxter, McCoist had joined a struggling club, the wrong club for his talents, and like Slim Jim, Ally McCoist might have been swayed by Sunderland's location on a map rather than a league table. Just a three-hour drive from Edinburgh and on a main train line, McCoist, like Baxter, saw it as pretty convenient in terms of spending time back home in Scotland. Ally didn't set the heather on fire at Roker Park, but there is no doubt had he persevered, he would have, as he is such a strong character, to say nothing about being a great player.

John Greig was persistent in his pursuit and was persuasive in the extreme, and ultimately Rangers bagged a bargain. McCoist remains Rangers' all-time top scorer, with 355 goals, a tally that is unlikely ever to be beaten. When Ally set up home in Sunderland, it wasn't long before he was being asked about a Scottish legend.

Super Ally says: 'I couldn't believe it, and I certainly didn't appreciate just how highly regarded Jim Baxter was until I had been there a few weeks and it soon became obvious. Everybody wanted to talk about him and they all wanted to know did I know him? Well, unfortunately I had to say I didn't know him, and I hadn't even seen him play, but I made a point of getting hold of some videos to educate myself and I soon realised why he was held in such high esteem. What a player. I would have loved to have played alongside him. I might even have got more goals – maybe even double the number of goals Derek Johnstone scored for Rangers!' Ally said that with his tongue in cheek, as it's always the topic of conversation when he and Derek get together. Great pals, great goalscorers.

McCoist was soon a Baxter fan. 'He was a genius. A superstar is not too high an accolade for him. We had a physio at Sunderland who had played with Celtic, Jackie Watters, and he kept a keen eye on the Scottish scene. Old Jackie was a real character. He used to smoke the pipe and you were peering through a cloud of smoke to see him when he was treating you. But he was always talking about great Scottish players and he raved about Jim Baxter.'

Watters served Sunderland as first-team physio for three decades. He actually made his Celtic debut against Airdrie in 1938, replacing the injured Malky McDonald, who later managed Jim Baxter in the dark blue of Scotland in that one international against Brazil at Hampden in 1966.

McCoist remembers chats with Watters in the treatment room. 'Watters was a Fifer too, and he would stop what he was doing and look skywards, as if trying to remember, then take a long drag on his pipe and recall, "Aye yous" – as in Rangers – "didnae hae many, but Baxter was yer best ever. He was some player!" I remember Jackie too used to stuff his pipe into the pockets of the long white coat he wore as he went about his job fixing niggles and strains. It wasn't the first time I had to tell him his coat was on fire!'

Like Baxter, McCoist broke his leg on foreign soil, his injury coming in a Portugal v. Scotland match in 1993. Remarkably, McCoist won the second of his European Golden Boot awards that year. He had fifteen glorious years at Ibrox, and his best goal haul in a match was four against Falkirk in 1992, but an old teammate of Baxter ribs him when he can.

'Yes, Davie Wilson never tires of telling me he got six in one game against Falkirk thirty years before my four, in 1962. I'm sure Baxter must have teed him up for at least five of them.'

In the middle of Rangers nine-in-a-row period, Ally used to enjoy Jim Baxter's company. 'I used to see him regularly in the lounges at Ibrox and, do you know this? My abiding memory of Jim is that he was such a happy man. He was always happy to see the boys doing well and was never short of words of encouragement. He used to tell the boys to enjoy themselves. "You've earned it," and he used to emphasise that *earned* line. He was never jealous, never talked about what players were earning by comparison to his day, but he constantly told us, "Look after yourselves, it's a short career." We used to meet up with him at the Steps Bar in Glassford Street. It was a haunt of the players in those days. It was an old-fashioned boozer where we didn't get any hassle and we were just treated like any other punter. I think that's why Jim liked it too, and we often played dominoes together there. He took very little to drink then, it was usually just orange juice.

'He was a gentleman and loved Rangers. The Steps was also a regular watering hole for Gazza when he was up here, but fortunately he and Jim never got together. In the interests of public safety that was a bonus. Can you imagine that pair getting together in their prime? On and off the park!

'Actually, with hindsight, I can see real similarities between Jim Baxter and Paul Gascoigne. Two geniuses who just loved to play football, and they had similarities in personality too – enough was never enough, and excess everything was the way they lived, but on the field they both came alive and that was all they wanted, the ball at their feet and a platform to show their skills. Two magnificent footballers.'

McCoist returned to Ibrox as assistant manager under Walter Smith in January 2007 and replaced his mentor in the Ibrox hot seat in 2011. He has the job of navigating Rangers back to the top of Scottish football. Like Jim Baxter, McCoist is in both the Rangers and Scottish Football Hall of Fame.

I bet there was some great chat over the dominoes in the old traditional Steps Bar public house.

27

WILLIE HENDERSON –
MY PAL STANLEY

'Jimmy was James Bond'

It's fair to say Willie Henderson and Jim Baxter were great friends. But they were more than that: they were kindred spirits. Willie was born in the Glasgow suburb of Baillieston, but was brought up in the Lanarkshire mining village of Caldercruix. The similarities between Caldercruix in the west and Hill of Beath in the east were obvious: both were formed from the rows and rows of dwellings that housed the workers from the local pits. These were people who had a phenomenal work ethic but were contented, and a genuine community spirit was also evident.

Jim Baxter joined Rangers when he was just twenty years of age, while Willie Henderson at the tender age of fifteen turned down more lucrative offers from Manchester United and Everton, among others, to sign for the Ibrox side.

From the day Willie walked through the doors of the hallowed ground to the day he said goodbye to his great friend as a pall-bearer at his funeral, their love for each other's company was evident, yet strangely they rarely socialised together away from football.

They were great teammates, who had the same sense of humour. They were both streetwise sons of miners. Willie once met legendary boxer Muhammad Ali, who looked at his face and reportedly advised him that with a face like his, he should have been the boxer and Ali should have been the footballer.

In that huge ten-man win over England in 1963, Willie Henderson was nineteen years of age and he was the provider for both of Baxter's goals in the 2–1 Scotland victory. Henderson was missing through an injury in 1967, when Scotland took on the Auld Enemy, but they paired up in between in April 1964, this time at Hampden, where a crowd of 133,000 saw the team in dark blue win by a single goal.

Henderson remembers it like it was yesterday: 'What a team performance that day! It was one going on seven or eight. Jimmy Baxter and John Greig were in midfield, with the late great John White. England had Gordon Milne, Bobby Charlton and Terry Paine up against them in there, but not a chance. Scotland dominated.

'These were great days for football in Scotland. I used to get nervous before games, but not Jim Baxter. Jim would be going round the dressing-room with not a care in the world. He would be looking for tickets or checking which horse he fancied a flutter on. When the game started, he could have been playing down the public park with his pals. That's how relaxed he was.'

Jim Baxter and Willie Henderson were a partnership like mince and tatties, or ham and eggs. They were quite perfect together.

'Jim Baxter was known as Jim to his family, and to those who probably didn't even know him, including the fans, he was also Jim. To his pals, he was Jimmy or Stanley, after Stanley Baxter, who was a popular Glasgow comic of that time. To Jimmy, I was always "Wee Man"!

'As I said, I used to get nervous before games. On this occasion we were in a Scottish Cup final replay. That was the night Ian McMillan got the match ball after Jimmy marched off the field with it.

'Celtic left out Wee Jinky [Johnstone]. What a bonus that was for us, and what a blunder by Celtic, but still I was anxious before the game. Stanley could sense that I was anxious. He said, "Wee Man, c'mon let's go for a wee walk."

196

'Hampden was empty as we strolled over the pitch a full hour or more before kick-off. Again, it was Wee Man. "I've got something to tell you," he said. "Wee Man, if by any chance we get a penalty with two minutes to go, I'll be taking it. I tell you something now, I'll be taking it. And I'll tell you something else. See when you see me put the ball on the spot, start walking up them stairs to collect the cup!"

'Relaxed? How could we fail when our star player was so emphatic about us lifting the cup. I felt ten feet tall and I knew we couldn't lose. We won 3–0. Ralphie Brand scored two and Davie Wilson got one. We didnae need a penalty from Stanley. What a night that was!

'Jimmy really was the man about town. He always dressed immaculately. Suits that were cut to perfection. Finest cotton or silk shirts, with a collection of ties that set the whole thing off. It was the time of James Bond 007. In 1962, Sean Connery was James Bond in *Dr. No*. Jimmy Baxter outshone Bond in the fashion stakes. In fact, at times I used to think Jimmy was James Bond.'

Henderson continues: 'Jimmy was always quick with a quip. I came into Ibrox one day in a brand-new light-grey suit, new blue shirt and dark-blue tie. I was feeling a million dollars. My bubble was quickly burst when Jimmy said to me, "Hello, Wee Man, have you joined the RAF?"

'Another time, after taking some financial advice, I made the mistake of saying to Jimmy: "You know, Jim, I've made investments. I've been told on good authority that I've to put my cash into bricks and mortar." Jimmy gave me "the look" and replied, "Wee Man, try paying for your steak wi' a brick." Priceless!'

It was the typical style of cutting humour from the football dressing-room. This was where Henderson and Baxter were most comfortable. Camaraderie meant everything to these boys.

'I thought I was pretty worldly-wise. It was 1964 and I loved the boxing. Before training one day I piped up that I thought the young pretender Cassius Clay would win the title and knock out Sonny Liston, who was the champion and had held the world heavyweight belt for two years. That fight went down in history as the fight of the decade. Anyway, Jimmy was less than impressed and immediately told me I was wrong, along with some other comments, like that I should be certified.

'There was no malice in it. It was just the way Jimmy saw things.

'Anyway, as it was, Cassius Clay dumped Liston in six rounds, as Liston refused to get off the stool to finish the fight and the world had a new heavyweight champion.

'I couldn't wait to get back to training on Monday to tell my big mate that I knew my stuff. I had hardly got through the doors when Stanley grabbed me, gave me a big bear hug and said, "Wee Man, yer a genius!" And he was laughing his head off.'

Willie Henderson is almost uniquely positioned to talk about Jim Baxter, as he was there for both of Slim Jim's spells in light blue. Like Baxter, Henderson left Rangers when he really didn't want to. Willie was at Ibrox for twelve years and found himself shipped out to play his football in South Africa when the club had a Cup-Winners' Cup final date in their diary. Henderson was twenty-eight years old when he was given a free transfer. It was a very sad way to end his Ibrox career, particularly as Rangers went on to win their one and only European trophy within weeks of his departure.

Baxter left for purely financial reasons in a period when Rangers showed no flexibility in their salary structure. Many years later, like Henderson, Baxter said he had never really wanted to leave.

Forty-two years after lifting his boots to play elsewhere, Henderson remains a Rangers icon and one of the most popular hosts in and around the various lounges and corporate boxes at Ibrox on matchdays.

The role of matchday host was one that Jim Baxter also enjoyed, and again, if it wasn't Baxter the fans wanted to chat to and have photographs taken with, it was Henderson. Both always had time for the fans and both had patience, no matter the circumstance. Working-class heroes, for sure.

Willie recalls one day at Ibrox when they were both working there. Again came the shout "Wee Man! Wee Man, I need a word! Quick, in here. Into this private box. It's empty," said Stanley. "Wee Man, I've got problems. Serious problems," he said.

'Now, when Jimmy Baxter tells you he's got problems, you fear the worst. It could have been anything. But no, this day his problems were his cholesterol!

'Jimmy wasn't in the best of health anyway, but he had been to the doctor and, after the usual checks, he was told his cholesterol was too high. "Too high?" I said. "Jimmy, how high is it?"

'He said, "It's 9.6!"

'I said, "Jimmy, you need to be careful, you're going to explode!"

'His reply was, 'Ah know, Ah know I've to change my diet, but, Wee Man, do you think it would help if I cut back my three bacon rolls in the morning to two? I'm happy to try it, but I canny gie up ma scone thick wi' butter and jam for ma lunch. That's essential.'

Sadly, by then Jim Baxter's health problems had begun to run much deeper than his high cholesterol.

Willie Henderson held his pal Jimmy in the highest possible esteem as a player. 'Anyone who plays for a Rest of the World team three times has to be very special. Jim was in the World select that celebrated the centenary of the FA in 1963; he was a key player in the select team that played in all white against Stanley Matthews' all-star line-up for his testimonial; and he was also selected by German World Cup-winning manager Helmut Schoen for an exhibition match in Stockholm. Jimmy Baxter mixed in so easily with the best players in the world because he was one of them himself.'

Willie himself was up there, too, in that company and was regularly in demand for special world star XIs. Willie, of course, was part of the side that sold out Stoke's Victoria ground for the Matthews testimonial, while he took centre stage in the match to commemorate the career of Benfica legend Mario Caluna. He was a star, too, in the benefit match for wayward Manchester United genius George Best.

The Best game was played at Windsor Park in Belfast in August 1988. The programme promised a mystery guest to complement the stars on display, who included Pat Jennings, Paul Breitner, Rudi

Krol, Liam Brady, Johan Neeskens, Johnny Rep, Trevor Francis and Ossie Ardiles. The mystery guest turned out to be none other than William Henderson, who was then forty-four years young and had been retired from professional football for nine years.

Was Willie a sideshow?

Not a bit of it. He wowed a packed Windsor Park and raised the cheer of the night when he trapped a spinning delivery with his backside.

Henderson and Baxter: showmen, for sure.

Willie and Jimmy Baxter had that bond, a special relationship, and to this day Willie has a tear in his eye when talking about his great friend.

Willie had his own issues to deal with, as did Jim, but deal with them they did. That's what heroes do. That's why James Curran Baxter and William Henderson, from good mining stock, were and will always be the kind of genuine heroes who never forgot their roots and never will.

28

BAXTER'S BEST BUD

'Stay away from Jim!'

Willie Johnston should be best remembered for scoring two goals against Moscow Dynamo when Rangers won the European Cup-Winners' Cup in 1972, but his escapades with the Scottish international squad on World Cup duty in Argentina in 1978 are what people often relate to when 'Wee Bud' is the topic of conversation.

Willie picked up the nickname 'Bud' in the Ibrox dressing-room when he came to training one day resplendent in a long winter overcoat with a fur collar. It was exactly the same style as the trademark coat worn by popular music hall entertainer Bud Flanagan. Hence, Willie was christened Bud by his Rangers teammates and it stuck.

Willie is still known as Bud to this day, but in his early days at Rangers he was Billy – Wee Billy – the 'Billy' moniker to ensure that there was no confusion with Rangers' other Willie, another raiding winger, Willie Henderson.

Henderson played on the right, while Johnston was like Baxter a 'lefty', operating on the opposite flank. As did Henderson, Johnston arrived at Rangers before his 16th birthday.

Willie has clear recollections of that first day in late 1962. 'When I joined the ground staff in November, I wasn't due to celebrate my 16th birthday for about another six weeks. I hadn't even been to Ibrox before I turned up that first day. I went in through those magnificent front doors: that was some experience in itself for a wee laddie from Fife. The problem was my train had been late and here I was on my first day at Rangers turning up late. I was met by Joe Craven, to whom I said I was reporting for training. He was one of the trainers and he said that they were expecting me, then he sorted me out with my kit. Old Joe told me to get changed, then pointed me in the direction of the Albion, which was our training ground, just over the way from the stadium. I ran across the road and couldn't wait to get started. I was told to find Bobby Shearer or Eric Caldow, who would sort me out. It didn't take me long to find them, as they were with Billy Ritchie and Norrie Martin. George Niven was there, too. Three goalkeepers and the back kicks from Rangers' first team.

'I was a winger, but I wanted to get going and be part of the group. Well, Bobby and Eric, with the goalies, were practising taking by-kicks. I was to join them. They were thumping the ball from the six-yard line to the half-line and more, where I could hardly launch it thirty yards! They were having a wee competition to see who could kick it the furthest and I certainly couldn't compete with that lot. After about twenty minutes, and me thinking is this what professional footballers do all day, Jim Baxter came over. I'll never forget what happened next.

'Jimmy said, "Are you the wee boy from Cardenden? Fae Bowhill? Come wi' me, son. You'll learn f**k all with that lot!" Jim marched me to the other end of the training pitch, where Ralph Brand, Jimmy Millar and Davie Wilson were lining up loads of balls right along the eighteen-yard box. "Right," said Jim, "Three wi' yer right and three wi' yer left. See how many times you can hit the crossbar!" Not score, mind you, hit the bar!

'Oh, and then Jim threw in: "We are all in for half a crown!"

'That was a fortune for me, but Brand, Millar and Wilson were all up for it and, of course, Jim cleaned up. Almost every time, he just pinged it off the woodwork. No problem, left and right foot. I think he hit the bar five times out of six. Jim was in the money again, as he

202

reminded the other three that he would be collecting his winnings after training.

'Some people say Jim's right foot was for standing on, but believe me it was much better than people thought. But the left was a wand. He could do anything with a ball with that left foot.'

Surprisingly, Willie Johnston, for all his pace and outrageous speed, had to be patient before he made his Rangers debut. That was probably down to the quality of natural wide players at Ibrox at the time, as, other than Henderson and Wilson, Craig Watson, who was a very close pal of Jim Baxter and Derek Trail, were very capable wingers but found first-team football difficult to secure because of the quality of players competing for places.

Willie had only played for Scot Symon's first team five times, in fact, when he was thrust into the Rangers team for the 1964 Scottish League Cup final against Celtic. Johnston had not yet turned eighteen and remembers the build-up. Again, Jim Baxter used a psychological line to help calm the nerves of the teenager. It was a wee story that had worked so well a year earlier to help Willie Henderson before an old firm game in another cup final and he trotted it out again when he saw how nervous Willie Johnston was around one hour before kick-off at Hampden.

Willie recalls: 'I was down in the toilets, chain-smoking to try and calm my nerves. Jim came in and I said I was feeling sick. It may have been all the fags, but Jim said, "C'mon out on the pitch wi' me for five minutes." Out we went and he said, "See if we get a penalty and it's in the last minute, I'm taking it, and when you see me put the ball on the spot get yersel' up the stairs and collect your medal and the cup."'

Jim Baxter captained Rangers in that cup final and recognised his responsibilities.

It had been an effective ploy to get Willie Henderson in the right frame of mind – Rangers won the Scottish Cup that night after his pep talk – and it proved its worth again, with Willie Johnston delivering the goods on the park, as Rangers beat Celtic 2–1 and another piece of silverware was destined for Ibrox.

There is an interesting follow-up to that game, as it was reported that Symon had promised his players a bonus of £500 each to win the trophy. When the wages were duly paid, Willie Johnston noticed his take-home pay had only been boosted by £50, not the £500 he expected. Willie made his way to the manager's office to see if a mistake had been made but was rebuffed by Symon, who told him, 'Too much money can turn a boy's head!' He also told him to steer clear of Jim Baxter!

Willie confirms this: 'Yes, it's true, Scot Symon, who always called me Billy, said, "Stay away from Jim, Billy. You don't want to be going to some of the places that Jim visits." Jim had his bad side, if that's what you could call it, but he was great with me and he had a heart of gold.

'He sometimes picked me up when he was back in Cowdenbeath, and when he did everbody in our street turned out to see him. That was how big a celebrity he was! Jim treated me like his wee brother and he looked after me. In my first games, he talked me through them when he was playing in behind me. He treated every game like a training game and if he had any nerves he never showed them. Those were some days. Happy days. Jim may not have been the best example to the young players coming through, if you are talking "off the park", but nobody can say that when it comes to "on the park". He never stopped offering me advice and kept trying to point me in the right direction, which basically meant that when you were playing with him, you had to give him the ball as often as possible. If he shouted for it and you didn't give him it, you were in trouble!'

There remains a myth that Jim Baxter sat on the ball at Wembley. It just didn't happen. Keepie-uppie, yes. Sit on the ball, no.

But Willie Johnston *did* sit on the ball in an Old Firm game. Johnston had tormented Celtic all day down the left flank and, when in space, and no Celtic player looked to close him down, Wee Bud sat on the ball and incensed his opponents. Definite shades of his mentor. Several Celtic players eventually did charge in, but Johnston took a touch before passing the ball to a teammate in light blue. The fans loved it, Celtic hated it. New Rangers boss Willie Waddell wasn't too happy either, and later fined Johnston £40 for bringing shame to the club and being disrespectful of his opponents.

That fine clearly wasn't a huge deterrent to Willie, as he repeated his 'sitting on the ball' show against Bayern Munich, no less, at Ibrox in the semi-final of the 1972 European Cup-Winners' Cup.

Baxter and Willie Johnston shared the same outlook on football, and life in general. Willie remembers that terrible night in Vienna when Jim Baxter broke his leg.

'I was only a couple of yards away. Jim had nutmegged the boy, then nutmegged him again, then whack! You heard the crack. Everyone knew it was a break. The game was all but over, too. He had been majestic that night and I remember our tactics. Scot Symon said, "Billy, I'm playing you at outside right tonight." I said I can't play on the right, and he replied, "It's all right, just do it for ten minutes, then swap with Davie Wilson." Symon continued, "Anyway, just get the ball to Jim as quickly as you can." That was a sad night and the break had a real negative effect on Jim's career.'

Willie remembers regular European nights, and Jim was always great company. 'I can't remember where we were, but I was just young and rooming with big Roger Hynd. We were at the usual after-match banquet and everybody was bored when the word reached us: "Party in Jimmy's room – pass it on." Now, all round the hall you could see people whispering and passing on the message: *Jimmy is having a party in his room*. I said to big Roger, "We can't go, it's just for the big players" – we had been warned off again by the boss. The Alexander Brothers and Callum Kennedy, I remember, were there, for whatever reason. They weren't in kilts and singing their usual Scottish songs, though, but Roger and I decided we should just go to our own room. We were hardly there ten minutes, and not yet in bed, when Jimmy Millar knocked on the door and said we had to come to Jimmy's room. So we went along and I remember it was bedlam, plenty of girls were there too, and my abiding memory is everybody was drinking Dimple whisky. Jimmy was on the bed and enjoying himself. I can't tell you exactly what he was doing, but he certainly looked to be having fun!'

Johnston was a real character. Even during his second spell at Rangers, he used to have a ball boy primed and ready for him with a lit cigarette that he would collect in the tunnel at half-time and head straight to the dressing-room toilets with it to get his nicotine kick!

Willie left Rangers, and after a spell in Australia he joined West Bromwich Albion, where he had seven great years with the West Midlands club. 'I played with some great midfielders over the years, including Johnny Giles and Bryan Robson, but when Jim Baxter was on the ball, nobody could touch him; he worked much harder than people remember, too.'

Willie retired from football in 1985, with his 40th birthday on the horizon, and again, in an uncanny similarity, like Baxter he made his living in the pub game after hanging up his boots.

Willie and Jim met up fairly regularly at Ibrox in later years, and Willie remembers Jim's health fading. 'We always met up when I was through for games, and he wasn't looking good. It was obvious he was ill again, but he never lost that sense of humour. A few of the lads told me he was just the same in hospital and at home near the end. I didn't visit him then. Maybe I just wanted to remember him how he had been all those years before, when he had looked after me like his wee brother. He was unique. He was just such a great guy.'

29

NOT THE GREATEST –
SIMPLY THE BEST

'The ultimate Rangers legend'

As of September 2014, only ninety players in the history of Rangers Football Club have been honoured in the official Hall of Fame. The names of these heroes are displayed proudly on the Hall of Fame board, which sits at the top of the famous marble staircase.

The inductees of 2014 included Nacho Novo and Fernando Ricksen. Another, Lee McCulloch, wore the iconic number 6 on the back of his light-blue shirt. As others elected to move on when Rangers were repositioned in the bottom tier of Scottish football following liquidation in 2012, McCulloch chose to stay. The number 6 jersey was, of course, the shirt of preference of Jim Baxter, who himself had been part of the Rangers Hall of Fame since its inception by Sir David Murray in 2000.

The criteria for recognition and inclusion are: service to the club, appearances made, honours won, international caps gained while with Rangers and, the final category, 'exceptional ability'. All are taken into consideration by a panel which, over the years, has included John Greig, Ally McCoist and club historian David Mason.

Jim Baxter was internationally recognised as an exceptionally gifted footballer and a firm fans' favourite, but was he the greatest player ever in Rangers' history? It's a question worthy of debate when you consider the quality of players to have adorned Rangers blue over the years. While John Greig MBE was voted 'the Greatest Ever Ranger' in 1999 by the club's supporters, and has a statue in his honour at the corner of the Main and Copland Road stands at Ibrox, was he the best on the field? Greig, like Baxter, was part of that sensational all-conquering Rangers team of the 1960s, but he was a different type of player to Slim Jim and, of course, his recognition was a very worthy reward for a lifetime as a one-club man.

Voting will always be subjective when it comes to who has been Rangers' greatest player over the various eras, and any nomination will be influenced by the maturity of those who have watched Rangers as the years have passed. For me, Baxter was the best, but there would be a huge list of candidates for the title of Rangers best player ever.

Baxter's Rangers career was relatively short compared to that of many others, but if we were to look at the impact he made in those five years first time around after signing from Raith Rovers, he would challenge anybody for the 'best player ever' title.

Who else would be a contender? A select list would surely include players from almost every era in the history of the football club.

In chronological order:

R.C. HAMILTON, 1897–1908, 209 appearances, four league titles, two Scottish Cups. Hamilton was Rangers' top scorer in nine successive seasons and their first player to break the hundred goals barrier. A genuine prolific goalscorer who was known for his direct style.

DAVE MEIKLEJOHN, 1919–36, 563 appearances after signing from Maryhill Juniors. Converted a penalty goal against Celtic in the 1928 Scottish Cup final to give Rangers the trophy for the first time since 1903. Sixteen caps for Scotland and an ever-present in Rangers sides for eighteen successive seasons. A colossus and a real no-nonsense defender who never played for any other club but Rangers. Captained the side the day Celtic goalkeeper John Thomson was killed during a game in 1931.

ALAN MORTON, 1920–33, 440 appearances as a player, nine league titles, three Scottish Cups. Polar opposite of Gascoigne: served as a director at Rangers for forty years until his death, aged seventy-eight. His portrait greets those coming through the doors before they take their first step on the marble staircase. A star in the Wembley Wizards Scotland side that beat England 5–1 in 1928. A left winger who could deliver precision passes and outwitted full-backs for fun.

BOB McPHAIL, 1927–40, 408 appearances, nine league titles, six Scottish Cups. McPhail scored 261 goals for Rangers, 230 in the league, and was only overtaken by Ally McCoist in 1997. Went on to coach the Rangers second string, but as a player he formed a deadly partnership with his wingman, Alan Morton. Lightning quick and alert to any half chance. Fleet of foot and very adept in the air.

WILLIE WOODBURN, 1937–55, 325 appearances, four league titles, four Scottish Cups, two League Cups. The Second World War curtailed his career, which was prematurely ended by a sine die suspension by the SFA following a head-butting incident in a match against Stirling Albion. That ban was lifted three years after it was imposed, but it was too late for the giant defender to come back to professional football. A player ahead of his time, who organised Rangers' defence with distinction and always tried to play it out from the back.

JOCK 'TIGER' SHAW, 1938–53, 242 appearances, four league titles, three Scottish Cups; later to serve the club as a trainer, and helped the development of youngsters, including John Greig, Sandy Jardine and Willie Henderson. The nickname 'Tiger' says it all. He had a huge desire to win and was an accurate passer of the ball.

WILLIE WADDELL, 1938–55, 301 appearances, four league titles, two Scottish Cups; later to serve as manager and general manager. He was the man who transformed Ibrox Stadium in the wake of the 1971 disaster. As a player, he was a speedy, direct, strong-running winger who set up goals for his centre-forward, Willie Thornton.

GEORGE YOUNG, 1941–57, 428 appearances, six league titles, three Scottish Cups, three League Cups. Captained Scotland on forty-eight occasions and was the first man to represent Scotland fifty times. Young missed only five games between 1948 and 1953. Young was the lynchpin in one of the most frugal Rangers defences ever. A huge imposing centre-half who struck fear into opponents. Nicknamed 'Corky' after the lucky charm champagne cork he carried in his shorts pocket going into every game.

SAMMY COX, 1945–55, 370 appearances, four Division A titles, three Scottish Cups, one league cup; like Baxter, a left-half, but he was pretty much an all-rounder. Played to the left of George Young in that invincible half-back line. A cultured and talented player, with great vision.

IAN McCOLL, 1945–60, 526 appearances, seven league titles, five Scottish Cups, two League Cups. A skilful right-half in the Iron Curtain defence. A real student of the game and reliable in the extreme. McColl later managed Baxter, with Scotland and at Sunderland.

RALPH BRAND, 1954–65, 317 appearances, four league titles, three Scottish Cups, four League Cups. Scored 206 goals. A mercurial front man who formed such a profitable trio with Davie Wilson and Jimmy Millar either side of him. Scored all types of goals and had the gear change to leave defenders flat-footed.

WILLIE HENDERSON, 1960–72, 426 appearances, two league titles, four Scottish Cups, two League Cups. A teenage sensation at Rangers and the provider of a mountain of goals for a succession of front players at Ibrox. Teased his opposition full-back with sight of the ball before skipping away from them as if jet-propelled, then delivered the kind of service to Millar, Brand, Wilson, Forrest, McLean and Ferguson, among others, that strikers dream of.

JOHN GREIG, recognised as the Greatest Ever Ranger; 1961–82, as a player: 755 appearances, five league titles, four League Cups, six Scottish Cups. Captained Rangers to their only European success in 1972, versus Dynamo Moscow. A born leader on the park, with an incredible will to win. Covered every blade of grass and never gave anything less than 100 per cent. A wing-half who tackled like a lion and passed pretty well too. Replaced Jock Wallace as manager of Rangers and struggled to achieve success. John resigned in 1983, but returned to the club in 1990 and served in a variety of roles before resigning as a director in 2011, when Craig Whyte was in office.

SANDY JARDINE, 1964–82 as a player, three league titles, five Scottish and League cups, a European Cup-Winners' Cup winner; scored that wonderful goal in the semi-final against Bayern Munich on the way to Barcelona. A supreme technician who epitomised a modern footballer of the '70s. Pacey and dedicated, with a real eye for a goal. A teammate of Baxter and his first training partner. Later came back to work at Rangers in a number of positions, right up to his untimely death in 2014.

DEREK JOHNSTONE, 1970–83; and a brief second spell, 1985–86: 546 appearances, a European winner when still only eighteen; three league wins, five Scottish Cups, five League Cups. Scored the winner against Celtic in the 1970 League Cup final when he was just sixteen. Notched a total of 210 Rangers goals and remains the club's fifth top-scorer of all time. Would have scored more, but didn't take penalties. Equally comfortable as a centre back. Wonderful touch, elegant in possession and a terrific header of the ball.

DAVIE COOPER, 1977–89, 540 appearances; recognised by the club as having scored Rangers' greatest ever goal. That goal came in the 1979 Drybrough Cup final, when he went on a run before drilling the ball into the net after lifting the ball over four Celtic players and waltzing round them en route to his shooting range. A naturally gifted footballer who, like Baxter, had a sensational left foot, whose close control made him look as if the ball was tied to his boot. Elegant in motion, he packed a powerful shot.

ALLY McCOIST, 1983–98, 581 appearances, ten league titles, nine League Cups, one Scottish Cup: Mr Goals! His record of 355 Rangers goals is unlikely ever to be beaten. Known as 'Super Ally' for obvious reasons; a fans' favourite and a supreme poacher, but he could link play too, as was shown when he played in midfield early in his career. A hugely intelligent footballer who was assistant manager under Walter Smith on his return to Rangers and is now guiding Rangers back to the top flight as manager in his own right. Known to his teammates as 'Hubcaps' under the assumption he used to steal them as a boy in East Kilbride.

RICHARD GOUGH, 1987–98 (split his two spells at the club with a brief spell at Kansas City Wizards in 1997), 427 appearances, three Scottish Cups, six League Cups. Once a Ranger always a Ranger, they say. Rangers first £1 million signing and of course skipper in that nine-in-a-row league-winning period. The picture of him holding the trophy aloft at Tannadice, despite missing the winning game through injury, with Alan McLaren being deputised as captain, remains an iconic image. A fitness fanatic and a cultured defender who never knew when he was beaten. Failure was not in the Gough vocabulary. He ensured his players delivered, as he took on the mantle of the manager on the park.

BRIAN LAUDRUP, 1994–98, 151 appearances; scored a rare headed goal to clinch nine-in-a-row at Tannadice. A Walter Smith signing for £2.3 million from Fiorentina. Sensational close control and blessed with blistering pace, he lit up the Scottish game but perhaps fell short on the European arena.

PAUL GASCOIGNE, 1995–98, appearances 104; another 'character' perhaps in the Baxter mould after a fashion. He only wanted to play football. Scored a stunning treble to single-handedly demolish Aberdeen 3–1 in 1996, giving Rangers the title. A truly flawed genius who again, like Baxter, loved to laugh and was always up for fun. Gascoigne was a sensation in his short time at Rangers, with strength, guile and a change of pace that left opponents in his wake. The Rangers fans loved him and he loved being a Ranger.

DAVID WEIR, 2007–12, 231 appearances, three league titles, two Scottish Cups, three League Cups. Came to Rangers as a stop-gap defender in 2007, aged thirty-six, and stayed for five seasons. Played in Rangers' fourth-ever European final, replaced Barry Ferguson as skipper and was a Rangers captain in every sense of the word. A huge influence in the dressing-room. A defender not blessed with great pace, but what he lacked in speed he made up for in guile. The Rangers fans took him to their hearts.

A list of true Rangers greats, but how many of them actually got the fans on the edge of their seats – or, in days before all-seated stadia, for whom would the crowd surge forward fully focused on the action on the field and willing their heroes to score?

Baxter truly did.

Sure, McCoist, Gascoigne and Cooper would have too, as would have Waddell, Morton, McPhail and so on before them probably, but did any of them have the Baxter swagger? The defiance to convention with the shirt outside his shorts? Gascoigne and Cooper, perhaps.

Did any of these blue legends play keepie-uppie at Wembley? Did any of these players enjoy the incredible record of success that Baxter could point to in Old Firm games? Certainly not.

Baxter passed through Rangers all too briefly first time round, and many well-respected football connoisseurs believe that Rangers would have won the European Cup the season of the tragedy and broken leg in Vienna had things ended differently.

Jim Baxter is the ultimate Rangers legend.

How many other Rangers players over the years have been called into World select XIs, as Baxter and Willie Henderson were on more than one occasion? Did any other Ranger see an international cap auctioned for £10,000, his Wembley jersey sold for £17,500? All the confirmation anyone needs to deduce Baxter was very special.

Only twenty-four goals, but how many assists in 254 Rangers appearances? His medal collection of three league titles, three Scottish Cups and four League Cup wins remains hugely impressive and a phenomenal achievement in such a short period of time. It was intense for Rangers, and Baxter was a man in a hurry to enjoy success from the day he joined from Raith Rovers.

Jim Baxter was world class.

John Greig is indeed a worthy recipient of the title of Greatest Ever Ranger, but when it comes to Rangers' greatest ever player ... well, James Curran Baxter has no peers.

AFTERWORD BY WALTER SMITH

My playing career was just about starting at Dundee United as Jim Baxter's was coming to a close. But before I signed for Dundee United, it's well documented that I was a Rangers fan and attended as many games as I could.

In the 1960s, Rangers had a fantastic team, with a lot of really good players. Jim Baxter was just one of them. He had fantastic ability and real character to carry it off. That's what struck me about him. He had confidence galore, and that kind of persona about him that, allied to an extreme level of ability, made him quite fantastic to watch.

One game in particular I remember as a fan was the 1964 cup final. Rangers were up against a quite exceptional Dundee team. It was some game, some cup final, and Rangers won it with two very late goals, if I remember correctly. But Baxter was at his brilliant best. He was magnificent, in fact. Baxter gave that level of performance regularly and going to watch him play was a thing I really enjoyed doing.

I don't know how I would have managed Jim Baxter. It would have been a challenge, that's for sure.

At Ibrox, I was lucky enough to meet him at a few games after he had finished his playing career, but as a player – I don't know, you can only manage people properly once you have started managing them and found out, or attempted to find out, what makes them

215

tick. I certainly wouldn't have been frightened by the prospect of managing him at his peak. I was never frightened to manage players, even some with big reputations, and a few whose reputations were gained for their off-the-field lifestyle. And of course Jim Baxter had that kind of reputation.

I think I would have handled it OK. Whether Jim would have handled it OK is a different matter.

I managed Paul Gascoigne and he respected the way I operated with him. It wasn't easy, but that's maybe the way with a genius – and Gascoigne and Baxter are in that category.

I don't think there is any doubt that there are uncanny similarities between Baxter and Gazza. Paul was another of these boys blessed with a huge amount of ability – Jim Baxter played football the way Jim Baxter played, and Paul Gascoigne played football the way Paul Gascoigne played, that was it, and both were never really taught anything; they both had an incredible level of ability and played so instinctively. Common traits that made them special.

Baxter, and Gascoigne, for that matter, will go down in Rangers history as two of the finest players to wear the jersey. Jim Baxter was ahead of his time and is up there with the true greats of the world game.

Walter Smith, OBE

APPENDIX 1

ERIC DAVIDSON POEM

Jim Baxter inspired not only Kevin Raymond to put pen to paper, but also well-known after-dinner entertainer Eric Davidson, who scripted his own tribute to his hero in a poem written after Jim died in 2001.

Eric came from Midlothian mining stock. His family understood the hardships and dangers of pit life. They were also huge fans of Rangers Football Club, with Jim being the all-time idol of the Davidson family.

Jim Baxter – A Miner's Son fi Fife

In the spring o' '67, when Wilson was in power
And miniskirts and love were all the rage
The whole world was to witness Scottish football's finest hour
When a tall slim genius took the centre stage.

The stage of course was Wembley, England's hallowed ground
Where the year before Alf Ramsey's men stood tall.
With Hurst and Moore and Charlton, they thought they were
   the best around.
OK, they were the World Cup holders after all.

Ah, but Bremner, Law, McCalliog, they weren't scared o' their elite
And with his keepie uppie Baxter took the pish!
You see, God looked down upon him, sprinkled gold dust on
   his feet
And every Scotsman got his greatest wish.

He'd signed for Glasgow Rangers, a miner's son fi Fife.
He said it was like being in a dream;
His scintillating passes cut defences like a knife.
With magical finesse, he reigned supreme.

Along wi' Bobby Shearer, Eric Caldow, Jimmy Miller,
   Ralphie Brand,
Wee Willie Henderson flying doon the wing,
They played a type of football that was the finest in the land.
Will we see their likes again? Well, here's the thing!

It seems to me those days are gone, when the youngsters
   learned their trade
In the Govan streets and stoorie miner's raws
Wi' a piece and jam in either hand each day and night they played
In their worn oot rubber's kickin their tanner ba's.

You hardly see the laddies playing under street lights ony mair
Or jerseys used as goalposts on the ground.
They'd rather play computer games, watch *Big Brother* or *Millionaire*.
Is it any wonder great players can't be found?

So here's to when these men were kings, who played a game so rare
Who took on Europe and the world wi' grace
And the miner's son fi Fife, whose genius, arrogance and flair
Helped put Scottish football in its rightful place.

Eric's poetry is a feature of his annual one-man show at the Edinburgh Festival. Eric was delighted to have his poem feature in this Jim Baxter biography as his own small tribute to Scotland's greatest-ever footballer. You can see more of Eric's work at www. ericdavidson.co.uk.

APPENDIX 2

FANS FOR THE MEMORIES

SANDY HOME: A lifelong Jambo, Sandy always made a point of making sure his dad took him to Tynecastle when Rangers visited, so he could drool over Slim Jim's talent.

'Baxter was a magician. A wizard with the ball, but so unselfish if a teammate was in a better scoring position. He never seemed to have a bad game, which usually meant Hearts losing. But you didn't mind so much, because you'd been entertained by a genius.

'One memory that sticks out was during a cup game at Tynecastle. Jim got the ball on the halfway line and ran like the clappers down the wing. About a foot from the byline, halfway between the goal and the corner flag, he stopped dead, leaving the defender to run past him and off the pitch. He then hit the ball right into the postage stamp. I've still no idea how Baxter scored from there.

'In another match a cross came over to the corner of the eighteen-yard box and Baxter just thumped it on the volley straight into the net. The way he would do keepie-ups or wee flicks to get past opponents was a joy to watch – even though it was my team he was dancing round. The ball seemed to be glued to his feet. The best honour I could pay him is this: my dad always loved Willie Bauld but regarded Jim Baxter as a more skilful, quicker player.'

BILLY YOUNG: From Falkirk, he has watched Scottish football for more than fifty years: 'Baxter had swagger, but it masked a footballing elegance which only a few players are blessed with. He was something special.'

GEORGE: A Celtic fan from Livingston: 'When I was between twelve and fourteen, my team could not get near Rangers and Baxter made them tick. It's no coincidence that when Baxter left in 1965 Celtic overtook them as the best team in Scotland and went on to dominate.'

ALAN CARMICHAEL: From Motherwell, he has supported Rangers for sixty-two years: 'My school was right next door to Fir Park and my first game was Motherwell v. Rangers on a Wednesday afternoon, as they had no floodlights. I got lifted over the turnstile that day. My favourite Baxter memory is the 1963 Scottish Cup final replay after a dismal 1–1 draw. Rangers, led by Slim Jim, ripped Celtic apart. Baxter waltzed through the game with a repertoire of flicks and contempt for Celtic. Nutmeg after nutmeg, playing at walking pace, he roasted and tortured Celtic, as their fans left early in droves as they couldn't bear the torment. Baxter was a truly world-class player who put on a virtuoso performance that night.'

WULLIE: A lifelong Rangers fan from Dundee: 'Baxter was Simply the Best! What a sight he was, running at teams with the ball, defences in panic and Ibrox rising in expectation.'

ALLY GOURLAY: A lifelong Raith Rovers fan: 'I never got to see him play in the flesh, but seeing what he did not once but twice at Wembley on DVD is just awesome. The stories are a bit legend about him, too. I actually used to bump into him in the Coaledge Tavern in Crossgates. The pub was owned by ex-Rangers player Alex Smith, but Jim used to visit and catch up with Willie Butchard from his Primrose days. He never forgot his roots.'

BRIAN PROUDFOOT: A Sunderland fan and long-standing season-ticket holder originally at Roker Park and now the Stadium of Light: 'When we signed Baxter, we thought we were getting a gem. We did, but he didn't shine as often as he should have, as we just didn't have enough good players who were on the same wavelength as him.'

STEVEN GRAHAM: A Rangers fan from Gourock: 'I first saw Baxter when he was a Sunderland player and he was back in Glasgow for Scotland against Italy in 1965. Scotland won 1–0, with John Greig scoring, but Baxter was Scotland's inspiration. He could have excelled in any company and of course he did.'

ALEX COPELAND: Emigrated to Canada in 1967 and still never misses a Rangers game on TV as a member of Toronto #1 Rangers Supporters Club: 'I moved to Canada after the Berwick Rangers defeat, I think that was about far enough. I had the privilege of watching Jim Baxter playing at club and also international games. Who can forget the Wembley games, especially the 3–2 victory on the heels of England winning the World Cup? And all the many cup finals – Hampden was almost like our second home. We were winning everything at that time, thanks to Jim Baxter and company. Baxter was a true Scottish genius on the park and we will never see the likes of him again. Slim Jim will live forever in the hearts of the folks who saw him. Thanks for the memories, RIP Slim!'

RONNIE SLOAN: Aged sixty-eight, a Mansfield-based Nottingham Forest fan: 'Baxter was past his sell-by date when we got him, but there was the odd flash of outrageous skill. Sadly, he was more often starring on the front pages of the papers than the back.'

JOHN CHRISTIE: Aged sixty-seven, a Celtic fan from Coatbridge: 'I hated seeing Baxter in light blue as much as I loved seeing him in the dark blue of Scotland. He was the player everyone admired, although at the time back in the 1960s I would never have admitted it.'

JOHN McCULLOCH: Born in the same year as Baxter, he is Dad to Rangers captain Lee: 'When Jim Baxter was at his peak, I was in the navy and was nicknamed "Slim" after Baxter, as I played left-half in the navy team. Scot Symon never clamped down on him, no matter what he got up to, including bevying up until a few hours before a game! He set up more goals than he scored, but what a player. He had that flaw though, where drink was concerned, and he thought two laps of the track was a hard shift by way of training. I remain immensely proud that my son Lee has captained Rangers and wears that iconic number 6 shirt, walking in the footsteps of a legend like Jim Baxter.'

IAN WILKIE: A member of the Big Apple Bears and a resident of New York: 'I was brought up in Coatbridge and remember Jim Baxter's wedding day. I had a good spot in front of the car and came away a wealthy boy. It was the only 'scramble' I ever remember with silver in it! I was in awe of Baxter because of all the talk from the adults about what a player he was, but I remember when he came back to play the second time (against Clyde, I think). Ibrox was full of hope, but when he ran out the tunnel he looked like my dad with a moustache. He must have been some player in his heyday, though!'

TOM PORTEOUS: A retired bank manager from Bargeddie: 'I used to go to record hops in Garturk Church in Coatbridge and it was next to where his girlfriend lived. We gave up with the dance and used to polish his car when he appeared. I went to every game on the Whifflet supporters' bus, and while Ralph Brand was my favourite, Baxter was the guy that made us tick. That was the best Rangers team I have ever seen, and I include the Souness teams in that, and it was largely down to Slim Jim.'

PAUL FARROW: A Sunderland fan from Chester-le-Street: 'When he came to us, we were convinced we could win the league, but we maybe needed another two players of his standard. He was sublime at times, and at other times just looked as if he couldn't be bothered. Baxter seemed to keep things in reserve for the bigger games. He will go down in history, though, as one of our best ever players and he's still talked of fondly down here yet.'

ROBERT BROWN: From Airdrie, he got his first Rangers season ticket in 1959: 'Baxter remains my all-time favourite and we have had some great players over the years, from Gascoigne to Barry Ferguson, but Baxter was out on his own. He made the ball talk at times. If I was to be critical, he didn't score enough goals, but he made plenty for others.'

DEREK HAMILTON: From East Kilbride, he was a twenty-year-old when Baxter joined Rangers: 'Quite simply, he should never have been sold. He was Rangers and you only have to look at the number of trophies we won when he was in Scot Symon's team. Baxter left, that team broke up and we handed the initiative to Celtic.'

PETER SAMPLE: From Nottingham: 'We won two European Cups under Brian Clough and that was not one but two miracles. It was another miracle that Baxter ever played for Forest. He seemed to go through life from one bar-room scrape to another. He was a major disappointment, especially when we had been told he was the man that would win us the championship. Some hope. I was at Wembley in 1967 supporting England and I left wondering: was that the same Jim Baxter that ruled that day who hardly tried a leg in my home-town team?'

JIM WHITE: From Bathgate, a lifelong Raith Rovers fan and former director of the club: 'We knew we had something special on our hands when Jim Baxter made the breakthrough as a teenager, and we also knew we wouldn't hold on to him for long. When we won at Rangers, it was inevitable that he would end up there. It was the right move for him at the time, but it was his next moves that defied logic. After Rangers, Jim should have been going upwards to bigger teams, Manchester United or abroad, not tin pot outfits like Sunderland. Bad decisions on both transfers, and he lost that spark of brilliance that came with a belief of invincibility. What a player. We were lucky to have him and so were Rangers.'

KENNY OLSEN: From Newton Mearns: 'Baxter was different class. Nothing more needs said. Different class.'

APPENDIX 3

EPIC BAXTER TALES

Some epic self-told Jim Baxter tales that will remain timeless and equally funny, no matter how many times they are told.

On Bert Herdman, his Raith Rovers manager: When we won at Ibrox in 1959, Andy Leigh coaxed the captain, Big Willie McNaught, to go and ask for an extra bonus. Big McNaught and Andy agreed he should ask for a tenner for each player. The full-timers were on about £17 per week then, and I was only on £7. Well, we had just beat the Rangers at Ibrox. Willie asked the manager, who had a bit of a stutter, and he said he would speak to his board. After the game we went to the Kenilworth Hotel, as we always did after a game in Glasgow, and we would usually get a high tea. The manager hadn't come back, so Big McNaught captured him and said, what about our bonus? Herdman replied, it's all sorted, you've got your extra bonus, you can all go *à la carte* instead of a high tea! It was 1959 – I had no idea what *à la carte* was! I thought it was a dug running at Shawfield.'

On getting his first cap for Scotland: 'I had only been at Rangers six months and I got called in to the Scotland team. It was well known then that if you played for Rangers or Celtic, you would get capped. Six months before then I couldn't get a bird at the Palais. Then when

226

I came to Glasgow, the birds were throwing themselves at me. I suppose it was to be expected, when you were as good-looking a young guy as I was!'

On his nickname, Stanley: 'I got it at Ibrox. Everybody had a nickname. Bobby Shearer was "Captain Cutlass" and he went off his head if you called him Bobby. I was Stanley, after the comedian Stanley Baxter. Obvious. But I often used to wonder, did Stanley Baxter's showbiz pals call him Jim?'

On Harold Davis: 'He was a hard man all right. In a game against Third Lanark, he gave the ball away and then won it back; he was good at that. Then he gave it away again. It was against Symon's instructions – "Just give it to Jim or Ian, and they'll deliver it up front" – so I gave Harold the verbals. We were in the dressing-room at half-time and Big Harry came up and lifted me off the deck by my shirt and said, "Don't you f*ck*n ever do that again or I'll plant you." I was scared, for sure, and so was Scot Symon. He was shouting, "Harold, Harold, put Jim down!" I didn't make that mistake again!'

On beating Celtic: 'I used to love beating Celtic and I had some record against them. There was something special about winning Old Firm games and it was great for the fans. It made or ruined the fans' weekend. I had a great record against Celtic and I used to wind up Big Billy McNeill during games. I would say, that'll be me getting letters galore on Monday morning fae the wives of Celtic fans, thanking me for sending their men home early again because their team was getting beat. Big McNeill used to go crazy!'

On his lifestyle: 'I didn't burn the candle at both ends. I burnt it in the middle as well. It was some size of a candle!'

On Willie Henderson: 'One night in Glasgow, two birds came up to Willie and asked for his autograph. He said, "Me? I'm no Willie

Henderson," and one of the girls said, "Well, if you're no Willie Henderson, yer ugly enough to be him." Poor Willie!'

On winning: 'I played in seven cup finals and I won them all. That's some record.'

On who were the better team: 'Rangers of Ritchie, Shearer, Caldow, Greig, McKinnon, Baxter, Henderson, McMillan, Millar, Brand and Wilson, or the Lisbon Lions? No contest! Old Jimmy Millar would have his teeth out and would have had Big Billy [McNeill] running scared, and me and Wee Bertie [Auld] would be going at it in midfield, kicking lumps out of each other but plotting to meet up for a few later. It would have been some game, but no contest. We all would have had a good night out after it, though!'

APPENDIX 4

FOOTBALL CARD COLLECTABLES

Baxter was a popular card to collect and there were a few that had his image on one side and a brief detail of the player on the reverse. Players cards have proven to be real football collectables over the years.

Nigel Mercer, from Tasmania, has a massive collection, spanning nearly fifty years of world football. Nigel has eighteen cards from various sources in his collection that are dedicated to Jim Baxter. It's a pleasure to describe some of them below that depict Baxter's career from 1965 to 1980. Visit Nigel's Webspace on Facebook to see his full collection.

Reddish Maid, 1965–66, card 1
'Having recently joined Sunderland, Jim Baxter's clever half-back play will be seen in England. Joined Raith Rovers before becoming a world-class player with Glasgow Rangers.'

A&BC Chewing Gum, Footballers 1966–67, card 74
'Sunderland left-half. Capped thirty times for Scotland, Jim recovered from a broken leg sustained in 1964 to regain his place in the Scottish team last season. He can perform at either wing-half or inside forward. Jim cost Sunderland £95,000 when they transferred him from Glasgow Rangers in May 1965. Height 5' 10½". Weight 11 st. 10 lbs.'

A&BC Chewing Gum, Footballers 1968–69, card 101

'Signed from Sunderland in December 1967 at a fee of £100,000, Baxter has been capped thirty-four times for Scotland. An elegant mid-field player, he started with Glasgow Rangers and joined Sunderland for £95,000 in May 1965. At his best at wing-half, but has the skill to play in the attack either at inside-forward or "up front".'

FKS Wonderful World of Soccer Stars 1968–69, sticker 183

'Brilliant if unorthodox schemer who joined Forest in December last year for £100,000. Started with Raith Rovers and cost Rangers £17,000 in June 1960, then moved to Sunderland.'

The Sun, Soccercards, 1978–79, card 212

'From £100,000 to a free transfer in just eighteen months, that is the sad story of Jim Baxter. One of Scotland's greatest wing-halves. Won thirty-four Scottish caps and made 347 Scottish and English league appearances. Began with Raith, moved to Rangers in 1960, in five years Jim won three League titles, three Scottish Cup and four League Cup winners medals. Broke his leg v. Austria in Dec. 1964. Moved to Sunderland (£72,000) May 1965 and £100,000 to Forest in Dec. 1967. Free transfer to Rangers, May 1969.'

APPENDIX 5

STATISTICS

JIM BAXTER'S CAREER

Season	Club	League Apps	League Goals	League	Final Pos	Scottish Cup	League Cup	Europe	Scotland caps/gls
1957–58	Raith Rovers	3	1	Scot Div 1	7th	Round 2	Section	–	–/–
1958–59	Raith Rovers	26	0	Scot Div 1	14th	Round 1	Section	–	–/–
1959–60	Raith Rovers	32	2	Scot Div 1	11th	Round 1	Quarter	–	–/–
TOTAL for Raith Rovers		**61**	**3**						
1960–61	Rangers	27	1	Scot Div 1	Champions	Round 3	Winners	CWC RU	4/0
1961–62	Rangers	29	2	Scot Div 1	2nd	Winners	Winners	EC QF	6/1
1962–63	Rangers	32	4	Scot Div 1	Champions	Winners	Semi	CWC R1	7/2
1963–64	Rangers	26	4	Scot Div 1	Champions	Winners	Winners	EC RQual	4/0
1964–65	Rangers	22	6	Scot Div 1	5th	Quarter	Winners	EC QF	3/0
TOTAL for Rangers (1st spell)		**136**	**17**						
1965–66	Sunderland	35	7	Eng Div 1	19th	Round 3	Round 3	–	6/0
1966–67	Sunderland	36	3	Eng Div 1	17th	Round 5	Round 2	–	3/0
1967–68	Sunderland	16	0	Eng Div 1	15th	Round 3	Round 4	–	1/0
TOTAL for Sunderland		**87**	**10**						
1967–68	Nottingham Forest	22	2	Eng Div 1	11th	Round 4	Round 3*	FC R2*	–/–
1968–69	Nottingham Forest	26	1	Eng Div 1	18th	Round 3	Round 2	–	–/–
TOTAL for Nottingham Forest		**48**	**3**						
1969–70	Rangers	14	1	Scot Div 1	2nd	Quarter	Section	–	–/–
TOTAL for Rangers (2nd spell)		**14**	**1**						
TOTAL for Rangers (overall)		**150**	**18**						

* played before Baxter joined Forest in December 1967

232

Transfer fees

June 1960, Raith Rovers to Rangers £17,500 (Scottish record at the time)

May 1965, Rangers to Sunderland £72,500 (highest fee paid to a Scottish club at the time)

December 1967, Sunderland to Nottingham Forest £100,000

May 1969, Nottingham Forest to Rangers free transfer

Scotland Internationals

9 Nov 1960	Scotland	5	Northern Ireland	2
3 May 1961	Scotland	4	Ireland	1
7 May 1961	Ireland	0	Scotland	3
14 May 1961	Czechoslovakia	4	Scotland	0
26 Sep 1961	Scotland	3	Czechoslovakia	2
7 Oct 1961	Northern Ireland	1	Scotland	6
8 Nov 1961	Scotland	2	Wales	0
29 Nov 1961	Czechoslovakia	4	Scotland	2
	(played in Brussels)			
14 Apr 1962	Scotland	2	England	0
2 May 1962	Scotland	2	Uruguay	3
	(one goal)			
20 Oct 1962	Wales	2	Scotland	3
7 Nov 1962	Scotland	5	Northern Ireland	1
6 Apr 1963	England	1	Scotland	2
	(two goals)			
8 May 1963	Scotland	4	Austria	1
	(abandoned after seventy-nine mins)			
4 Jun 1963	Norway	4	Scotland	3
9 Jun 1963	Ireland	1	Scotland	0
13 Jun 1963	Spain	2	Scotland	6
7 Nov 1963	Scotland	6	Norway	1
20 Nov 1963	Scotland	2	Wales	1

11 Apr 1964	Scotland	1	England	0
12 May 1964	West Germany	2	Scotland	2
3 Oct 1964	Wales	3	Scotland	2
21 Oct 1964	Scotland	3	Finland	1
25 Nov 1964	Scotland	3	Northern Ireland	2
2 Oct 1965	Northern Ireland	3	Scotland	2
9 Nov 1965	Scotland	1	Italy	0
24 Nov 1965	Scotland	4	Wales	1
2 Apr 1966	Scotland	3	England	4
18 Jun 1966	Scotland	0	Portugal	1
25 Jun 1966	Scotland	1	Brazil	1
22 Oct 1966	Wales	1	Scotland	1
15 Apr 1967	England	2	Scotland	3
10 May 1967	Scotland	0	USSR	2
22 Nov 1967	Scotland	3	Wales	2

Record v. Celtic

20 Aug 1960 – League Cup section match
Rangers 2 (Millar 36, Brand 61)
Celtic 3 (Carroll 15, Divers 25, Hughes 44)

3 Sep 1960 – League Cup section match
Celtic 1 (Chalmers 2)
Rangers 2 (Davis 48, Brand 70)

10 Sep 1960 – Scottish League
Celtic 1 (Chalmers 89)
Rangers 5 (Scott 2, Millar 65, Brand 78, Wilson 84, Davis 86)

2 Jan 1961 – Scottish League
Rangers 2 (Brand 62, Wilson 80)
Celtic 1 (Divers 28)

16 Sep 1961 – Scottish League
Rangers 2 (Christie 5, Baxter 88)
Celtic 2 (Divers 28, Fernie 48)

9 Apr 1962 – Scottish League
Celtic 1 (Hughes 43)
Rangers 1 (Wilson 78)

8 Sep 1962 – Scottish League
Celtic 0
Rangers 1 (Henderson 84)

1 Jan 1963 – Scottish League
Rangers 4 (Davis 12, Millar 68, Greig 70, Wilson 80)
Celtic 0

4 May 1963 – Scottish Cup final
Rangers 1 (Brand 43)
Celtic 1 (Murdoch 45)

15 May 1963 – Scottish Cup final (replay)
Rangers 3 (Brand 7, 71, Wilson 44)
Celtic 0

10 Aug 1963 – League Cup section match
Celtic 0
Rangers 3 (Forrest 29, 62, McLean 56)

24 Aug 1963 – League Cup section match
Rangers 3 (Wilson 38, Brand 54pen, Forrest 61)
Celtic 0

235

7 Sep 1963 – Scottish League
Rangers 2 (McLean 52, Brand 65)
Celtic 1 (Chalmers 11)

1 Jan 1964 – Scottish League
Celtic 0
Rangers 1 (Millar 65)

7 May 1964 – Scottish Cup quarter final
Rangers 2 (Forrest 44, Henderson 46)
Celtic 0

5 Sep 1964 – Scottish League
Celtic 3 (Chalmers 35, 50, Hughes 56)
Rangers 1 (Wilson 82)

24 Oct 1964 – League Cup final
Rangers 2 (Forrest 52, 62)
Celtic 1 (Johnstone 69)

13 Aug 1969 – League Cup section match
Rangers 2 (Persson 48, Johnston 50)
Celtic 1 (Hood 8)

20 Sep 1969 – Scottish League
Rangers 0
Celtic 1 (Hood 49)

APPENDIX 6

TRIBUTES

On the day of Jim Baxter's funeral, www.glasgowguide.co.uk published the following tributes from the world of football on their website. Many thanks for their permission to share them here.

DENIS LAW (Scotland teammate): 'It's a very sad loss for everybody. It's just a shame to see him go. He turned on the class in the 1967 game against England and was the best player on the park that day. To beat the world champions on their own ground was mainly down to Jim Baxter. He was a wonderful player, a lovely passer of the ball and it's very sad to lose the man. We have lost two of the great players from that side now, with the death of Billy Bremner a few years ago.'

ERIC CALDOW (Former Rangers captain and Scotland teammate): 'He loved football – all he could talk about was football; he was just a genius. He was arrogant, but he wanted to win. That left foot of his … nowadays it would be worth £20 million, just for the left leg alone!'

BILLY McNEILL (Former Celtic captain): 'He was a typical cheeky, confident type of character. But he had this enormous ability and I think Rangers spotted that more quickly than anyone else. He will be sadly missed by every Scottish football fan.'

ROBERT McELROY (Rangers historian): 'Every single member of that team was a good player, but without Baxter they were just a good team; with Baxter, they were exceptional – he could almost defeat a team single-handedly. His very presence on the park was almost worth a goal a start to Rangers.'

BOB CRAMPSEY (football historian): Referring to Baxter's ball-juggling antics at Wembley, as Scotland defeated the then World Cup holders England 3–2 in 1967: 'That's a defining moment for almost every football fan in Scotland, irrespective of where their club allegiance lies. Baxter going up and down that left wing at no great pace, keeping the ball off the deck, with 90,000 people there was phenomenal. England had no idea what to do about it and Baxter was not about to solve that problem for them – it was a wonderful moment. Almost from the word go he became a cult figure and he achieved almost messianic status. I would seldom use this word about football, but I think Baxter was loved and loved in the totality. Fans weren't blind to what others might have seen as faults. They knew he liked a drink, that he liked to stay out late, and they knew he wasn't a dedicated pounder of the track, but they liked the package. I think more than anything else, he was the player they would have liked to have been.'
Bob Crampsey died in 2008, aged seventy-eight.

SANDY JARDINE (Rangers and Scotland teammate): 'Jim was a wonderful player who had outrageous skill and huge confidence in his own ability. People band on about the phrase "world class", but Jim genuinely was a world-class player. Jim could have played at any time and anywhere because of his skill level.'
Sandy Jardine died in 2014, aged sixty-five.

ANDY MITCHELL (Scottish Football Association spokesman): 'Jim is one of Scottish football's all-time greats. Two of his greatest performances were in a Scotland shirt – scoring two goals against

England in 1963 and the famous moment when he played keepie-uppie in 1967. That is one of the great moments in his career, but he had so many other great games and performances for club and country, and he will be sadly missed.'

GORDON BROWN (Chancellor of the Exchequer at the time) 'One of my earliest memories of football is supporting Jim Baxter at Stark's Park. He was one of the greatest players Scotland ever produced and went on to represent his country with great distinction. I last saw Jim just a few weeks ago in Glasgow, where as always his well-known sense of humour made the evening one that everyone present will never forget. The courage he should in his final months was a mark of the man. Like every other Scotland fan, I will mourn and miss Jim Baxter and will never forget what he contributed to our game.'

CRAIG BROWN (Former Scotland manager): 'He was an all-time great in Scottish football. When we won at Wembley in 1967 to become "world champions", Jim was instrumental in the victory.'

KENNY DALGLISH (Former Scotland, Liverpool and Celtic star): 'My lasting memory of him will be of Wembley in 1967. To keep the ball up just when it looked as though Scotland were going to beat them was beyond belief.'

JIM McLEAN (Former Dundee United manager and chairman): 'Today we lack the creative ability that he had in abundance. I played against him but did not get a kick of the ball.'

Some great names with some great memories of a truly great player.

Author Tom Miller has a wealth of experience reporting and broadcasting on Scottish football and has worked for Rangers TV as their match commentator for the last seven years. Tom can also be

239

SLIM JIM

regularly heard on talkSPORT and Radio Clyde, and was previously involved in *Scotsport*.

In 1963, Tom was captivated, listening to Jim Baxter and his Scottish team beat England at Wembley, with the wireless commentary still vividly recalled as it brought the game to life.